Interactive Visualization

Insight through Inquiry

Bill Ferster

Foreword by Ben Shneiderman

The MIT Press
Cambridge, Massachusetts
London, England

MIT Press books may be purchased at special quantity discounts for business or sales promotional use. For information, please email special_sales@mitpress.mit.edu or write to Special Sales Department, The MIT Press, 55 Hayward Street, Cambridge, MA 02142.

This book was set in Stone Sans and Stone Serif by Toppan Best-set Premedia Limited. Printed and bound in the United States of America.

Library of Congress Cataloging-in-Publication Data

Ferster, Bill, 1956–
Interactive visualization : insight through inquiry / Bill Ferster ; foreword by Ben Shneiderman.
  p. cm.
Includes bibliographical references and index.
ISBN 978-0-262-01815-9 (hardcover : alk. paper)
1. Information visualization—Data processing. 2. Web-based user interfaces. 3. Inquiry (Theory of knowledge) I. Title.
TK7882.I6F47   2013
006.7—dc23
2012008686

10 9 8 7 6 5 4 3 2 1

For Susan, Margot, and Mike

Contents

Foreword

The sound and light shows at the Egyptian pyramids or Jerusalem's Damascus gate delight and inform viewers by revealing historical episodes, architectural triumphs, and human dramas. Visual presentations have always attracted viewers because they offer insights about the world around them and make the invisible visible.

Palladio's classic architectural drawings, Dürer's copper engravings, and Leonardo's portraits enabled comprehension by telling stories in attractive ways. Similarly, Mercator's cylindrical maps, Playfair's economic charts, and Snow's cholera map of London complemented visual appeal by revealing patterns that supported decision making. Cultural treasures such as Mayan temple painting and Hiroshige's prints of the road from Edo to Kyoto are valued because they reveal how different cultures saw the world around them.

These hand-drawn inspirational masterpieces encouraged visual literacy and stimulated the development of better ways of seeing the world. Dramatic changes came with powerful optical imaging devices such as telescopes, microscopes, x-ray machines, and magnetic resonance imaging. These devices enabled astronomers and biologists to probe the physical world, supporting their understanding of the cosmos, microcosmos, and human anatomy.

These breakthroughs were controversial in their time, often meeting angry opposition from those whose worldview was challenged or resistance from those whose existing expertise was undermined. The path to widespread acceptance often took decades, requiring refinements to improve quality, demonstrations to clarify utility, and simplification to enable broad comprehension.

In the twentieth century, photography, movies, and animations became dominant forms for understanding our world and telling stories. Early in the twenty-first century, interactive computer-based information visualizations offer new opportunities to reveal patterns, show relationships, and support decision making. The worldwide enthusiasm for information visualization during the past two decades adds new opportunities for increasing understanding of previously invisible social, political, economic, and historical processes. Early information visualizations such as genealogical trees, military maps, diplomatic timelines, or trading networks hinted at the potential to show human dramas in meaningful ways that accelerate pattern finding, relationship discovery, and policy making.

The excitement is most profound among natural and social science researchers, where molecular biologists are charting genomic pathways and sociologists are viewing community formation in real time. Similarly, financial analysts track global stock markets to detect fraud and insider trading patterns, while pharmaceutical analysts make drug discoveries by filtering massive chemical datasets. The explosion of visual analytics for demographics, epidemiology, business management, political analysis, and social network analysis offers bold new opportunities.

A growing number of creative historians, literary analysts, and other humanities scholars recognize that interactive information visualizations can reveal patterns, show relationships, find clusters, detect gaps, and identify anomalies to support scholarship and education. Their efforts have naturally generated resistance and opposition from some, but the compelling visual presentations and important insights are gaining acceptance rapidly.

The increasing availability of online data complemented by rapidly improving tools has broadened interest dramatically. The compelling opportunities for creative humanities research attracts innovative scholars and students, who extract insights from data and present them in comprehensible visualizations. They add to the experiences of those who know that the goal of visualization is insight, not pictures. The thrill of discovery is what drives these innovators who are trying to make sense of complex human dramas, historical trajectories, creative writing, or artistic expressions.

Of course, not all visualizations are good, honest, or useful. As with any emerging technology, some information visualization practitioners violate established principles of statistical analysis, accurate reporting, and perceptual psychology. Unfortunately, even well-intentioned researchers can be more attracted to visual appeal than meaningful results or to attractive animations than comprehensible insights. Higher quality visualizations will come from improved tools, better guidelines, and more effective education. The vigorous debates over these issues advance scholarship and raise quality.

Bill Ferster's book on *Interactive Visualization: Insight through Inquiry* is a valuable contribution to the growing literature on visual analytics. His digital humanities orientation gives a fresh perspective on existing guidelines, principles, theories, tools, data analysis processes, and more. He adds his own ASSERT framework, which steers students to effective inquiry by getting them to:

- Ask a question.
- Search for evidence to support the question.
- Structure that information to answer the question.
- Envision ways to answer the question using the data.
- Represent the data into a compelling visualization.
- Tell a meaningful story using the evidence to answer the question.

This framework and Ferster's diligently assembled collection of resources constitute a useful and readable guide that opens the door for an increasing variety of humanities scholars and students to enter the world of interactive information visualization. Ferster deftly integrates wisdom from visualization leaders such as Wurman, Tufte, Few, Spence, and others, while addressing quantitative versus qualitative data, perceptual issues of design for static and dynamic visualizations, and the multiple arts of critical thinking, storytelling, and persuasion. Ferster's tantalizing introduction provides an invaluable collection of diverse visualization examples, as he broadly scans the tools for data gathering, data cleaning, statistics, programming, and internet services, while also addressing universal usability.

Some humanities scholars fear that statistical analyses, data-based research, and flashy visualizations will somehow shift attention to computer-based manipulation and away from human analysis. Some data mining and machine learning promoters mistakenly reinforce the belief that algorithms reveal truths and are above reproach. Countering these shallow models with richer understandings of the unique human capabilities for reason, inquiry, insight, discovery, and creative contributions will encourage humanities scholars to produce new insights and contribute to important current debates about the power and limits of technology.

Computers have no more intelligence than a wooden pencil. The growing recognition is that people are not computers and computers are not people. The unique human capacity for rich forms of reflection, principled advocacy, nuanced contextual understanding, and critical thinking is enhanced by powerful tools to sift through voluminous data, while seeking meaningful insights. As time goes by, the differences between humanities-based insights and computer-based algorithms will become clearer, accelerating the development of both disciplines and the collaboration between them.

Humanities researchers who adopt visual analytics tools are likely to find new ways to support passionately held theories and make creative leaps that advance their scholarship. At the same time, computer scientists who take on the challenges of humanities research, could invigorate their discipline with complex data structures, novel algorithms, and innovative user interfaces.

Ferster's book contributes to bridging these disciplines and offers engaging examples that will be appreciated by even wider audiences. His book also will give many readers the knowledge and confidence that they can create interactive visualizations to tell their own stories, reveal unnoticed patterns, and support further exploration by users.

It's an exciting time. Opportunities for innovation are abundant. There's much work to be done. Let's do it!

Ben Shneiderman

Preface

Interactive visualization is emerging as a vibrant new form of communication that spans many fields of interest from history and the humanities to finance and science. In addition to the varied subjects used as topics, interactive visualization permits the modeling of dynamic expressions of data and information that draw from a number of disciplines to inform the final representation, including design, psychology, perception, computer science, statistics, human interface design, and literature.

A number of excellent books and papers address individual facets of visualization, and this book reflects their influence and contribution by synthesizing the history and current research in the field into this single volume, which is organized around issues in *creating* interactive visualizations.

I first became involved with interactive visualization at the Virginia Center for Digital History (VCDH) of the University of Virginia. VCDH had been actively developing Web-based digital history scholarship beginning with Ed Ayers' groundbreaking *The Valley of the Shadow* project[1] in the 1990s and continuing with a number of historical projects with topics ranging from Jamestown, nineteenth-century railroads, and the Civil Rights movement. As diverse as the subject matter, resources, and methods of discourse were, they all shared a common set of characteristics: to make primary source documents digitally accessible and dynamically supportive of historical inquiry that encourages individual discovery.

In response to the shared goals of these projects, and with support from a grant from the National Endowment for the Humanities, we developed a Web-based authoring tool. *VisualEyes* has provided an opportunity for us to think about the overarching ideas in creating interactive visualizations that rely on information-rich elements to communicate directly with viewers. These ideas were further refined over a number of years by a series of seminars taught by myself and the historian Scot French and religious studies professor Kurtis Schaeffer, in which undergraduate history

1. http://valley.lib.virginia.edu.

students researched, designed, and implemented a series of compelling interactive visualizations.[2]

In the course of developing many interactive visualizations on a wide variety of topics, we developed the ASSERT model to help support scholars and students through the process of creating their projects, and it has proven a useful tool. The ASSERT model consists of six components that provide a scaffold for visualization designers to explore meaningful questions through visual representation and interaction.

This book uses ASSERT as the backbone on which the disparate facets involved in creating and understanding interactive visualizations are connected. Part III contains a number of tutorials on the basics of using spreadsheets, the Internet, statistics, accessibility, and teaching using project-based learning techniques that may prove useful.

What This Book Explores

This book is an introduction to the field of interactive visualization through the lens of the ASSERT model. The history, theoretical basis, and practical elements of creating interactive visualization projects are explored within that framework. Because the tools and technologies for developing visualizations are constantly evolving, those elements are discussed independently from any given tool or technology. Thus, it is not a "how-to" book on creating interactive visualizations but offers guidance to some of the important concepts required to build projects using the tools appropriate to each project, its designer, and the final audience.

The assumption is that detailed descriptions of tools and techniques will become outdated almost as soon as they are written, but the principles of inquiry, design, and usability have long traditions that are informative when viewed from a more abstracted level. This book attempts to describe concrete projects and ideas from that level, to offer the reader insight into the processes operating in all visualization projects, regardless of how they are ultimately realized.

Some of the ideas explored are the inquiry process used in the social sciences, the importance of understanding the target audience, how information can be found and structured and analyzed to facilitate that inquiry, and how that information can be visually represented to tell a story that answers a question asked by the designer and the audience.

The multidisciplinary nature of interactive visualization makes it unlikely that designers will have extensive knowledge in all of the requisite components, so the book covers the basic principles of inquiry, data structuring, information design, statistics, cognitive theory, usability and human factors, working with spreadsheets, the Internet, and storytelling.

2. www.viseyes.org/class.htm.

This book is designed for undergraduate and graduate students and working designers who want to explore the guiding principles behind developing compelling interactive data-driven visualizations. It does not require any prior programming, design, or statistical experience.

I would like thank the many people who have helped me put together this book by reviewing, copyediting, and offering guidance: Rafael Alvarado, Kay Buchannan, Jean Cooper, Max Edelson, Elizabeth Fanning, Stephen Few, Margot Ferster, Susan Ferster, Scot French, Roger Geyer, Dov Jacobson, Marc Leepson, Robert Nelson, Lynn Rainville, Kurtis Schaeffer, Randy Shifflet, Bill Strum, and Andrew Torget. I would also like to thank the people who generously offered illustrations of their work to include, and, finally, the students in our undergraduate classes who helped me hone the ASSERT model over the years.

I About Interactive Visualization

Interactive visualization is the process of letting primary sources of information communicate directly with a viewer to support inquiry in a visual, compelling, and interactive manner.

1   Introduction

. . .how like the needle information is. It always has a point and needs an eye.

—Thomas F. Gilbert

Print-based information visualization has been used effectively for centuries to marshal multifaceted data in the service of making a point visually. The advent of interactive computer graphics, the Internet, and readily available sources of data extends that rich tradition and introduces a new kind of expression, *interactive visualization*. This innovative medium has the potential for sustaining a meaningful virtual dialogue between scholars and their audience, using data as the liaison. This chapter introduces the emerging field of interactive visualization by exploring the following topics:

- What is information visualization?
- Why visualization is valuable
- A brief history of visualization
- Information graphics in journalism
- Theoretical models for interactive visualization
- Descriptive models for interactive visualization
- Prescriptive models for interactive visualization
- The ASSERT model for interactive visualization

What Is Information Visualization?

In 1854, an epidemic of cholera spread through the Soho section of London, killing hundreds of people in a matter of weeks. London was overcrowded by the influx of people to the city from the country, and sanitary services could not keep up with the population. The streets were literally a cesspool of human waste, and the city leaders assumed that the constant odor in the air was the cause of the outbreak.

A London anesthesiologist named John Snow used data from a local priest, Henry Whitehead, and London city epidemiologist William Farr to geographically map the

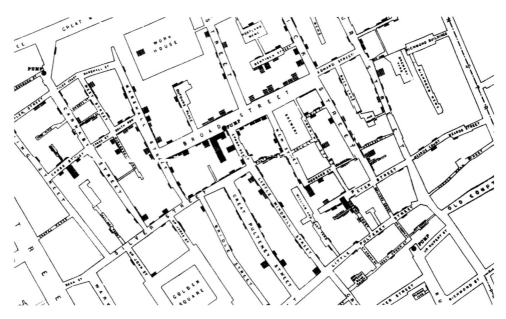

Figure 1.1
Portion of John Snow's cholera map (image courtesy John Snow Archive and Research Companion).

spread of the massive cholera outbreak in London. Snow plotted the deaths of cholera victims on a simplified map of the afflicted Soho neighborhood (see figure 1.1) to convince authorities that cholera was waterborne and that the outbreak emanated from an infected water pump on Broad Street.

The visualized data that Snow presented helped turn the tide from the airborne miasma theory of how disease spread to the modern germ theory and provided early evidence of visualization's power to persuade (Johnson, 2006; Tufte, 1997).

Early efforts such as Snow's simple but effective map have been growing and are taking full advantage of the new technologies afforded by computers, the Internet, statistics, and computer graphics, known as *interactive visualization*. Interactive visualization is a subset of a larger field known as *information visualization*, which is also sometimes referred to as informatics, that crosses the disciplinary boundaries of computer science, design, statistics, psychology, cognition, neuroscience, and the basic sciences. The early researchers Stuart Card, Jock Mackinlay, and Ben Shneiderman's definition of information visualization is the most often cited description of this nascent field: *The use of computer-supported, interactive, visual representations of abstract data to amplify cognition.*

Implicit in this definition is the potential for information visualization to externally increase understanding by (1) increasing the number of resources available to the viewer while remaining cognizant of the limits of human working memory, (2) reducing the need for time-consuming and tedious searching, (3) enhancing pattern recognition to detect meaningful trends and conditions, (4) using the properties of the human perception system to effectively communicate meaning, and (5) allowing the user to directly interact with the information to construct his or her own understandings (Card, Mackinlay, & Shneiderman, 1999).

Information visualization involves the *reduction* of raw information, such as data, into simpler graphical elements that use *spatial variables*, such as position, size, shape, and color, to reveal visual relationships and patterns implicit but hidden within the data. "The goal is to discover the hidden structure of a (typically large) dataset" (Manovich, 2010).

A good visualization can tell a rich and profound story using primary source data to answer meaningful questions about a topic. This aligns with the research practices used by other disciplines such as history and the social sciences and provides an opportunity for scholars to share research in this new medium in other forms beyond the written word.

This is not to say that the medium in which an argument is presented has no effect on the ultimate perception of the message (McLuhan, 1964). Writing has its own internal structures, such as linearity, sequence, syntax, abstraction, and cultural heritage, that can cast a profound effect on meaning. Different media types will be better suited to representing particular subject matter and characteristics than others. The popular musician Elvis Costello[1] cleverly described the difficulty matching an argument with its medium of expression by explaining that "Writing about music is like dancing about architecture" (Staley, 2003).

Genres of Visualization

Different groups create visualizations for a variety of reasons. Scientists use visualization to graphically communicate scientific phenomena, historians use visualization to explain and further explore what people do, and journalists use infographics to clarify and communicate complex ideas to the general public. This book uses the term *visualization* as a broad category encompassing both static and interactive visualizations. *Data* and *information* are used interchangeably to represent the reality-based elements involved. The examples discussed are often rooted in historical visualization, but the ideas demonstrated are common to all types of visualization.

---

1. This quote has been attributed to other people than Costello, including Martin Mull, Laurie Anderson, Frank Zappa, Steve Martin, and Miles Davis. I'm sticking with Elvis on this one.

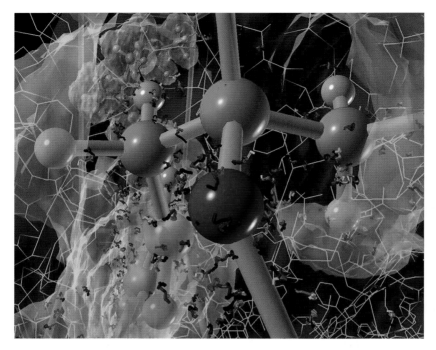

Figure 1.2
Molecular visualization by Benjamin Grosser, University of Illinois.

Scientific Visualization and Simulations

Scientific visualization is a subset of visualization that uses quantitative data to create graphical images of scientific phenomena. It can help explain the underlying dynamics that data represent so opaquely when represented only as a table of numbers. Three-dimensional renderings of molecules (see figure 1.2), weather patterns, and MRI imagery allow researchers to visually explore these rich datasets and gain insights that otherwise might not be obvious.

In addition to the goal of describing phenomena, one of science's roles is to predict aspects of nature from a theoretical foundation. Scientific visualizations in the form of *simulations* do not necessarily need to rely on real-world data but can use mathematics such as differential equations to generate data based on theoretical models that interactively play "what if" scenarios and graphically display the results.

Historical Visualization

In our work with historical visualization at the University of Virginia, we define interactive visualization as *the process of letting primary sources of information communicate*

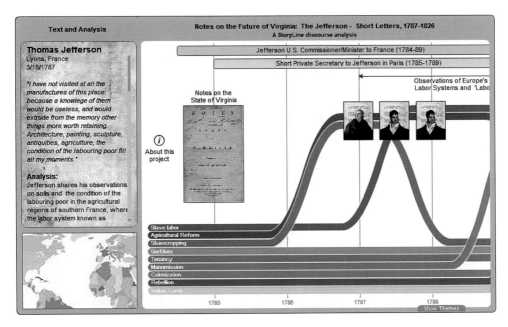

Figure 1.3
Screen shot from VisualEyes "Notes from Virginia" project (image courtesy Scot French).

directly with a viewer to support inquiry in a visual, compelling, and interactive manner. The primary sources of information for historical study can take many forms, including photographs, maps, drawings, letters, legal documents, numeric data consisting of weather, population, demographic, and financial data, newspaper accounts, and almost any product of human effort. The method for communicating the material can be equally varied, from charts, timelines, maps, animations, three-dimensional (3D) renderings, and movies (see figure 1.3). The means of interaction with those data can range from dynamic textual queries on a database to fully immersive 3D environments.

Infographics

Infographics is a subset of information visualization. It is often used by newspapers and magazines to explain complex processes in an attractive, clear, and direct graphical depiction using charts and illustrations in a highly aesthetic manner (see figure 1.4). Typically rendered as two-dimensional static images with high production values, many journalistic infographics are often accused of oversimplifying complex issues and choosing aesthetics over truth.

BIKE-OPOLIS

The battle over which North American city is the best for biking is fierce and—most likely—unresolvable. We can tell you which cities' residents make the largest percentage of their commutes by bike.

Portland, Oregon, you can keep on gloating.

NEW YORK: 0.7%
CHICAGO: 1.1%
WASHINGTON, D.C.: 1.7%
TORONTO: 1.7%
SAN FRANCISCO: 2.5%
VANCOUVER: 3.0%
MINNEAPOLIS: 3.8%
PORTLAND, OR: 3.9%

A COLLABORATION BETWEEN
GOOD AND CHRIS KORBEY

SOURCE: "Cycling and Walking for All New Yorkers:
Path to Improved Public Health,"
by Professor John Pucher, Rutgers University

BIKE BY REPUBLIC BIKES:
www.republicbike.com

Figure 1.4
Infographic for *GOOD Magazine* (image courtesy Chris Korbey: http://chriskorbey.com).

Interactive Visualization

Interactive visualizations are another subset of information visualization and share most of its features. Specifically, they add the ability for the end user to interact dynamically with the visualization in a reflexive manner. This interaction can allow the user to limit or expand the data being explored, to selectively contrast differing datasets together, show change over time, or zoom into the data for more details. Because of the large number of possible combinations for user interactions, interactive visualizations can be generative, meaning that they can potentially provide insights into the information beyond what the visualization's designer had originally intended.

This interaction is made possible by the ever-rising capabilities of computer graphics technology on inexpensive personal computers. The spread of this technology into mobile devices such as cell phones and hand-held tablets will undoubtedly provide new opportunities for people to graphically interact with data and reveal unanticipated but often fascinating insights.

Why Visualization Is Valuable

Information visualization is useful in both organizing and making sense out of data, particularly when there is a lot of it. We are limited in the amount of analysis we can do by looking at raw data, but when those data are visually structured, we are better able to understand complex and multidimensional relationships, prompting connections that may have not been otherwise apparent. We do this by taking advantage of our brain's massive parallel processing capabilities that the human visual system affords.

Numbers alone do not always tell the full story but often are a good place to start. To find that story, statisticians use very precise mathematical techniques to describe the relationships among groups of numbers, such as the *mean*, the *variance*, and the *correlation*. For the most part, these techniques accurately provide a good representation of the underlying phenomenon the data represent, but that is not always the case.

In 1973 the Yale statistician Frank Anscombe created four unique datasets that generated identical means, variances, and correlations but that, when graphed, showed very different shapes (figure 1.5). In a real dataset, these graphs would have shown very different distributions of the samples and suggested very different underlying dynamics. Clearly, the statistical measures did not accurately portray the underlying phenomenon very well in this case. Reading clockwise in figure 1.5, the datasets are normally distributed, a very linear relationship with one outlier, a very linear relationship with one anomaly, and, finally, a curvilinear relationship (Tufte, 1983).

The visual system is a powerful pattern-recognizing mechanism that can instantly discern patterns that are unmediated by mathematics. Data-driven visualizations harness that innate human ability toward a deeper understanding of their meaning.

A Brief History of Information Visualization

The visualization of information in a graphical context has been practiced for centuries, with an ever-increasing sophistication and reliance on empirical data. Leonardo da Vinci's 1487 drawing *Vitruvian Man* (figure 1.6) directly communicated the correlations of the ideal human proportion using the figure of a man circumscribed within a perfect circle.

By the eighteenth century, merchants and governments collected progressively more quantitative data about their world. This information was typically stored in

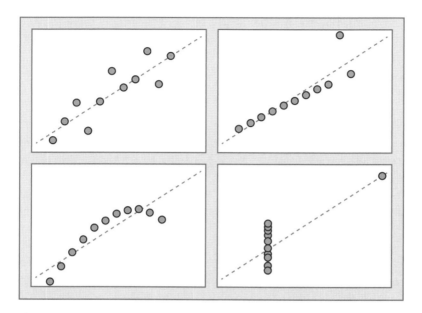

Figure 1.5
Anscombe's Quartet. Each dataset has the same base statistics but represents a different phenomenon.

massive tables of numbers, making interpretation difficult at best. The Scottish social scientist William Playfair (1759–1823) devised a number of now-familiar graphical devices such as pie, bar, and line charts (figure 1.7) that are able to quickly communicate tabular data with clarity using this much more accessible form (Tufte, 1983).

Although she is known mainly for her work as a nurse, the writer and statistician Florence Nightingale was a key figure in using statistical graphics to convey insight into the role that inactivity, malnutrition, and inadequate sanitation had on soldier deaths during the Crimean War. She kept detailed records and used those data to expand on Playfair's pie charts to create rose diagrams (figure 1.8), now known as *coxcombs* (Spieglhalter, 2008).

The use of graphs and charts to visualize quantitative data became more commonplace with new advances in statistical analyses. Representing even the simplest of these new ideas such as the range, median, and quartiles as numbers was not immediately intuitive. However, techniques to visually represent them through the use of new charting types, such as the pioneering statistician John Tukey's *box and whisker* plots (figure 1.9), provided depth to the data.

For example, this simple graphical device conveys the basic descriptive statistical facts of a dataset in a single glance. The box's *height* is mapped to the lower and upper

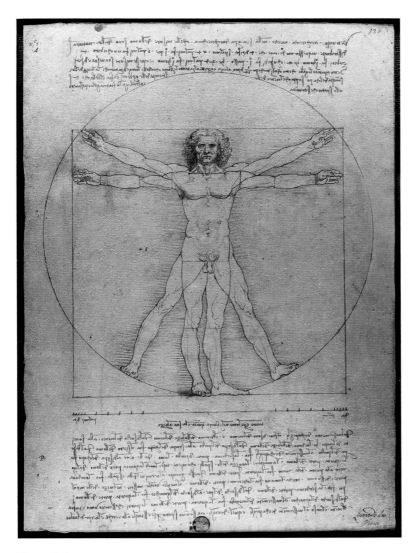

Figure 1.6
Leonardo da Vinci's 1487 Vitruvian Man.

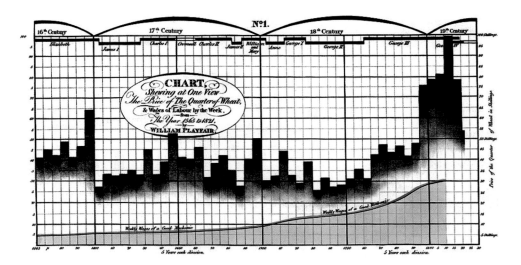

Figure 1.7
Early chart by William Playfair.

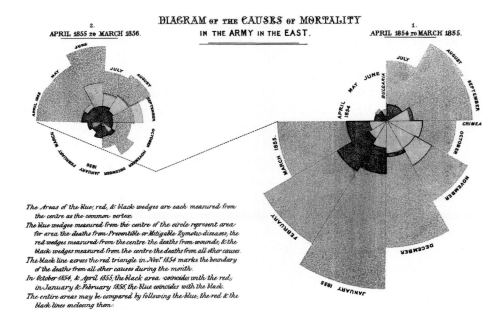

Figure 1.8
Florence Nightingale's 1855 coxcomb chart.

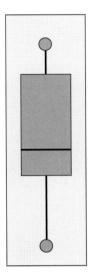

Figure 1.9
John Tukey's box-and-whisker graph.

quartiles, the *line* within the box shows the median, the middle of the box shows the *mean average*, and the two *whiskers* on top and bottom show the range of data.

In the beginning of the eighteenth century, the English geologist and former canal builder William Smith created what has been called "the map that changed the world" (figure 1.10). It was the first published geological map of Britain, where the different geological layers were represented as an overlay to the underlying geography using information Smith garnered from extensively traveling across England (Coppock & Rhind, 1991). This remarkable map helped introduce the concept that maps could be used to convey other information aside from geography.

Two-dimensional maps took a turn away from geographic accuracy and toward increased utility in 1931, when a draftsman working for the London Underground drew a map (figure 1.11) in his spare time that forever changed the way subway maps were drawn. Harry Beck ignored the actual distances between stops and the geographic placement of lines, stations, and crossing points in favor of making the map more usable for its riders and increasing its communicative impact (Spence, 2001).

The Impact of Computers
The advent of computers that are capable of drawing sophisticated graphics provided a new opportunity for both designers and statisticians to experiment with a new medium of expression, one that could render complex graphics based on large sets of data to create data-rich graphical visualizations beyond the static drawings of the previous centuries.

Figure 1.10
The map that changed the world.

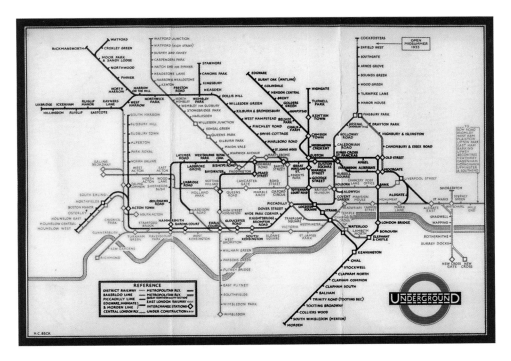

Figure 1.11
Harry Beck's London Underground map (image courtesy and copyright TFL/London Transport Museum).

Animators such as the legendary abstract film artist John Whitney experimented with algorithmically creating and animating imagery using the computer. After years of creating abstract films using analog techniques (figure 1.12), Whitney adopted the digital computer as a tool to produce a mesmerizing relationship between music and visual design and became IBM's first artist in residence in 1965.

As processing speeds increased at exponential rates of growth and rendering techniques grew in sophistication, computers were being used to render realistic models of complex scientific phenomena in three dimensions. The Jet Propulsion Laboratory's James Blinn introduced the general public to computer animation with the simulations created for the Voyager project 1978. These simulations provided photorealistic depictions of Voyager, an unmanned spacecraft, approaching various planets in its travels through space (figure 1.13)—something not possible to actually witness first hand.

With both the rendering fidelity that was increasing and the increasing processing speed of the computer, people were able to interact with the graphics being rendered in more meaningful ways. University of Utah computer science professors David Evans

Figure 1.12
Frame from John Whitney's film *Matrix III* (1972).

Figure 1.13
3D computer simulation of Voyager 2 by Jim Blinn.

Figure 1.14
Image from Evans and Sutherland simulation.

and Ivan Sutherland introduced a new genre of computer tool, the simulator, in which people had an immersive interaction with the computer in applications such as flight simulators and combat games (figure 1.14).

However, computer graphics were beyond the grasp of nonprogrammers to create until commercial companies such as Genigraphics produced systems for making presentation slides and computer-aided design (CAD) systems for engineering and architectural drawing such as CADAM, both of which were available on expensive and dedicated minicomputers. The confluence of the personal computer and accessible software such as AutoDesk's *AutoCad* and MacroMind's *Director* has brought powerful tools within the reach of casual users.

The computer gaming industry has had a tremendous impact on the development of software and hardware, driving the ever-increasing power and capabilities of modern computer graphics. The large gaming marketplace has created a critical mass accelerating innovation in high-performance/low-cost rendering chips such as NVIDIA and advances in software rendering developed by game producers.

It is important not to underestimate the potential the computer has for the sophisticated interactive communication of information. Rather than be passively content with the visualization designer's decisions of what data elements are compared, contrasted, transformed, aggregated, shown, or hidden, a good visualization now involves a *dialogue with data* that can enable a viewer to generatively explore data directly to develop insights not dictated by the designer.

The Impact of the Internet

The Internet and the open-source ethos of free accessibility have made data more widely available for instantaneous download. A wealth of freely available information from US Census data from 1790 to worldwide geographic, economic, and political data to real-time social media data from services such as Twitter can be instantly downloaded and used without any requirement for permissions from the provider. These data are increasingly being used by interactive visualization producers to provide powerful tools for information and inquiry.

Google and other Internet companies have added simple *application programming interfaces* (API) to their popular online services such as maps that encourage people to create geographically based visualizations called *mash-ups,*[2] which layer data and maps together in ways that are easier and more accessible to a mass audience than previous GIS[3]-based desktop systems. This visualization connects real-time police crime reports and plots them on a map (figure 1.15) where users can select the kinds of crimes to view during any given time period.

Other freely available APIs offer a wide range of web-based tools that programmers with little effort or experience can use to create timelines, such as MIT's SIMILE project. These tools have access to online images using *Flickr* and any number of charting and visualization APIs including *Processing, ProtoVis,* and *Prefuse,* all of which are freely available for anyone with even a modest level of programming skill to incorporate into his or her Web site.

Recently, a new genre of Web sites has emerged that make it easy for people who do not know how to create Web sites or programs to produce sophisticated visualization using their own data. These *Web-apps* make it easy to upload datasets and make a variety of compelling visualizations that can be shared worldwide. IBM Research's

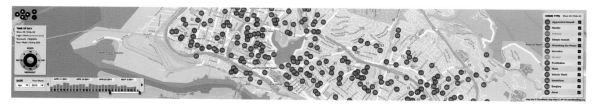

Figure 1.15
Oakland Crimespotting, courtesy of Stamen Design.

2. Image courtesy SpotCrime.com.
3. Geographic Information System (GIS).

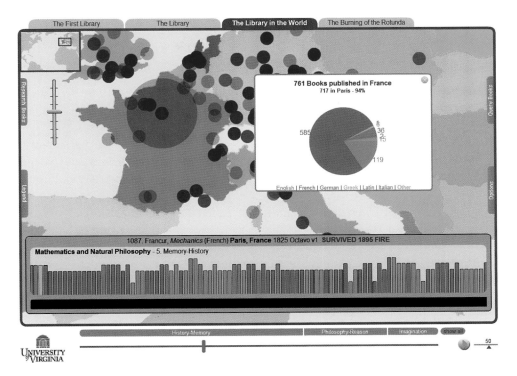

Figure 1.16
Screen shot from VisualEyes project.

ManyEyes[4] project allows users to share and visualize their own datasets using simple Web-based tools to create network diagrams, charts, tree-maps, word clouds, and geographic maps (figure 1.16). Other tools such as *Tableau*[5] and our own *VisualEyes*[6] allow for sophisticated data-driven interactive visualizations to be rapidly created by nonprogrammers.

The University of Virginia's Sciences, Humanities and Arts Network of Technological Initiatives (SHANTI) SHIVA project[7] provides access to a number of Web-based services from sites such as Google, Kaltura, Flickr, and MIT to provide data, charts, maps, videos, and images together in a simple-to-use interface where the elements can interact with one another (figure 1.17). The resulting visualizations can easily be linked to or embedded in Web pages or WordPress blogs.

4. www-958.ibm.com/software/data/cognos/manyeyes.

5. www.tableausoftware.com

6. www.viseyes.org

7. www.viseyes.org/shiva

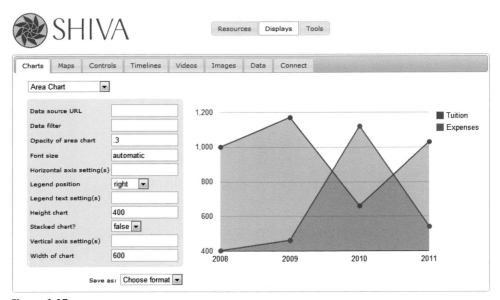

Figure 1.17
Screen shot from SHIVA project.

Networks

In his influential book, *Pattern Language*, the architect Christopher Alexander asserted that the design of the urban landscape was not the product of top-down, hierarchical mandates, but a more organic bottom-up process that reflected an "invisible mesh of interconnections" forming the basis of a network (Alexander, Ishikawa, & Silverstein, 1977; Lima, 2011). This concept resonated with the emergence of a topology of data and inspired new ways to visualize the Web-like connections between network data (figure 1.18). This new shape of information could potentially reveal much about the interconnections between people and ideas.

The need to find patterns within larger sets of data prompted a large amount of research into techniques for effectively visualizing huge datasets and showing the relations between individuals and groups of members. Going beyond traditional scatter plots, these network diagrams highlight the connections and try to illuminate relationships between members.

Visualization in the Academy

The emergence of the personal computer in the 1980s and the highly graphical user interfaces of Unix, Macintosh, and Windows (all inspired by Xerox PARC's work) offered an accessible platform for a new direction for information visualization that was truly interactive to a large audience. An interesting mix of academic disciplines

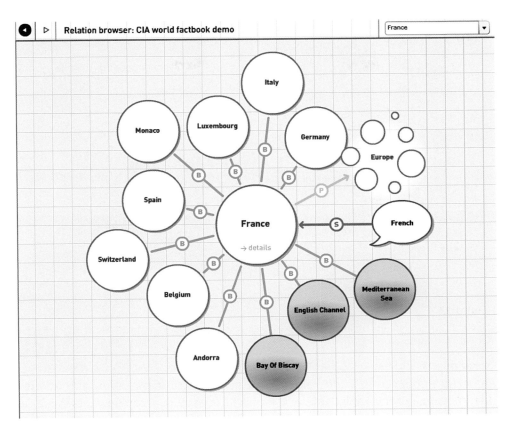

Figure 1.18
Radial network map using data from the CIA *Factbook* (image courtesy Mortitz Stephaner).

from statistics, psychology, computer science to design are crossing boundaries to create new tools, techniques, and projects. Universities around the world have established centers to keep pace with the rapidly unfolding new developments in processing speed and storage capacities.

The University of Maryland's Human Computer Interaction Laboratory,[8] founded in 1983 by Ben Shneiderman, has had an extended history of innovative projects that have consistently pushed the bounds afforded by the personal computer revolution and the increasing availability of large sets of raw data. Research at the Laboratory has spawned a number of influential academic and commercial projects for interactive data visualization, including a toolkit for graphically querying and analyzing datasets called *SpotFire* and a mapping method called *Treemaps* for displaying large link-node

8. http://hcil.cs.umd.edu

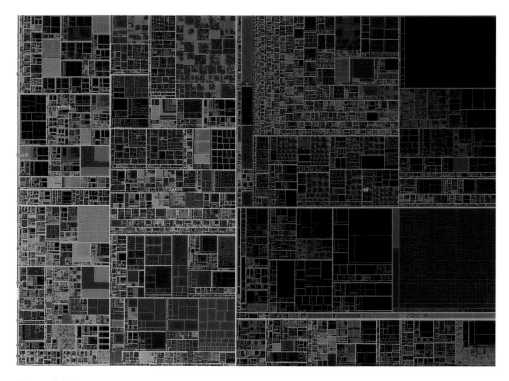

Figure 1.19
A tree map (used with permission of University of Maryland Human–Computer Interaction Lab).

diagrams (like the directory of a hard disk drive) (figure 1.19) that has been widely adopted for displaying data such as the makeup of the national budget.

The University of Virginia has had a long tradition of innovative research in the digital humanities beginning with the founding of the Institute for Advanced Technologies[9] (IATH) in 1993, which pairs humanities faculty members with technological support to create groundbreaking projects that cross multiple disciplines from the mapping of witchcraft accusations during the 1692 Salem witch trials (figure 1.20) to the *Temporal Modeling Project* that graphically plots time-related data in literature.

The historian Ed Ayers's *Valley of the Shadow* project (figure 1.21) began at IATH and eventually gave rise to a major digital history center, the Virginia Center for Digital History (VCDH). Most recently, Virginia launched a digital humanities center, the Sciences, Humanities and Arts Network of Technological Initiatives (SHANTI), which supports the *VisualEyes* interactive authoring tool developed by the author.

9. www.iath.virginia.edu

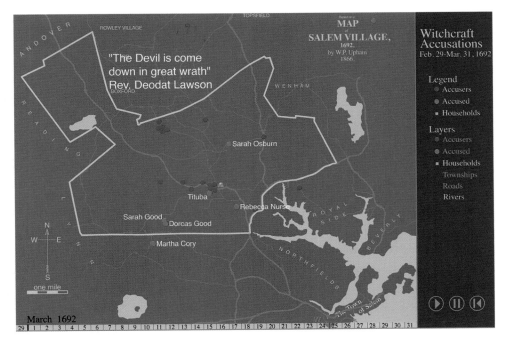

Figure 1.20
Map of Salem witchcraft accusations (image courtesy Ben Ray/IATH).

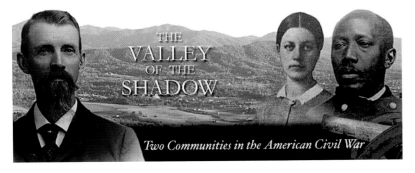

Figure 1.21
The University of Virginia's Valley of the Shadow project.

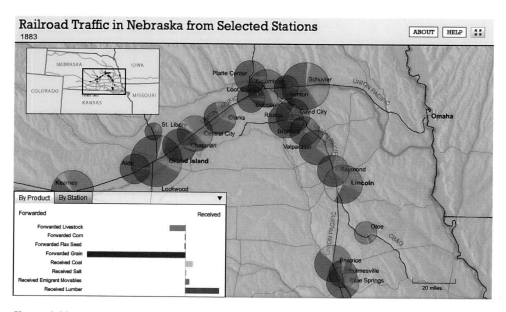

Figure 1.22
Screen shot of Stanford's Spatial History project.

Stanford's *Spatial History Project*[10] focuses on visualization and history with innovative software that interactively connects historic maps and data (figure 1.22). The project looks at history with a geography-based interface that connects temporal historic data to information such as the growing role of railways to a growing country.

The *Stanford Visualization Group*[11] develops innovative data visualizations and tools to represent data. They have created a number of interactive visualization toolkits including *flare, prefuse,* and most recently the popular Javascript-based *protovis* and new tools for structuring data like *Wrangler* (figure 1.23).

Information Graphics in the News: Visual Journalism

The popular newspaper *USA Today* pioneered the use of high-profile information graphics in the 1980s in its daily national newspaper. These visually bold charts and graphs, called *infographics*, provided simplified but visually engaging views of data-driven issues such as weather, politics, and demographics and ushered in the advent of a new field: *visual journalism*. The paper was often criticized for sacrificing visual aesthetics for simplicity and using the images as page fillers. To help maintain the

10. www.stanford.edu/group/spatialhistory
11. http://vis.stanford.edu

Figure 1.23
A streamgraph visualization by the Stanford Visualization Group.

integrity of visual journalism projects, an alliance of over 100 designers and journalists worldwide have endorsed a six-point checklist[12] from Harvard University's Neiman Foundation for Journalism (Cairo, 2011).

It is the venerable *Gray Lady*[13] that has led the field of innovative information graphics in both the print and online editions of the *New York Times*. Its online work has dramatically raised the bar of journalistic interactive visualization by consistently providing usable interactive visualizations that utilize state-of-the-art research in both theory and technique. A good collection of the web-based information visualizations can be found at this Web site.[14]

The *Times* has an eclectic staff of 25 editors, artists, 3D modelers, journalists, designers, statisticians, cartographers, and computer programmers who develop cutting-edge infographics to bring data to life for readers of the daily paper and Web site. Speaking at a design conference in Copenhagen, *Times* Graphics Editor Amanda Cox explained the goals[15]: *"We reveal patterns, provide context, and describe relationships . . . to create a sense of wonder."*

Models for Information Visualization

A model is an attempt to describe a complex real-world phenomenon or process by abstracting its important aspects into a more concise and generalizable description. Models are "a set of interrelated guesses about the world," and a successful model can reduce the number of factors involved to remove confusion but still be able describe the true situation (Lave & March, 1993).

12. www.niemanwatchdog.org/index.cfm?fuseaction=Showcase.view&&showcaseid=152
13. A nickname for the *New York Times* because it has more words than pictures.
14. www.smallmeans.com/new-york-times-infographics/
15. Video of Amanda Cox's talk at New Media Days 2010: http://newmediadays.dk/amanda-cox

Visualization models generally fall into three camps:

• *Theoretical* models that try to offer insight as to the fundamental issues at stake.
• *Descriptive* models that create taxonomies of the elements that characterize their fundamental attributes.
• *Prescriptive* models that provide a framework to scaffold scholars through the process of creating and evaluating information visualizations.

This book is organized around a prescriptive model developed by the author called ASSERT, but it was informed by a long tradition of models outlined in this section. The ASSERT model uses six steps to scaffold the design of inquiry-based interactive visualizations: *ask a question* that one might be interested in the answer to; *search for evidence* to support the exploration of that question; *structure that information* in a meaningful way to explore the question; *envision ways to answer the question* using that structured data; *represent that evidence* in a way that provides answers to the question and the opportunity to explore the data; and, finally, *tell a story* that uses the structured information that can offer insight into the question.

Theoretical Models

A frequent criticism about information visualization is that it lacks the theoretical bases of more mature disciplines. In response, visualization researchers have started identifying some of the theoretical foundations that support the effectiveness of information visualizations, particularly in education settings. Most research to date has focused on the visualization techniques (the strategy) rather than the more foundational scientific underpinnings (the why) behind efficacy, but a number of potential influences are beginning to surface.

Abstraction

Rudolf Arnheim (1969) described graphic abstraction as "a means by which a picture interprets what it portrays." The level of detail is presented prima facie, but its interpretation is in the eye of the beholder. Therefore, there are two dimensions to abstraction: the level of mimetic (realistic) detail in the image itself and the way in which it can be interpreted, ranging from ideas and symbols to specific instances of particular things. The image and interpretation scales are inversely correlated so that highly realistic and detailed imagery tends to produce specific and nongeneralizable associations, whereas more stylized graphics speak to broader ideas and situations.

Arnheim believed that the process of cognition could not be detached from the act of perception, that these two operations were inseparably linked into one simultaneous operation of understanding, and that the process of abstraction is a critical element involved in that comprehension. Abstraction is firmly rooted in specific perceptions and knowledge, and it involves the extraction of salient traits from one or more of these real situations.

These traits must be generative in nature, meaning they are not merely descriptive but can build an image that invokes understandings beyond the traits themselves, like Aristotle's principle of *entelechy*, in which the forms (abstractions) can generate new instances of particulars. It is this abstraction that enables the rich multidimensionality that interactive visualizations can offer beyond the single dimensional thread of the conventional written narrative.

Interactive visualizations are, at their heart, abstractions of the data and phenomena they seek to represent. The maps in figure 1.24 represent a continuum from a realistic, highly mimetic depiction, an aerial photograph of Manhattan from Google Earth, to a hand-drawn but still accurate 1865 topographic map from the David Rumsey Collection[16] and, finally, a highly stylized but informationally accurate map by Alexander Cheek[17] showing the neighborhoods of Manhattan.

The degree of that abstraction is an important design question and is dependent on the message to be communicated. The aerial and drawn maps convey a high sense

Figure 1.24
Degrees of abstraction in lower Manhattan (neighborhood map courtesy Alexander Cheek).

16. www.davidrumsey.com
17. www.alexandercheek.com

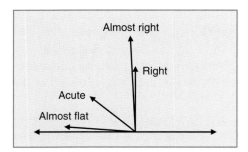

Figure 1.25
Mileposts along the continuum.

of accuracy and are useful for locating a point exactly, whereas the more stylized maps give an overall sense of where Manhattan neighborhoods are in relation to one another. A higher level of abstraction can help isolate and communicate an overarching or more generalized idea than a less abstract version might.

Continua

Although most measurements taken in the world are continuous in nature, our perceptions of them are not. We tend to reference known "mileposts" that divide the continuum into discrete parts. For example, an angle moves smoothly from 0° to 180°, but we often refer to the angles in phases, (i.e., flat, almost flat, acute, almost right angle, etc.) rather than their exact angle because they are more meaningfully, but inaccurately, abstracted this way (figure 1.25).

This idea is contrasted by the *sorites* or *heap paradox* posed by Eubulides,[18] a philosopher and contemporary of Aristotle. He showed his students a pile of sand and all could agree it was a heap of sand. Eubulides then asked if he removed one grain, was it still a heap? They still agreed it was. He then asked if he continued to remove grains until the pile was gone, could the students identify the step at which the sand ceased to be a heap? The "fuzziness" of this position shows how arbitrary the categorization process in continuous data can be (Kosko, 1993).

These abstractions alter how we make sense of the world and are important to keep in mind when we design visualizations of continuous phenomena. Scott McCloud (1994) wonderfully illustrates[19] this point by showing the degree to which people can generalize the actions of the figure being drawn on multiple continua: complex to simple, realistic to iconic, objective to subjective, and specific to universal. The simpler

18. Sometime incorrectly attributed to Zeno, who used it as the basis of his own paradox about size.
19. Image courtesy Scott McCloud, *"Understanding Comics: The Invisible Art."*

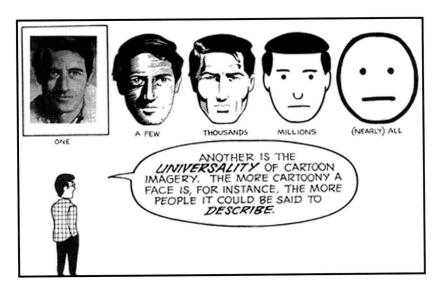

Figure 1.26
Continuum of representation detail.

(i.e., more abstract) the representation, the more the viewer can see the drawing as more broadly generalizable, and the more detailed the representation, the more likely the drawing will be viewed as an instance of a particular item or phenomenon (figure 1.26).

Cognitive Load Theory

Cognitive load theory (CLT) has emerged as one of the most important factors in understanding, learning, and overall attention. Research suggests that memory is comprised of two primary structures—*short term* and *long term*—both of which are controlled by a central executive. Long-term memory is where instruction goes once it is actually learned by the user; hence, the aim of all instruction is to alter long-term memory, but information must first pass through short-term memory (Sweller, 2005). Short-term memory is able to hold up to seven items (plus or minus two) and, equally important, is able to contrast, combine, or manipulate no more than two to four elements at a time. This is sometimes referred to as *working memory*. In addition, all the contents of working memory are lost within 20 seconds without rehearsal (Miller, 1956).

These limitations in short-term memory have profound effects on how people are able to understand concepts, see patterns in data, and extract relationships between elements. To overcome this issue, people have developed strategies that connect the limited short-term memory to the larger long-term memory by grouping disparate

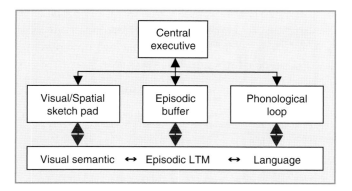

Figure 1.27
The cognitive load theory (adapted from Sweller, 2005).

items together into a group, called "chunking" (e.g., telephone area codes), and immediately connecting new data to already known information (e.g., linking to stories, schemas, and frames of reference).

CLT posits that there are three separate distinct stores of short-term memory: a *visual/spatial sketchpad,* which stores perception of two- and three-dimensional objects; a *phonological loop,* which stores audio and language-related (verbal) input; and an *episodic buffer,* which temporarily integrates the other two (figure 1.27). Certain kinds of information can be cross-encoded. For example, on-screen text is presented and processed visually, but it may be encoded verbally (Baddeley, 1992).

One of the primary goals of information visualization is to present information in a comprehensible manner. Designers of visualization must respect the limitations and make use of the affordances suggested by CLT about people's ability to accept information in order to reach that goal.

Multiple Representation/Multimedia
Research and theory on the use of multimedia in general suggest some benefits of using multiple representations of information to facilitate understanding. Because the auditory/verbal and visual channels by which information can be absorbed are relatively independent, the limited capacity of short-term memory might be increased by targeting information delivery simultaneously to both. The basic premise of multimedia learning is that people learn more deeply from words and pictures than from just words alone. But adding images and sound alone will not enhance learning—instructional messages should be designed for the way the mind works to take advantage of the potential by targeting the appropriate short-term memory component for that type of information.

Multimedia cognition literature suggests that using both auditory and visual channels will result in higher content retention than using any one channel alone when performed properly. Richard Mayer (2005) outlined the following principles that describe some of the characteristics involved in multiple-channel learning:

1. *Multimedia principle*   People learn better from words and pictures than from words alone.
2. *Split attention principle*   People learn better when words and pictures are physically and temporally integrated.
3. *Modality principle*   People learn better from graphics and narration than from graphics and text.
4. *Redundancy principle*   People learn better when the same information is represented in multiple formats.
5. *Segmenting, pretraining, and modality principles*   People learn better when information is broken into segments, when they know the names of the main concepts, and when words are spoken rather than written.
6. *Coherence, signaling, and spatial/temporal contiguity principles*   People learn better when extraneous material is excluded, when pictures and text are close to each other, and people learn better from graphics and narration.

These principles can help designers develop visualizations that build on the benefits of multiple representation and multimedia by adding a contextual modeling layer to *"provide a powerful inscription that promotes learning conversations, can be flexibly manipulated, and build on existing metaphors and representations"* (Gordin & Pea, 1995).

Distributed Cognition

Distributed cognition stands in opposition to the conventionally held notion that all thinking and understanding is performed within an individual's mind. The theory suggests that artifacts, such as paper, web pages, and tools serve as external scaffolds for internal cognition. In this view, "Google makes us smarter"[20] by providing an environment in which individual minds are supported and carried further by the vast information provided, so that thinking becomes a joint activity working with knowledge both "in the head" and "in the world."

The ability of the computer to rapidly provide closely linked multiple representations in various forms facilitates its role in enabling forms of distributed cognition. This has the result of enlisting the computer to further reduce the cognitive load requirements and increase the combined ability to understand complex information. The visualization and the interaction act as a bridge between internal and external

20. An allusion to Nicholas Carr's article "Is Google Making Us Stupid?" *Atlantic Magazine,* August 2008.

representation, with cognition as the emergent property of that interaction (Liu, Nersessian, & Stasko, 2008).

Mental Models

People construct mental models that abstract the facts about a specific situation so they can later be compared to new experiences and offer insight into the issues and relationships operating in both cases. A successful visualization should be able to guide the viewer to infer relationships, patterns, and alternative possibilities beyond the explicit goals of its designer, something that had not yet been considered in the design.

These mental models are not necessarily visual or logical in nature but provide an imagistic representation of the world in which visual characteristics are blended with conceptual and physical features extracted from perception (Pylyshyn, 2002). This abstraction makes mental models useful tools for problem solving, as they have been encoded with the temporal, spatial, and causal relationships of a concept, and they become a template for understanding (Rapp, 2005).

The ability of mental models to internalize and generalize conceptual understanding is the "holy grail" in education and allows people to transfer their internal representations about one situated experience to another. People integrate new experiences with information they already know, and that integration is mediated by mental models that frame previous experiences (Bransford, Brown, & Cocking, 2000).

Descriptive Models

Descriptive models were developed to simplify some facets of the complex world and organize them according to some factors that help describe that environment. These simplifications allow people to compare similar situations with one another. There are a number of attempts to create taxonomies or organizations of the elements that characterize their fundamental attributes and overarching qualities. Descriptive models are useful ways to categorize specific instances of the real world so they can be evaluated with other but comparable situations.

Bertin's Storing, Communicating, and Processing

The late French cartographer Jacques Bertin formalized a rich description of information visualization elements into a comprehensive theory encompassing perception, information analysis, and graphical theory. His *Semiology of Graphics* (Bertin, 1983) provided information visualization research with an empirical foundation of the rules of graphic communication. Bertin maintained that graphs have three primary functions—*storing, communicating,* and *processing* information—and offered guidelines for the effective marshaling of data through visual representations.

Shneiderman's Task by Data Type Taxonomy

Ben Shneiderman (1996) described a *Task by Data Type Taxonomy* in which the nature and structure of the underlying data dictate how the data should be visualized. He proposed seven basic ways to describe the structure of data relative to the way is could be visualized:

1. *One-dimensional* data types are nominal (named) lists of elements and are typified by documents and names.
2. *Two-dimensional* data types include maps, images, and other kinds of spatial displays that utilize the height and width factors to convey information.
3. *Three-dimensional* data types represent the real-world dimensionality of three space like molecular data.
4. *Multidimensional* data include an arbitrary mapping of multiple related factors, each with the same number of items represented, such as census information and weather factors.
5. *Temporal* data have some set of values arranged by the time dimension and are often rendered as timelines and line charts.
6. *Tree* data are hierarchical collections of items that have some relationship to one another, such as a family tree and computer disk directories.
7. *Network* data are similar to tree data, where the items have a distinct relationship to one another, but the structure is not strictly hierarchical and is typified by the graphs of social networking tools such as Facebook and Twitter.

The idea of a task taxonomy was expanded a decade later by his colleagues, who defined *low-level tasks* (sort, filter, cluster, etc.), *topology-based tasks* (node relations), *attribute-based tasks, browsing tasks, overview tasks,* and, finally, *high-level tasks* (Lee, Plaisant, Parr, Fekete, & Henry, 2007).

Stanford's Visualization Zoo

Stanford University researchers Jeffrey Heer and colleagues described a taxonomy of visualization display types based on the nature of the underlying data, much like Shneiderman's Task by Data–type taxonomy, with five basic categories:

1. *Time series* data are best represented by index charts, stacked-data graphs, small-multiple graphs, and horizon graphs.
2. *Statistical distributions* can take advantage of box and whisker, q-q, and stem-and-leaf and scatter plots.
3. *Maps* take advantage of spatial dimensions and include process maps, cartograms, and choropleth maps.
4. *Hierarchies* are best represented by node-link diagrams, tree graphs, and tree maps.
5. *Networks* show organization through force-directed graphs, arc diagrams, and matrix views.

These categories provide a useful way to organize style of visualizations based on the topology of the data that drive them while being cognizant of the issues of effective visual encoding into the human perceptual system (Heer, Bostock, & Ogievetsky, 2010).

Prescriptive Models

Prescriptive models seek to provide support in the creation, understanding, and evaluation of visualizations. These models provide an overarching vision of how the individual components can work together to achieve the visualization's goal while providing guidance as how to actually accomplish that goal. Prescriptive models are not procedures such as recipes, which are step by step and followed in sequence toward a goal, but provide generic guidance in the processes that can prove useful.

Shneiderman's Visual Information-Seeking Mantra

Interactive visualization pioneer Ben Shneiderman offered the "Visual Information-Seeking Mantra" for use as a starting point for designing interactive visualizations, particularly those with large amounts of data: *overview first, zoom and filter, then details on demand*. In his oft-cited paper first introducing the statement, he wrote the mantra 10 times in a row to underscore how valuable he and his colleagues had found it when developing some of the earliest examples of interactive visualization.

The overview step, much like an establishing shot in a feature film, provides an overall contextualization of the entire dataset and makes it possible to seek out overall patterns. The ability to *zoom* in on a subset of the data containing items of interest while *filtering out* extraneous features allows focus on a particular subject and is amplified by the ability to show additional *details on demand* (Shneiderman, 1996).

Van Ham and Perer's Search and Expand

Sometimes, the amount of data being explored is too large or too varied to make an overview of the data meaningful or even technically possible. The *search, show context, expand on demand* model stands in contrast to Shneiderman's *Visual Information-Seeking Mantra* by reducing the dataset *before* an overview is provided.

This is done by initiating the process with a search or some other user interaction method to create a more manageable and potentially meaningful subset of the dataset, called a *degree of interest*. This subset can be presented as an overview to provide context, and the user is then free to expand the context and/or further explore the subset in more detail depending on interests (van Ham & Perer, 2009).

Chi's Data State Reference

Xerox Parc researcher Ed Chi's *Data State Reference model* takes a data-centric view of the visualization process, beginning with the raw data. Those data pass through three stages in a linear pipeline: *analytical abstraction* (generating metadata: data about data), *visualization abstraction* (extraction of visualizable elements), and finally, the *view* (end product of mappings). Each stage is ushered to the next phase by *transformation operators*, which transform the *data*, the *visualization* of the data, and the *visual mapping* of the data. This model is useful by creating a taxonomy in which a wide variety of visualizations can be evaluated together (Chi, 2000).

Spence's Selection, Encoding, and Presentation

Citing Marcel Proust as the inspiration for his model, *"The real voyage of discovery consists not in seeking new landscapes but in having new eyes,"* Robert Spence (2001) outlined a progression, in which raw data pass through *selection, encoding,* and final through *presentation* on the way to the viewer, who then has the ability to manipulate those three steps to make meaning. This changes the locus of control from solely the visualization's designer to a more collaborative relationship among the data, the designer, and the viewer.

Fry's Acquire, Parse, Filter, Mine, Represent, and Interact

Ben Fry, developer of the popular Processing[21] visualization programming language, described a framework for visualization that starts with the collection of data with the goal of answering a question using that data. The procedure to answer the question follows a seven-step sequence:

1. *Acquiring* the data initiates the process, where raw data or information is obtained in a digital form and made available locally or through an Internet connection, such as US Census data.
2. *Parsing* is the process of structuring the raw data from its native format into something that can identify the constituent parts, such as tagging or structuring data elements into discrete database fields or spreadsheet columns.
3. *Filtering* the data removes portions of the structured dataset that are not of interest. This filtering-out process can be done across multiple dimensions. For example, we may only want the census income data for the married men in California from 1920 to 1950.
4. *Mining* the filtered data will be useful in finding patterns that emerge using statistical methods, such as correlation and regression. For example, we may want to compare incomes of men and women using the census data and see if that correlation changes over time.
5. *Representing* the data visually makes it possible to communicate the patterns found in the mining step by using tables, graphs, network diagrams, and a host of other visualization techniques.

21. www.processing.org

6. *Refining* that representation to make it more engaging by iteratively revisiting the earlier steps in the procedure in light of insights gleaned by later steps.

7. *Interacting* with the visualization adds options to manipulate the representation, allowing the user to change how and what data are being represented, making it easy for them to discover new relationships or better understand the ones being presented.

This model is a pragmatic sequence for converting raw data into an interactive visualization and has been evidenced in Fry's many excellent visualization projects. Even though it is not explicitly mentioned by name as a step, he believes that all visualizations should begin with a guiding question (Fry, 2004).

Roam's Back of the Napkin

Visual thinking consultant and author Dan Roam has developed a framework for solving business problems using drawn images that is a useful model for framing the visualization process as well. The *Back of the Napkin* model refers to simple drawings to describe ideas, often made on the back of a restaurant napkin. It looks at problems through an iterative loop of *looking, seeing, imagining.* and *showing*:

1. *Look*   The process of gathering and selecting information with an open attitude by *gathering* data relevant to the problem, *deploying* that information in a manner that supports observation and reflection, *establishing* the dimensions to explore the data by (i.e., who, what, when, etc.), and finally *classifying* the information to determine what parts are important to the problem at hand.

2. *See*   Processing the information relevant to the problem to refine its definition and scope into the six ways to see: *who/what, how much, where, when, how,* and *why.*

a. *Who* and *what* help define the objects of our inquiry by offering both names and descriptions of the items in our topic and their observable characteristics.

b. *How much* helps quantify those characteristics into numeric terms so the objects can be compared with one another and have statistical techniques applied to them.

c. *Where* helps situate the objects in the world to provide external context and with each other to help expose part-to-whole relationships between them.

d. *When* provides the critical temporal context that can help expose causal relationships both among the objects themselves and with the larger world they exist in.

e. *How* explores the cause-and-effect relationships and is more explanatory and deductive than Roam's first four proposed ways of seeing. *How* can be thought of as the sum of the "Four W's" (i.e., how = who/what + how much + where + when).

f. *Why* provides the entry portal to begin asking questions with the evidence suggested by the other five ways. *Why* asks us to synthesize the information collected and reflect on it in the larger context of our topic.

3. *Imagine*   Identifying patterns and components in the data identified and envisaging ways to convert them into graphical representation. This is done by rating them on a set of five continua, called SQVID (unfortunately pronounced *squid*):

a. *Simple or elaborated:*   The degree in which the data being represented requires a complex or simple solution. The ultimate goal is to make the complex understandable, not just simpler. The objective is to provide the proper amount of complexity that properly represents the problem without overwhelming the audience.

b. *Quality or quantity:*   The degree to which the problem is qualitative or quantitative or both. Some problems lend themselves to one or the other, but the richest descriptions of human endeavors will typically contain both methodologies.

c. *Vision or execution:*   The degree to which the problem is represented prescriptively or descriptively.

d. *Individual or compared:*   The degree to which individuals or groups will best represent the problem.

e. *Delta or absolute:*   The degree to which differences in the data are reflected as change in relation to themselves over time or with others, versus concentrating on the actual values of the underlying data.

4. *Show*   The process of choosing an appropriate technique of representing the data/problem, graphically rendering that technique, and presenting the results for others.

This model is not a formal model in the academic sense but, nonetheless, is a useful lens to look at visualization problems through and provides a systematic methodology for generating and evaluating projects (Roam, 2008).

Elements of User Experience

User-experience designer Jesse James Garrett (2003) has proposed *Elements of User Experience,* a model with a user-centered perspective for developing Web-based projects. The model has five "planes" ranging from the more abstract *Strategy* to the more concrete *Surface* (figure 1.28).

1. *Strategy*   Where user needs and objectives are defined. This is an explicit exploration of the specific goals to be achieved by the project from both the designer's and the user's perspective, hopefully with some measure of success. The users are carefully profiled, and a strategy is developed to satisfy them.

2. *Scope*   Where functional specification and content requirements are set. The strategy from the first plane is translated into specific features and functionality to meet the user's expectations. Decisions are made on what to include and what to ignore in terms of functionality and content.

3. *Structure*   Where the interaction design and information architecture are accomplished. The disparate pieces of content and functionality need to be merged into a

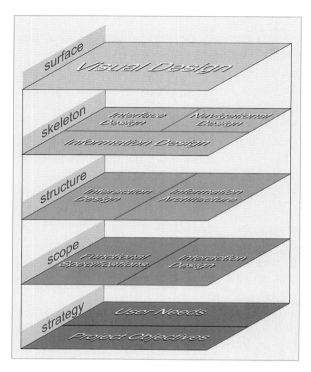

Figure 1.28
The elements of user experience (adapted from Garrett, 2003).

cohesive design. Appropriate metaphors and conceptual models are developed, and the information is organized in an understandable manner.

4. *Skeleton*   Where the interface, navigation, and information design are actually performed. These three design elements must work closely with one another, interface design answering "how" issues, navigation design informing "where" issues, and information design presiding over the "what" communication problems.

5. *Surface*   Where the visual design is performed. This is the culmination of the previous planes where content, functionality, interaction, and aesthetics meet the end user.

Garrett's model has been widely adopted in the graphics design and interactive experience communities and is equally applicable to data-driven inquiry-based interactive visualizations.

The ASSERT Model
We have developed the ASSERT model (figure 1.29) to support the creation of visualizations that are accessible, insightful, educational, compelling, and that build on the

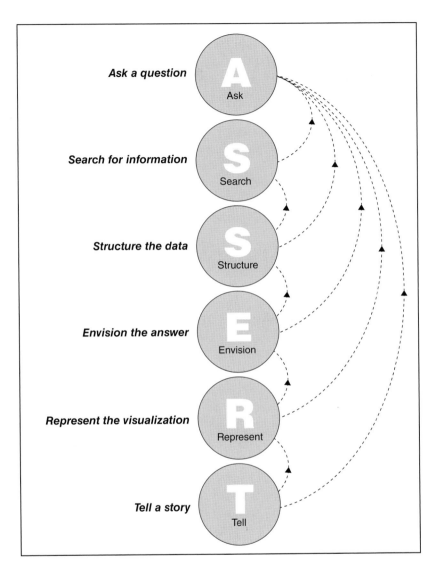

Figure 1.29
The ASSERT model.

traditions of historical and social science research. It has evolved over a number of years in the context of developing historical visualizations at the Virginia Center for Digital History (VCDH) for museums, historians, and civic organizations and teaching a series of undergraduate history seminars where creating historical visualizations were the final deliverable of the course. Finally, the model has been successfully used in a cross-disciplinary cohort of faculty and graduate students from history, architecture, education, religious studies, art history, archeology, and anthropology.

This begs the question: With all of the models discussed above, why introduce yet another? ASSERT synthesizes important ideas introduced by these models and extends their scope. The other models typically addressed subsets of critical issues but did not deal with the complete developmental life cycle of interactive visualizations. Unlike its predecessors, ASSERT addresses the full scope development in a process-driven manner.

In the course of creating interactive visualization in the humanities, it became clear that a more holistic perspective would be useful. One that embraced the long-held inquiry-driven research traditions common to the sciences, humanities, and the social sciences; one that could scaffold the process from idea to execution in an iterative fashion; one that was able to freely cross between theoretical and practical bounds in its execution; and finally, a model that included the narrative element so crucial to create a compelling communicative experience.

The model has six components: *Ask* a question, *Search* for evidence to answer that question, *Structure* that information to answer the question, *Envision* ways to answer the question using available data, *Represent* the data in a meaningful visualization to answer the question, and, finally, *Tell* a meaningful story using that data to answer the question. It provides a scaffold for scholars and educators to pose meaningful questions through visual representation and interaction.

1. *Ask a question.*   Good visualizations are driven by good questions. The goal is to ask specific questions about the topic that can be answered by accessible and reliable data. In addition, questions should be able to address why you or anyone would care if you answered them and who the intended audience is for the project.

2. *Search for evidence to answer the question.*   For each of the questions that are being explored it is important to find good sources of information that could answer that question and be aware of each source's strengths and limitations: Is it accessible? Is it illuminating?

3. *Structure that information to answer the question.*   Information in its raw form needs to be abstracted and structured in order to tell a compelling story. The data may need to be transformed, pared down, sampled, or have statistical methods applied in order to be useful as a data source in a visualization.

4. *Envision ways to answer the question using the data.*   This is an exploratory process to develop ways of answering the questions identified using the data found and struc-

tured in the earlier design phases. It involves looking at the relationships in the data to the research question and within parts of the data.

5. *Represent the data in a compelling visualization.* The visible product of the entire visualization process is its *representation* and is where users will interact with the information presented. Creating that representation is a careful blend of *science, art,* and *display technology.*

6. *Tell a meaningful story using the evidence to answer the question.* Storytelling is one of the primary ways we make sense of the world. A good visualization answers a question using primary source evidence to tell a story. That story should be meaningful and able to address the significance criteria (the "so what?").

The model offers a prescriptive framework to apply traditional research methodology used in many disciplines for developing interactive visualizations. The steps and sequence need not be slavishly followed. As in all creative endeavors, there are multiple paths to a successful project, but the framework provides an overarching scaffold for the process. Most steps benefit from iteration to previous steps as more information is uncovered and other options are further explored.

ASSERT is a holistic model in which all of the constituent parts relate to the whole and, in a perfect world, would be considered together. The reality of our humanity forces us to work serially on what is in truth a parallel problem. The model helps scaffold this process. As designers work longer with visualization projects, the individual steps will begin to join, ones that work well in particular situations will emerge, and new strategies will be adopted as needed. The ASSERT model provides a useful starting point to structure the process.

Summary

This chapter explores some definitions of what interactive visualization is, such as Stewart Card's *"The use of computer-supported, interactive, visual representations of abstract data to amplify cognition,"* and why it is a valuable addition to just analyzing numeric data, as illustrated by *Anscombe's Quartet.* There are several genres of visualizations created to serve different groups and purposes from scientists to journalists.

People have been using graphics to visualize information from the time of Leonardo da Vinci and before. William Playfair introduced the world to pie and bar charts in the mid-eighteenth century, John Snow's cholera map effectively used mapping to persuade people toward the germ theory in the mid-nineteenth century, and Harry Beck's iconic subway map helped the use of maps as geometric as opposed to only geographic displays.

The computer has played a big role in the evolution of more sophisticated graphics generated by sources ranging from the video artist John Whitney to the spacecraft animations of the Jet Propulsion Laboratory's Jim Blinn and highly realistic

3D simulations by Evans and Sutherland. The Internet has brought a wealth of freely available data, resources, and tools are easy for anyone to use for sophisticated explorations, analyses, and compelling, graphically rich data-driven presentations.

Universities have been on the forefront in information visualization research beginning with the University of Maryland's Human Computer Interaction Laboratory work in interaction usability and display of large data sets, the University of Virginia's Institute for the Advancement of the Humanities work in pioneering the digital humanities, and Stanford University's work in display techniques and accessible visualization tools. The efforts of *USA Today* and the *New York Times* have advanced the use of visual journalism and the development of a new genre of information display, the infographic.

A number of theoretical models provide a good foundation for interactive visualizations. Theoretical models such as the issues of abstraction, the cognitive load theory, and multimedia theory offer useful guidance. There are many descriptive and prescriptive models that inform the prescriptive ASSERT model developed by the author.

The ASSERT model should be thought of more as a web or a circle with links than a straight line and assumes that iteration between phases will be common. Starting at any stage can be useful, but ultimately, a clear question to ask (and hopefully answer) is essential.

The following chapters explore creating interactive visualizations through the lens of the ASSERT model using the six steps that define it and exploring the various issues involved in the design and production of interactive visualizations.

II An Assertive Approach to Visualization

This section is organized around the ASSERT model, which uses six phases to guide the design of inquiry-based, data-driven interactive visualizations: Ask a question; Search for information; Structure that information; Envision the answer; Represent the visualization; and, finally, Tell a story.

2   Ask a Question

A prudent question is one-half of wisdom.
—Francis Bacon

Good visualizations are driven by good questions. Crafting solid questions is traditionally the first step in embarking on any research project, regardless of its delivery medium. The goal is to ask specific questions about the topic that can be answered by accessible and reliable data. In addition, questions should be able to address why you or anyone would care if you answered them, and just who is the intended audience for the project.

This chapter introduces the choosing of appropriate paths of inquiry for interactive visualization by exploring the following topics:

- Questions for visualizations
- Defining the audience needs and capabilities
- Narrowing the scope
- Turning topics into questions
- Brainstorming techniques
- Mind/concept mapping
- Generating questions from questions
- When questions come second

At this stage in the design process there are no bad questions, but not all questions can or should ultimately be explored. Discarded questions often lead to other questions or provide a foundation for others to expand on. Leading design firm IDEO founder Tom Kelley (2001) calls these opportunities to "build and jump." Questions can *build* an incremental foundation for developing new ideas or provide a way to use previous questions as contrasting ideas to *jump* to alternative queries.

The questions should serve as a "mantra" to guide the subsequent phases and be used as a test for inclusion or rejection of a source or method. If the item does not help answer the question, it most likely will dilute any potential explanatory power of items that do. These discarded sources or methods may lead to new questions to be asked in an iterative fashion.

Identification of the target audience for the project will have a profound effect on all aspects of the research question. Different topics and scopes will appeal to different constituencies. K–12 students' interests, attention spans, and degrees of prior knowledge about the topic will vary and may be more didactic, in contrast to a scholarly audience, who want to create new knowledge (Presnell, 2007).

Defining the Audience

An interactive visualization is a conversation between its designer and its user using data as the language. In many ways the process is similar to a college seminar, with specific content provided in support of ideas searching for understanding. The presentation can be didactic, where the instructor/designer provides the material for consumption and adoption, or more exploratory, where the information is presented in a manner that encourages self-discovery. No matter which side of the continuum that the visualization aims for, it is important to have a good understanding of who its audience will be, what they know already, what they want to know, and how they forge understanding.

Audience Needs and Capabilities

The needs and capabilities of a middle-school social studies student and a postgraduate history scholar vary enormously. Although it is certainly possible to create a visualization to serve both audiences, its creation requires a conscious and deliberate understanding of a number of factors: the audiences' background knowledge and need for detail, what they want to know, their degree of computer navigational skills, their degree of statistical knowledge, the availability of technology, their values and beliefs, their need for sensitivity to content, and various accessibility issues.

Their Background Knowledge

The background knowledge of your audience is probably the single most important element in producing a successful visualization. Assuming that users will possess requisite information will eliminate or frustrate those who do not. Providing too much detail will discourage an audience that already knows that information and make it difficult to present more nuanced aspects of the information.

One of the tenets of exemplary instructional practice of any form is to evaluate what people know with respect to the basic knowledge about a topic and meet them where they are. This is, of course, easier to do in a small seminar environment than it is in a 300-student lecture hall, but the interactive networked nature of web-based technology makes the goal more attainable in information visualizations.

Visualizations are adaptive, however, and can rapidly provide wide overviews in terms of time, space, and information to help those with a limited background knowledge navigate in the same information space as experts provided that the project offers good navigational tools to easily focus in or broaden out the view. Visualizations should also take advantage of the wealth of contextual information available on the Internet, from Wikipedia to scholarly articles, all freely available with a simple mouse click.

The Information They Want to Know

Not all audiences are interested in the same quantity or level of detail as others. To some degree this disparity can be mitigated through the various representational techniques used to render interactive visualizations, but those choices need to be made consciously. A visualization targeted to people searching for their own genealogical backgrounds would need more detail on the individual level than an epidemiological visualization on the spread of cholera in the eighteenth century, where aggregated group data are more likely to be useful in providing insight.

Visualizations targeted for K–12 educational purposes need to be aware that, because of the dominance of standardized testing in the wake of the "No Child Left Behind" legislation, schools are increasingly covering only the "greatest hits" versions of many topics. The result is that teachers may be reluctant to take advantage of a visualization that explores the same subject but uses less iconic people and events.

Their Content Sensitivity

The language and beliefs of previous eras often do not match the sensibilities of the times we live in. Designers of visualizations need to be sensitive to issues such as race, gender, and religious beliefs to encourage effective communication, particularly in educational contexts.

This issue was highlighted recently when a version of Mark Twain's classic *Huckleberry Finn*[1] was published with all 219 references to the "n-word" replaced by the word "slave" because of many teachers' reticence in assigning this classic piece of literature for fear of offending students. There has been much debate on both sides, with purists saying the "cleansing" degrades the work and other educators praising it because it allows them to more confidently assign the book in the classroom.

Their Availability of Technology

The availability of Internet bandwidth varies greatly across the country and the world. While high-speed access is generally available in large cities and universities, rural and home access are often much slower, providing an important decision point for

---

1. *Adventures of Tom Sawyer and Huckleberry Finn* (The NewSouth Edition, Alan Gribben, ed.).

Internet-based visualization designers. Should the visualization depend on the need for high bandwidth and limit the potential audience, or should performance be sacrificed to meet the lowest common denominator, making it more accessible? Again, technology can mediate this by providing both high- and low-bandwidth versions of the visualization for the user to choose from, albeit at higher development costs for the designer.

Some computing environments, such as libraries and schools, have content restrictions that block certain Web sites and types of media. It is common to have Web sites such as photo-sharing sites and .mp3 audio files blocked from access, so relying on some of these resources can prove problematic. These "locked-down" computers often place other restrictions, such as not permitting users to download any plug-ins that might be needed, and such restrictions present the visualization designer with another design dilemma: whether to gain the functionality of a plug-in that might provide illuminating interactive 3D views or an alternative display such as a noninteractive movie, or whether to forgo the experience altogether to encourage access.

Additionally, many of the leading interactive visualizations have been developed in Adobe's popular *Flash* format. The introduction of Apple's iPad and its current inability to run *Flash*-based movies and applications have presented a new problem for designers, who want to operate on this new exciting delivery platform.

Personifying the Audience

Once a determination of the baseline audience has been made for a visualization, it can be useful to better understand and even personify its members to help better connect to their capabilities and needs. There is a long tradition in the graphic and industrial design communities of creating fictional users, called *personas,* that characterize and personalize an individual in the targeted audience. Designers have found them invaluable in focusing their attention away from their own needs to those who will use their products.

Designer and author Nancy Duarte, who worked with former vice president Al Gore to design the powerful and persuasive presentation used in the movie *An Inconvenient Truth*, offers the following seven questions to designers of presentations that can help make their presentations come alive by developing hypothetical *personas* that describe the audience's core characteristics (Duarte, 2008):

1. *What are they like?*   Personifying the audience with names, ages, desires, fears, and educational and income levels can help make the process of understanding what kinds of visualization are likely to be effective to them.

2. *Why are they paying attention?*   Try to ascertain why the audience is most likely to be looking at the finished visualization. Does it solve a problem, entertain, or provide understanding of an issue, and why?

3. *What keeps them up at night?*   What does the audience care about, have strong beliefs about, or have any deficiencies in their understanding of that needs to be addressed?

4. *How can you solve their problem?*   See if any understandings provided by the visualization provide insight into any audience issues.

5. *What do you want them to do?*   This has more to do with your goals for the audience but it is useful to define what changes in understanding you want to achieve in the context of this particular audience.

6. *How might they resist?*   There may be resistance to overturning currently held knowledge and beliefs. Being cognizant of those issues will alert you to places where more convincing and/or detailed data need to be presented.

7. *What is the best way to reach them?*   Think about strategies that acknowledge the insight gleaned from the first six points and present data in a format that will serve audience needs.

Narrowing the Question's Scope

It is critical is to narrow the scope of the topic so that a meaningful (and presumably answerable) question can be found. It is not that big scopes are necessarily meaningless, but often enlightening individual differences can be masked by the tyranny of the average. In addition, the practical reality of dealing with huge scopes can make the research process painfully time consuming and expensive.

A topic is probably too broad if it can be stated in four or five words, and Booth, Colomb, and Williams (2003) recommend adding nouns (i.e., the contribution) derived from verbs expressing action (i.e., to conflict, to describe, to develop) to the topic, so the topic "The history of the Civil War" becomes "The contribution of the economic value of slavery to the Civil War."

The narrowing can be done on one or more dimensions, such as time, location, or other attributes that might constrict the topic into a manageable size. By restricting the topic to a specific time period (i.e., 1850–1855), a specific location (i.e., South Carolina), a specific population (i.e., enslaved males), or any other factor or combination of them, it may be possible to develop nuanced questions that might not have been otherwise apparent.

It is often useful to deconstruct the topic into its constituent parts and examine their relationship to one another (people, location, politics, economy, environment, etc.) and see if any interesting questions arise from their interaction. For example, *"Did the ratio of men and women in the enslaved population in South Carolina have any effect on the 1850 economy?"*

Looking at the history of the topic can offer insight into some of the underlying fundamental questions that can be explored. Examining the changes over time of one or more aspects in the topic can offer questions as to why something changed or stayed the same (Booth et al., 2003).

Of course, it is possible to focus a question too finely, such that it can never be answered because there is not enough information available to support it, it degenerates into a simple yes/no outcome, or the result has no real meaning that people might care about. As Albert Einstein famously said, *"things should be as simple as possible, but not simpler.*

Turning Topics into Questions

Once a general topic of interest has been identified, it can be difficult to extract specific questions that are suitable for visualization. The following techniques can be useful tools to distill focused questions out of general topics.

Strategies for Generating Questions

In general, questions that offer more complex answers than a simple "yes" or "no" tend to be more interesting pursuits. Rather than "Was slavery the cause of the Civil War?" pose a more probing question such as "What degree of economic advantage did slavery offer the South to maintain it?" Questions that draw on known data have the best chance of being meaningfully answered.

Questions can center on how a particular theme fits in with the broader topic area, its history, similarities, and differences. Can the topic be explored by comparing multiple perspectives on it?

There are a number of techniques for methodically generating and assessing the quality of research questions, and these include:

- The three-part query
- The journalist's five Ws (and an H)
- K-W-L

These strategies can help overcome the inertia in starting a new project by providing a structure with which to explore the topic in a more systematic manner. These techniques can also be helpful in overcoming personal biases in exploring more options than initially came to mind. All strategies require a thorough analysis of the overall topic, which will help concentrate on information that is germane and ignore information that is irrelevant.

The Three-Part Query

A useful technique for constructing a research question is the *three-part query* approach for identifying a *focused topic*, the *questions* to ask about information needed to explore, and the *reason to care* about exploring it:

- *Topic* It is important to define the scope of the inquiry to help narrow the question toward something answerable. This narrowing can be done by quantity or quality: in limiting the topic by the number of potential subject areas with subsampling a larger group by (i.e., geography or time) or along some qualitative dimension (i.e., age, gender).
- *Five Ws (and one H)* The journalist's maxim of *"Who, what, when, where, why, and how"* is a useful construct to formulate a question about the topic. These modifiers help further focus the question along what specifically the visualization will explore within the defined topic.
- *Significance* What is the significance of answering the question? If the visualization is successful at answering a specific question about a particular topic, what is the value in its answer?

These three components should be able to be combined into a simple sentence that guides the visualization process as its "mantra" somewhat like this:

We are looking at [*topic*] because we want to find out [*who/where/when/why/ what/how*] in order for my audience to understand [*significance*].

For example:

We are looking at the *University of Virginia 1828 library* to find out *where the books were published* in order for my audience to *see the geographic spread of eighteenth century scholarship*. (Booth et al., 2003)

K-W-L
Another useful strategy for generating research questions is the *K-W-L* method, which is often used in secondary education.

- K asks what we already *know* about the topic.
- W is what we *want* to learn about the topic.
- L holds what we have *learned*.

These sections are typically laid out in a three-column chart on paper or on a whiteboard as shown in figure 2.1 (Ogle, 1986).

The process begins by brainstorming about what is known about the research topic in the K column, what might be interesting or illuminating that is not yet known about the topic in the W columns, paying particular attention to questions about items identified in the K column. The L column is less useful in the context of developing research questions for visualization than it is for students, but it can be used in an iterative fashion to become more items for the K column to generate more questions.

One variation to using the K-W-L is to replace the "we" with the target audience for the end visualization and put what the audience are likely to know about the topic

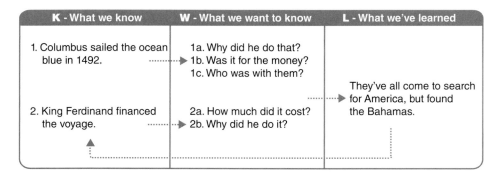

Figure 2.1
The K-W-L model.

in the K column, questions they might have about their preexisting knowledge in the W column. This approach can help focus the research questions toward the intended consumers and flush any issues with tacit knowledge only the designer might have.

Creative Problem-Solving Techniques

A number of frameworks are useful in generating ideas. One of the better known is *creative problem solving* (CPS). The goal of CPS is to generate a large quantity of varied and unusual ideas (called *options*) using a methodology that encourages quantity over quality and then systematically evaluates the options by focusing on them using an organized system of tools to appraise them for appropriateness to the problem and as a source to generate other options.

The CPS framework begins by identifying the broad goal in order to understand the problem to be solved. This is done by exploring the available data and framing the problem in similar terms to the three-part K-W-L query described earlier. Once the problem has been defined, options are generated using the tools listed below. It is important to defer judgment of the ideas at this phase and strive for quantity over quality and to capture all options for consideration.

Options in combination may be more powerful than any one option alone, so it is useful to try to connect ideas together to see if novel ideas emerge. CPS suggests[2] the following tools as helpful in generating ideas:

• *Brainstorming* Using the free association of ideas with no judgments attached to them. Whiteboards and Post-It® notes can be useful here. See the following section for more on the brainstorming process.

2. http://www.creativelearning.com/creative-problem-solving/about-cps.html

• *Force-fitting*   This involves using seemingly unrelated words and concepts about the problem to elicit new ideas or connections between existing ones.
• *Attribute listing*   Listing the core features may provide new ideas or insights about existing ones.
• *SCAMPER*   This is an acronym consisting of: *substituting* ideas and alternatives, *combining* options, *adapting* options in a new way, *magnifying* or *minifying* options, *putting* options to some other use, *eliminating* confusing options, and *reversing* or *rearranging* options.

After a sufficient number of ideas have been generated, they are then deliberately and explicitly evaluated with a positive (affirmative) perspective. Ideas are appraised for their novelty and appropriateness to the problem being solved (Treffinger, Isaksen, & Stead-Dorval, 2006).

Brainstorming

Brainstorming is a technique for generating a large quantity of ideas from a small group of people (figure 2.2). It was originally developed by a Madison Avenue advertising executive, Alex Osborn, in the late 1950s. The technique has been overwhelmingly

Figure 2.2
A brainstorming session at University of Virginia.

Figure 2.3
Ideas generated from brainstorming.

adopted by business and the design community over the last 20 years, in spite of some empirical evidence that it may not be as effective as individual thought (Furnham, 2000). That said, it remains a powerful technique to employ and is widely used by graphic and industrial designers the world over.

The basic goal of a brainstorming session is to provide an environment for a group of people (usually 4–8) to meet in a comfortable setting to come up with as many ideas as possible. The ideas should be as freewheeling as possible and not criticized, dismissed, or ridiculed. Quantity and variety are encouraged over a smaller number of practical ideas. All ideas are recorded for later discussion (figure 2.3), and participants are encouraged to build new ideas based on earlier ideas. What follows are some guidelines for conducting a successful brainstorming session:

1. Group size should be limited to four to eight people.
2. There should not be too much structure.
3. It should be a fun experience.
4. There should be no criticism or ridicule of ideas.
5. Quantity and variety trump quality and parsimony.
6. Ideas can be built on previous ideas.
7. All ideas should be recorded, even seemingly silly ones.

The industrial design firm IDEO has raised the process of brainstorming to a fine art in the industrial design world. The basic steps of the process are the same as those outlined above, but IDEO's founder Tom Kelly (2001) adds these "seven secrets to better brainstorming":

1. *Sharpen the focus*   Begin with a well-honed statement of the problem and use that as a way to keep people focused on the topic. Care should be taken not to focus so tightly that there is no room for discovery but not so loosely that the group is trying to solve world peace.

2. *Playful rules*   Discourage critiques and debates of ideas. IDEO puts signs on the walls saying "Go for quantity," "Encourage wild ideas," and "Be visual." The process should be fun.

3. *Number the ideas*   Give each idea a number, so people can refer to them quickly and the ever increasing count can serve as a target or motivating factor. Kelly considers 100 ideas an hour to be a productive fluid brainstorming session.

4. *Build and jump*   Ideas can and should *build* an incremental foundation for developing new ideas or a way to use previous ones as contrasting ideas to *jump* to alternatives. This allows for playful repartee between participants and increases the energy in the room.

5. *The space remembers*   Use Post-It® notes, papers taped to the walls, whiteboards, and other ways to envelop the space with the generated ideas. People's spatial memory will help recapture the spirit of the discussion in later discussions.

6. *Stretch your mental muscles*   It is often useful to do some warm-up exercises when the group has not worked together before. Fast-paced word-association games can help unhook participants from their outside distractions and help them "be here now."

7. *Get physical*   The act of drawing, creating models, and even pantomiming actions can bring energy into the room and spark new ideas.

Brainstorming in Larger Groups

Brainstorming works best when the group is small, but the *Charette procedure*[3] can be used to manage brainstorming in larger groups such as classrooms. The larger group is divided into any number of smaller groups containing five to seven people. Each group is instructed to brainstorm on a different variation of the topic for 10 minutes and write its ideas on large pieces of paper.

After 10 minutes, each group passes its ideas on paper to another group (figure 2.4), and its members add any further ideas to the paper. This process is repeated until every group has seen every other group's ideas and commented on them. The entire group is then reconvened, and the various ideas are discussed and refined.

Mind or Concept Mapping

Mind or concept mapping is a technique used to graphically show a collection of core ideas and their interrelations with one another (figure 2.5). A central theme is often shown with subordinate ideas connected by lines, offering insight into their relationships with one another.

3. www.extension.iastate.edu/communities/tools/decisions/charette.html.

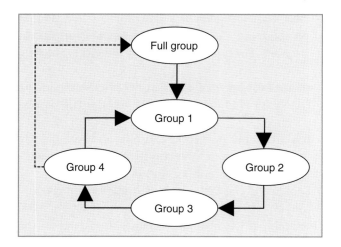

Figure 2.4
The Charette procedure for brainstorming in larger groups.

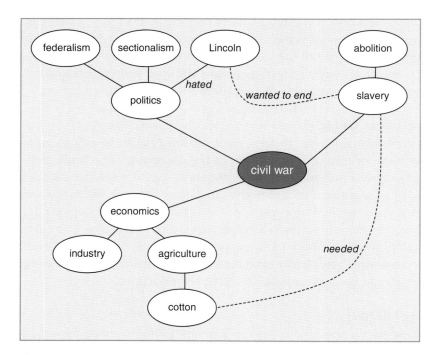

Figure 2.5
A concept map.

The process typically begins with placing an idea, called a *node*, in the middle of the page and using it to suggest ideas that are connected to it in some way. These ideas are drawn close to the original node, and lines are drawn between the two. The line can have a caption written alongside it to explain the type of relationship between the two nodes, such as "is a part of," "is related to," the four Ws+H (who, what, when, where, how) or other explanations to their connectedness. These newly added notes should provide inspiration to find other ideas that connect with it, until a rich map of the topic emerges, with an implicit structure that can reveal much about the topic and serve as a powerful catalyst for generating questions about the topic.

Mind/concept maps can be drawn by hand using a pencil and paper, but a number of excellent computer applications are available that automate the process and make it easy to rearrange nodes to accommodate the ever-emerging structure. Any number of commercial applications, such as *Inspiration*, are available, as well as a host of free applications available on the Web.[4]

Creating Concept Maps

John Kolko (2011) offers some guidelines for creating successful concept maps in the context of design synthesis: Start by creating a series of words that are important to the problem and that will form its core taxonomy or organization. The words should be nouns and verbs of the systems, actions, processes, people, organizations, and objects related to the problem space.

1. Write them on 3×5 cards, one card per concept.
2. Create a sense of structure to the cards by ordering them by level of importance (figure 2.6). Cards deemed to be a subset of another card should be indented and placed below.
3. Use this structure to begin to create the concept map, by moving the most important card to the center and group the next important cards below it.
4. Draw circles on a piece of paper to reflect the cards and draw connecting lines to show their new structure (figure 2.7). Label the lines by the kind of relationship set circles have to one other.

Generating Questions from Questions

The best source of new questions about the topic may come from questions already asked. This can be accomplished by drilling down deeper into the question, examining the question from multiple perspectives (i.e., northerners, southerners, slaves, and slave-holders), and asking the question from an opposite point of view.

4. See: http://en.wikipedia.org/wiki/List_of_mind_mapping_software.

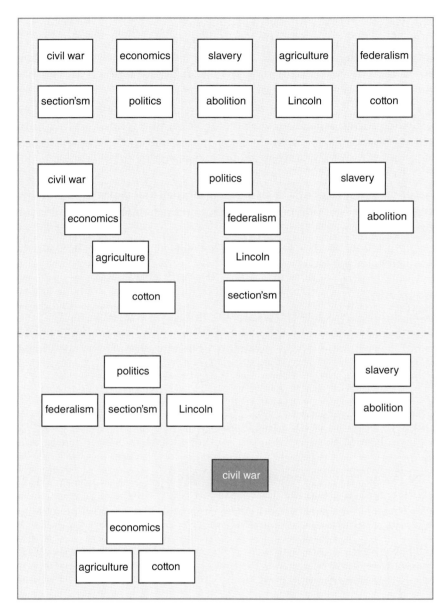

Figure 2.6
Creating a concept map (adapted from Kolko, 2011).

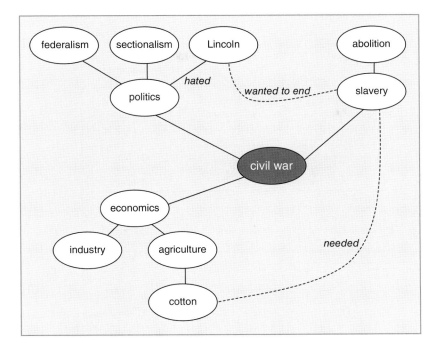

Figure 2.7
The finished concept map.

The iterative nature of questions generating questions is nicely illustrated in this drawing adapted from William Cronon's University of Wisconsin students Po-Yi Hung and Abigail Popp, who outlined a simple sequence (figure 2.8) to follow:

1. Look at an item of interest.
2. Ask one or more questions about that interest.
3. Pick a plan of action to answer those questions.
4. Using the results of that action, develop a new item of interest.

This new item of interest causes the whole process to repeat until enough meaningful questions have been raised.

When Questions Come Second

Not all visualization projects are initially driven by questions. In some situations the project begins with a unique set of data that is so potentially rich that the process begins by exploring the data first to find questions to further explore. Some of these datasets will require substantial structuring before any underpinning phenomenon is understood.

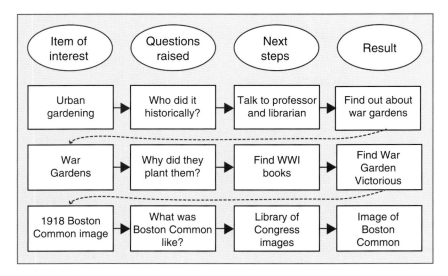

Figure 2.8
Generating questions from questions (adapted from Hung & Pop, 2008).

It is important to return to the formation of questions that will guide the exploration structuring and ultimately envision a representation of those data such that
meaningful insight can be gained. The questions can be very general at first and later
be refined as the data are explored.

For example, the political scientist Don Debats discovered mid-nineteenth century
voting records from the cities of Alexandria, VA and Newport, KY that identified who
the voter was and who he voted for. These data were unique because most voting
decisions cannot be uniquely connected to the people who cast them, offering an
opportunity to connect a wide array of information, such as tax records, census data,
geolocation, slave ownership records, and church information to their political cast-
ings. The relatively small size of these cities provided enough individuals to see meaningful trends without overwhelming the researchers. Debats used these data to develop
questions about what factors might have influenced these voting patterns.

Summary

This chapter looks at the importance of developing good questions to drive the design
of interactive visualizations. These questions can serve as a "mantra" to guide the
subsequent phases, be used as a test for inclusion or rejection of a source or methods,
and provide overarching guidance for the project.

It is critical to be aware of the *audience* for whom the visualization is intended. Middle-school students have vastly different backgrounds, content sensitivities, infrastructures, needs, and abilities than seasoned professionals, so it is important to understand the intended audience and target the questions and, ultimately, the visualization to meet the intended audience's needs.

Questions and topics can get too broad and be difficult or even impossible to answer in a meaningful manner. *Narrowing the scope* covered by one or more factors, such as the time period, geographic location, or gender can be a useful way to develop an answerable research question.

Many techniques can offer question seekers freedom from the tyranny of the blank page. These techniques, such as the *three-part query*, the journalist's chestnut, *the five Ws (and an H), K-W-L,* and *creative problem-solving* techniques, can all be helpful tools to generate usable questions. *Brainstorming,* a time-tested technique from the golden age of advertising, has been widely adopted in many design and business environments as a way to generate as many ideas as possible. Variations, such as the *Charrette procedure,* make brainstorming effective in larger groups, such as classroom settings.

Graphical mapping techniques such as *mind and concept mapping* are useful to come to a better understanding about the relationships among a collection of facts, concepts, and ideas. Questions themselves are also useful starting points for generating new questions, and finally, the data as well can suggest avenues for further inquiry.

The chapter that follows explores the kinds of data sources available to answer the questions raised here, where to find these, and how to evaluate their effectiveness.

3 Search for Information

Where is the wisdom we have lost in knowledge?
Where is the knowledge we have lost in information?
—T. S. Eliot

Effective and compelling visualizations tell a story relying on data to provide evidence directly to the user. This central role places great responsibility on the nature of the data on which conclusions are to be based. Great questions that cannot be answered because of a lack of evidence do not lead to successful visualizations, so finding sources of data is critical. This chapter provides guidance for the effective use of information sources with the following topics:

- Primary sources
- Secondary sources
- Tertiary sources
- Library resources
- Local resources
- Online resources
- Effective data

Types of Sources

The data for a visualization can take any number of forms: numeric information, such as populations and rainfall amounts, documents from public records such as court records, birth and death records, letters, diaries and other personal writings, photographs, drawings, and audio and video recordings used in oral histories, news coverage, and documentaries. These sources can be categorized into three types— *primary, secondary*, and *tertiary* sources—based on the origin of their information (figure 3.1).

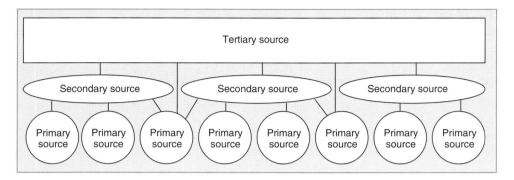

Figure 3.1
Primary, secondary, and tertiary sources.

Primary Sources

Primary sources are artifacts that were created at the same time as the person, event, or time period being considered and provide the basic evidentiary support for traditional historical inquiry. Examples of primary sources include letters and other correspondence, diaries, government and other official documents, newspaper articles, photographs, drawings, and audio and video recordings. The key issue is that the source was generated by a person at the event, who may have recorded the event, or a made a later recollection of the event. Empirical data, such as rainfall amounts, temperatures, and financial data can also be considered primary source data.

It is important to understand some of the subjective issues when using primary sources, as the source may have been produced with some inherent biases, such as an Englishman's observations during the American Revolution, or male biases concerning the intelligence of women in the nineteenth century. The reason the author wrote the source may have some bearing on how it could be interpreted.

Secondary Sources

In contrast to primary source documents, secondary sources are works by authors who were not present at the event in question and often rely on primary source documents as evidentiary proof using more subjective and analytical arguments. The generalization and synthesis often provide a more accessible overview to an event or situation. The importance in citing the primary sources used makes secondary sources an invaluable way to find references to the original documents.

Tertiary Sources

There is some debate about the line between secondary and tertiary sources, and definitions tend to vary by the context and discipline involved. Tertiary sources are works, such as encyclopedias, almanacs, bibliographies, directories, and of course the venerable Wikipedia, that draw on primary and secondary sources to provide authoritative synopses of historical events. Tertiary sources are invaluable in the beginning stages of research, as they present a broad overview of a topic and provide a list of secondary sources to consult for more detailed discussion on the components of that topic. This in turn provides access to the primary sources cited by those secondary sources.

Both secondary and tertiary sources can suffer from the same subjective biases that primary sources can. Information can be included or discarded from accounts for non-objective reasons, and material can be improperly characterized, so it is important to be able to know who wrote the text or collected the data and why that person did it.

Principal and Contextual Sources

There are two other ways to characterize sources used in visualizations, regardless of whether they are primary, secondary, or tertiary. *Principal sources* are those that relate directly to the topic of interest, and *contextual sources* provide more indirect evidence that may have a bearing on the topic but are not immediately connected with it. Good visualizations rely on contextual sources to provide information that supports the inquiry into the principal topic by triangulating multiple sources (viewpoints) to construct a persuasive narrative that the principal sources may not be able to tell alone.

For example, Charles Minard's 1869 visualization of Napoleon's march to Moscow (figure 3.2) uses the troop populations and geographical positions as principal sources to tell the story of the conflict, but the temperature is used as a valuable contextual source that helps explain the failure of the attempt.

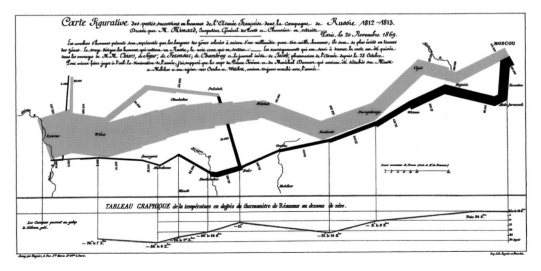

Figure 3.2
Charles Minard's map of Napoleon's march to Moscow.

Sources Can Suggest New Sources

Sources that have already been identified are a good place to get ideas for additional sources. When analyzing one source, it may be necessary to find additional information to help resolve issues and discrepancies in the data. This process can continue iteratively.

For example, when researching sources for a visualization of the 1895 University of Virginia Rotunda fire, first-hand reports mentioned that the wind direction had shifted, resulting in saving some important buildings. To verify this, weather reports for the day were obtained, and they indicated that there were no winds of any significance. To resolve the matter, students found records from an environmental study that suggested the winds were caused by the fire itself, creating a kind of combustion chamber.

Data as a Form of Evidence

Data serves the same role in a visualization as evidence does in a courtroom procedure. They both offer support to a hypothesis that the underlying phenomena are actually occurring. The clues support the lawyer's case, while data support the visualization's ability to persuade or explain. The historian David Staley suggests that *"evidence is something the makes something else evident."* It is the historian, or in our case, the producer of the visualization that identifies that a dataset should be viewed with an evidentiary status. The data is merely a proxy to the actual phenomena it claims to represent and needs to be understood in context.

When evidence is understood in relation to a specific inquiry, the data move from evidence *of* something to evidence *for* something, and insight can be inferred from that transition. When evidence can be placed in context with other pieces of evidence, those in turn equally context-dependent, stronger inferences can be obtained (Staley, 2007).

Sources of Information

Successful interactive visualizations depend on the availability of effective and sufficient sources of data to draw on as evidence. Secondary and even tertiary sources are a good starting point for finding relevant primary sources, particularly in the footnotes. It is not often that a simple Google search will provide a comprehensive survey of the available data, particularly for historical data, so a number of resources can be used, including libraries, museums, historical societies, courthouses, and public records. Some of these organizations have strong Web presences, but others will require personal visits to extract the desired information.

For example, when doing an interactive visualization[1] about the University of Virginia's first library, undergraduate students used a variety of sources. A comprehensive

---

1. Visualization: www.viseyes.org/library.

history of the library, which was housed in Thomas Jefferson's Rotunda, provided references for a number of primary sources including letters to and from Jefferson, invoices for books purchased, and a list of library fines, which included multiple infractions by Edgar Allen Poe. Discussions with the special collections librarians yielded the 1828 book listing, which was later hand-annotated to indicate the books that had survived the 1895 fire, and numerous other documents and drawings. You can view the complete research guide[2] online.

Library Resources

The digital age is a time of both opportunity and confusion for libraries and librarians. Economic pressures, the Internet, Google, and the wide-scale digitization of books are forcing libraries to look hard at their central mission and how they deliver it. Most libraries have embraced this new environment and have responded with services that combine the importance of physical books and structures with the opportunities afforded by more recent information media such as eBooks and databases. The assistance of a skilled reference librarian, particularly at universities and local libraries, can be invaluable in locating information resources for interactive visualizations.

Libraries hold a number of useful resources in addition to books, including microfilm and microfiche containing collections of primary source documents, letters, records, and newspapers. Research libraries have discipline-specific handbooks that chronicle the state of the art in those fields and are useful guides for finding additional resources, including tomes known as *handbooks*, which summarize the current thinking in a particular discipline.

Subscription Databases

Academic libraries provide access to subscription databases both on site and off site. Off-site access is restricted to the students, faculty, and staff at the university. However, in most cases, researchers who are not affiliated with the university can access the database on site at the library. Once the researcher has the citation, he or she will want to read the article cited. Access to the full-text articles could be in the form of print, digital format, or microform. These libraries will also have online catalogs the researcher can search to retrieve books, videos, datasets, geographic data, sound recordings, government information, manuscripts, diaries, and more. One often overlooked database resource is the database of doctoral dissertations and master's theses, which can provide a well-researched and up-to-date collection of references.

Most public libraries will provide access to subscription databases to their library card holders. Often the databases are available on site and off site for card holders. A researcher can search the database to retrieve citations to magazines, journals, news-

2. Research guide: www.viseyes.org/library/ResearchGuide.pdf.

paper articles, and dissertations. Although the public library may not provide online access to the full text, it may have the print version of the resource or offer an inter-library loan service that the researcher can use to obtain a copy of the article from another library. There may be a fee to use this service.

Special Collections

Many university libraries have extensive *special collections* divisions, which archive historical records, letters, rare books, and manuscripts that can provide information not typically available by any other means. Many special collections libraries will digitize documents on request and/or allow the photography of documents in their collections.

Finding Aids

Finding aids are comprehensive overviews of important library collections that have been compiled by scholars, researchers, or librarians that provide a portal to navigate through the large number of primary sources available. These documents offer over-views, biographical and organizational notes, detailed descriptions of the collections' contents, and the location of the material. The Library of Congress offers a large col-lection of finding aids for its collections[3] and has developed a standard called the Encoded Archival Description (EAD) that helps other institutions provide consistent finding aids to their patrons.

Public Records

Modern governments collect a surprising amount of data on their citizenry that is freely available to the public. Federal, state, and local governments are in the process of making even historic information Web accessible, but much of it still remains as paper documents that must be viewed in person. The US census is available online in various locations dating back to the first census of 1790, and the National Archives has many military records available from their Web site. The manuscript versions of the federal censuses provide the most detailed information on individuals and house-holds, but the government restricts access for 75 years to maintain individual privacy issues.

Local courthouses are a good source for many public records, including property deeds, tax records, birth, marriage, and death certificates, and voting records. Divorce and criminal and civil litigation records are available to be seen in person. When courts deal with equity issues in disputes, such as estates and divorce proceedings, a *chancery* (or *equity*) court is convened to adjudicate the matter. These chancery court records often contain depositions and can contain familial relationships and other valuable information.

3. www.loc.gov/rr/ead.

Local Resources

Local resources such as historical societies, county libraries, museums, churches, and genealogical groups rarely have large online presences but can offer a wealth of local information for historians, scholars, and genealogists. Genealogical groups are a good source about people and groups in an area, as are church, cemetery, and burial records. Many local newspapers and radio and television stations maintain archives of local events and are often receptive to questions on their material.

Historical societies and museums[4] collect, preserve, interpret, and provide local sources of information such as photographs, genealogical records, maps, scholarship on local topics, obituary files, and city directories. Before telephone books became popular in the 1940s, many cities published city directories that often listed inhabitants by name, occupation, and even race. Business listings usually include the proprietor and the type of business it was (i.e., barber, grocer, etc.).

Sanborn Maps

The New York–based Sanborn-Perris Map Company published a series of very detailed maps of many US cities from 1867 to 1970 to help insurance companies assess fire insurance liabilities. The maps have street names, railroads, individual lots and businesses, even water, sewer, and electrical lines. These are large and colorfully drawn maps available in many library special collections divisions and local historical societies. Digitized versions of the Sanborn maps are available from local sites, and the Library of Congress[5] makes 3000 maps from 15 states freely available online, but ProQuest[6] provides the complete set to libraries and universities on a fee basis.

Social Network Data

A popular source of data for interactive data visualizations has been social networking sites such as Twitter, del.icio.us, and MySpace. Many of these Web sites make it easy to capture the complex web of human interaction in a quantitative form that can be analyzed and visualized for meaning.

Online Resources

The Internet's current ethos of openness has made large amounts of high-quality data freely available online. This represents an unprecedented opportunity to link to excellent data sources to provide context and evidence for your particular research question. Many datasets are available as downloadable tables in common formats such as comma-separated values (CSV), *Excel*, and XML. Others online sources will require

---

4. A listing of historical societies by state can be found at www.daddezio.com/society/hill.

5. www.loc.gov/rr/geogmap/sanborn.

6. http://sanborn.umi.com.

that tables be cut and pasted from Web pages into spreadsheet applications such as *Excel* and Google *Docs*, which will automatically convert the Web page's data into a table. Some popular online data sources include the following.

Government Data

• *US Census Data*   The Census Bureau (www.census.gov) site is a goldmine of excellent data about US demographics.
• *US National Archives*   The US (and many other countries') National Archives is a good source for governmental and military documents and records as well as myriad other resources such as photographs and newsreel footage (www.archives.gov).
• *UK National Archives*   The UK National Archives allows searches for the records from a number of different databases. Searching is free, but there may be a charge to download documents (www.nationalarchives.gov.uk/documentsonline).
• *Historical US Census Data*   The University of Virginia Library (mapserver.lib.virginia.edu) has digitized and transcribed the tabular census data from 1790 to 1960 and made it searchable by data type and geography.
• *Data.gov*   The US government's experiment in transparency and participatory democracy Web site (www.data.gov) contains datasets and geospatial data in multiple formats.
• *World Bank*   A good source (data.worldbank.org) for international and OECD economic and health data downloadable in multiple formats.
• *US Court Records*   Records for Federal court cases since 1999 are freely available online from the government (www.uscourts.gov/CourtRecords.aspx). Many states and local courts have also put their more recent cases online.
• *ManyEyes*   A free data-sharing and visualization site developed by IBM (manyeyes.alphaworks.ibm.com) where individuals post a wide variety of datasets that can be downloaded as text files. VisualEyes can load these sets directly.

Datasets

• *Infochimps*   A commercial/free data-sharing site that has data from many sources, including social media providers, in multiple formats (www.infochimps.org).
• *Freebase*   Freebase (recently acquired by Google) is a rich source of Creative Commons[7] licensed structured datasets with some 20 million objects on multiple topics that are semantically linked and organized (www.freebase.com).
• *Google Ngrams*   Drawing on the millions of books digitized for Google Books, Google has made word frequency data available for search and download via their NGrams Viewer (http://ngrams.googlelabs.com).

---

7. A nonprofit that supports infrastructures that encourage digital sharing: www.creativecommons.org.

• *Google Public Data Explorer* Google has made available a large number of datasets containing US and world economic, health, business, political, and environmental data that can be graphed, downloaded, and interactively explored. They have just added the option to upload personal datasets to the collection (www.google.com/publicdata).

• *Azure Data Market* A Microsoft effort that provides both free and paid collections of data that can be easily downloaded into an Excel spreadsheet. (https://datamarket.azure.com).

• *DBpedia* DBpedia is a free service that uses the vast human-generated knowledge base of Wikipedia to provide a 3 million+-object structured database that can be mined for information about almost any subject (www.dbpedia.org).

• *Internet Archive* An ambitious site that archives snapshots of the World Wide Web starting in 1996 at regular intervals, as well as a host of documents, audio and video files, and images freely downloadable (www.archive.org).

• *Documenting the American South* The University of North Carolina at Chapel Hill provides access to digitized primary materials that offer Southern perspectives on American history and culture (http://docsouth.unc.edu/browse/collections.html).

• *Interuniversity Consortium for Political and Social Research (ICPSR)* The University of Michigan offers more than 500,000 digital files containing social science research data from political science, sociology, demography, economics, history, gerontology, criminal justice, public health, foreign policy, terrorism, health and medical care, early education, education, racial and ethnic minorities, psychology, law, and more (www.icpsr.umich.edu/icpsrweb/ICPSR).

• *Social Explorer* Social Explorer is distributed by Oxford University Press and provides easy access to demographic information about the United States from 1790 to the present. It is a subscription database but often freely available through local and university libraries (www.socialexplorer.com).

• *Pew Research Center* The Pew Research Center is a rich source of data on a wide range of issues, including Internet use, education, religion, social issues, and journalism (pewresearch.org).

• *GeoHive* GeoHive offers world statistical data on economics and population on a global and country basis and is freely available (ww.geohive.com).

Genealogy

• *Ancestry.com* Run by the Mormon Church, Ancestry.com has the largest collection of genealogical information available, some for free and others for a fee (www.ancestry.com).

• *Genealogy Commons* An open source site that provides much of the same type of information as Ancestry.com at no cost (www.genealogycommons.com).

Images and Maps

• *Library of Congress*   The US Library of Congress Web site has one of the largest collections of historic photos, maps, political cartoons, and artwork available. The American Memory project is the most accessible collection (www.loc.gov).
• *David Rumsey Map Collection*   Historic maps collector David Rumsey has made over 25,000 images of rare eighteenth- and nineteenth-century maps freely available for download in multiple resolutions (http://www.davidrumsey.com).
• *Perry-Castañeda Map Collection*   The University of Texas has scanned and made freely available over 44,000 maps, both historical and more recent maps from the CIA and other governmental entities (www.lib.utexas.edu/maps).
• *Flickr*   Literally millions of Creative Commons licensed images are freely available on this Yahoo! Web site (www.flickr.com).
• *The British Library*   The main catalog contains records for over 19 million books, serials, printed music, maps, newspapers, sound archive, and web archive items (www .bl.uk/reshelp/findhelprestype/catblhold/all/allcat.html).
• *The British Museum*   Search almost 2 million objects from the entire museum database (www.britishmuseum.org/research/search_the_collection_database.aspx).
• *USGS Geography*   The US Geological Survey is a good source for satellite and topographic maps in a number of freely available formats (http://geography.usgs.gov).

Books and Newspapers

• *Google Books*   The largest book digitization project with over 12 million volumes digitized and available for online reading, has as its goal the digitizing of all known existing books (according to Google, 129,864,880 books) by 2020 (www.books.google .com).
• *HaithiTrust Digital Library*   A partnership of universities and libraries provides a noncommercial alternative to Google books with over 8 million volumes digitized and available for online reading (www.hathitrust.org).
• *Chronicling America*   With funding from the National Endowment for the Humanities, the Library of Congress is making newspapers from 1860 to 1922 from multiple states freely available online (http://chroniclingamerica.loc.gov).
• *Newspapers around the World*   This site contains links to thousands of international newspaper sites **(**www.onlinenewspapers.com).

Effective Quantitative Data

Not all data are useful enough to be included in an information visualization. Information designer Stephen Few (2009) has compiled a list of traits that define what he termed *meaningful data*. Meaningful data are high volume, historical, consistent, multivariate, atomic, clear, dimensionally structured, richly segmented, and of known pedigree. Data that meet these requirements are more likely to yield insights when visualized.

We have found the word "meaningful" to be somewhat loaded with the expectation that the data alone portend meaning, before analysis or combination with other data sources, so we prefer referring to *effective* data. Effective data share most of Few's attributes as well as some additional characteristics:

• *High Volume* The visualization may not use all the data that are available, but having enough information to accurately represent the phenomenon increases the chances of being able to answer questions using it.

• *Historical* The ability of data to represent change over time makes it possible to infer some sense of causation from the same factors being examined at multiple times.

• *Consistent* An ideal dataset will use the same criteria for all measurements it contains, allowing for direct comparisons between samples taken at different times, circumstances, and locations.

• *Multivariate* The more independent aspects (a.k.a. variables) that can be extracted from the information, the richer that dataset is, and it allows for comparisons, contrasts, and other interpretations.

• *Atomic* The aspects should be examined and described at the lowest level of detail, but not so low as to lose meaning. We can always aggregate various aspects into "meta-aspects," but it is hard to take a combined variable and parse out its constituent parts. Remember Einstein's dictum, *"things should be as simple as possible, but not simpler."*

• *Clean* Data should be accurate, complete, truthful, and objective. As the saying goes, *"garbage in, garbage out."* Historical data unfortunately are often incomplete, which presents a challenge in using these data to objectively support arguments.

• *Structured* The aspects of the data should be separated into groups that make it easy to tell which part of the dataset relates to what aspect. It is also better if that dimensional structure gives us information about how the aspects relate to one another. Hierarchies and groupings aid in this process.

• *Sourced* It is useful, and sometimes essential, to know why a particular set of data was collected and by whom. Such a dataset will necessarily have a bias based on its origin and purpose that *must* be factored into our analysis and relied on.

• *Accessible* Data should be easily extracted from their source. Like shale oil, the more valuable the data are to you, the more effort you will be willing to expend to extract these data from their source.

• *Representative* The information should be a reliable picture of what it claims to represent. If it is wrong, at least it should be constantly wrong.

Not all these characteristics need be present to warrant inclusion into a project, but they increase the probability of the data being able to effectively answer the questions asked. The sources available may suggest new questions, or discourage the further exploration of current ones. In addition, not all sources of data are quantitative and can consist of photographs, media, letters, and other written documents.

Summary

This chapter explores the types of data resources that can be used in an interactive visualization. *Primary sources* are data taken directly from the event, such as a first-hand witness account or temperature readings. *Secondary sources* are books and other resources that aggregate the information from primary sources, and finally, *tertiary resources* such as encyclopedias pull from both primary and secondary sources to provide broad but shallow overviews of a topic.

There are many places to find data to use in visualizations. Libraries, museums, historical societies, courthouses, and government offices contain a wealth of information, but it most often must be obtained in person at considerable effort. Increasingly, even smaller organizations are digitizing their material and making it freely available online.

The Internet provides the largest collection of readily available data by far. Search engines such as Google are invaluable research tools for finding even the most obscure bits of data. Resource sites from the Census Bureau, Ancestry.com, The National Archives, and the Library of Congress make highly vetted primary-source data freely available for download.

Not all data are effective sources for a visualization. *Effective data* are of high volume, consist of multiple connected dimensions, are at the proper level—not too general and not too detailed—are clean in nature, properly structured into meaningful groups, have a known and trustworthy provenance, are easily accessible, and, finally, are representative of what they are purporting to represent.

The next chapter discusses how sets of data can be structured to be effectively used in a visualization so that meaningful insights might be attained.

4 Structure the Information

In all chaos there is a cosmos, in all disorder a secret order.
—Carl Jung

Information in its raw form needs to be abstracted and structured in order to tell a compelling story. The data exist to serve whatever purpose they were originally collected to serve and may need to be transformed, pared down, subsampled, or have statistical methods applied to them in order to be useful as a data source in an information visualization.

The structuring of data is an inherently subjective operation and represents conscious and deliberate decisions about which and in what manner data are to be used to answer the question. It is important to make those decisions as transparent as possible to the viewer so it is clear that the data were structured using a consistent methodology that can be easily understood.

This chapter explores the following topics:

- What structured data are
- Domain space abstraction
- Data selection
- Richard Saul Wurman's LATCH
- Qualitative and quantitative information
- Data-structuring tools
- Linked data and the semantic web

What Is Structured Information?

Structured information is data that are organized, which means that data are sorted and grouped together into meaningful groups, such as name, age, and gender. In contrast, unstructured information is data that are lumped without organization into

name	sex	age	grade
Bob	male	22	100
Ted	male	43	40
Carol	female	33	90
Alice	female	23	75

Figure 4.1
A simple table of data.

a single document, such as a Word file, with nothing separating the important elements. The following text provides an example of unstructured data

Bob is a male student aged 22. He scored 100 on the test. Ted is a 43-year-old male student who scored 40 on the test. Carol is a female student age 33 and scored 90 on the test. Finally, Alice is a female student, age 23. She scored 75 on the test.

If we wanted to know whether men scored higher than women, we would closely read the text and extract the gender and scores for each of the people. This procedure might work for small amounts of information, but imagine needing to find out this information if there were 400 people in the class. It would be very difficult to automate, as the computer would have a hard time telling the ages from the grades.

One solution is to *structure* the data. That is, if we know an item is a grade, we would put it in the "grade" group, and an item that is a name would go into the "name" group. These collections of structured information are called *tables*, and they are really no different than an ordinary *Excel* spreadsheet (figure 4.1). Both spreadsheets and tables consist of multiple rows of information, sorted into useful groupings in columns.

Each column is a grouping of related things, called a *field*. The first row defines the names of the fields, followed by any number of rows that contain the information for the fields. In this table, there are four people (Bob, Ted, Carol, and Alice) and four fields (name, sex, age, and grade).

Having the data structured makes it easier to make sense out of the information and ask it better questions. Google is essentially an unstructured search of the web. When we do a search, Google looks to see if any of our search words appear in a web page and then returns those pages if it does. An example of an unstructured search would be if you searched for "Tiger" Woods, the golfer. Your search results would include data about the golfer as well as about the feline predator. By comparison, a structured search would involve searching specified fields in a structured table. For example, to conduct a structured search for the occurrences of "Tiger" as a first name, you would indicate that you are searching for matches in a structured table's name field. Structure adds a level of semantic meaning to our searches.

Domain Space Abstraction

Initially, the data need to be abstracted from the *domain* space (i.e., process of collecting the census) into the kind of *quantitative* data required by typical visualization methodologies. Threats to the *validity* of this process that can influence the abstraction process, including *focusing* on the wrong data that are not germane to the problem or *encoding* the data such that they do not reflect the underlying process (Munzner, 2009).

The abstraction process yields quantitative and qualitative information of three broad types:

1. *Categorical data*, for which labels are assigned to provide identity (i.e., apple, orange, etc.).
2. *Integral data*, for which a number is assigned to the information to count, show order, and so forth.
3. *Continuous data*, which represent things that do not move in discrete steps, such as temperature, time, and money.

These different types lend themselves to particular statistical and visualization techniques (Bertin, 1983; Ware, 2004).

Information that serves as an effective source for information visualizations often is *multidimensional*. This means that a number of attributes can be attached to each item being represented, making for a richer description of the item. For example, the US census is a multidimensional set of information consisting of *categorical* data (race), *integral* data (number of people in house), and *continuous* data (annual income). By comparing subsets of these attributes, insights can be gleaned from exploring their interaction.

Data Selection

In the data-structuring phase, the appropriate portion of the data needs to be determined and selected for succeeding steps. Many information sets are large and cover times or areas that are not useful for the question to be answered, so a subset of the data needs to be extracted from the full set. This dataset can be:

• Defined by *minimum and maximum* values of a particular attribute, such as time and location;
• *Sampled by interval* (i.e., every fifth item is represented), *stratified* (i.e., 20 percent of samples in each county);
• *Aggregated* (i.e., data from all counties are averaged or totaled);
• *Clustered* by grouping attributes together by similar characteristics (i.e., *all men under 21 years of age*).

Within this selection process, look for data points that appear erroneous, are missing (a frequent issue in historic datasets), or are outside of expected bounds (outliers), and set rules for their removal from the dataset. These omissions and exclusions can have dramatic effects on the story reflected by the data, particularly with smaller datasets, so care must be taken to ensure that these defining decisions are explicit and consistently applied.

The data selection process requires specificity and care in order to clarify your dataset and maintain its validity. The decision to include or exclude sections of the potential dataset will have a significant impact on the final results. It is important to clearly document these selection choices so the viewer can properly evaluate their impact on the final visualization.

Organizing Information by Wurman's LATCH

Systematically organizing the information may help in structuring it into a more useful form for communicating meaning. The iconic and irascible information architect Richard Saul Wurman claims that, in the past 30 years, he has tried hundreds of different organizational schemes, but they always can be reduced down into five basic dimensions for organizing data through a system he calls *LATCH: location, alphabetization, time, category,* and *hierarchy* (Wurman, 1989, 1996).

1. *Location*   Geography or proximity, particularly when combined with time, is one of the most useful ways to organize information. Location can be concrete, such as a position on a map, a part within system diagram, or a step in a flow chart, or more abstract senses of space such as a grouping of images together to convey their relation to one another or a relative size in a drawing.

2. *Alphabet*   Alphabetizing along one or more factors is less useful in interactive visualizations, but it does provide a way to organize large amounts of data. Although "A" fits nicely in the LATCH acronym, this dimension represents any scheme in which information is organized by an arbitrary symbol, such as a number or table of contents index.

3. *Time*   Organizing things temporally allows for the suggestion of causality. This approach is most valuable when combined with other schemes, such as location. Time, of course, is often represented by graphical timelines and calendars.

4. *Category*   Classifying an item as a member of a group helps identify patterns in data. Groups can include distinctions such as color, gender, and other item attributes. Once categorized, the items can be counted and have a variety of statistical techniques applied to tease out patterns.

5. *Hierarchy*   The relationship of items according to one or more factors helps reveal the internal structure and relationships among data elements. For example, one kind of hierarchy would involve a simple ranking of an item's attribute, such as its size,

order of importance, or number. More complex hierarchies include family trees, organizational charts, and other kinds of relational data types.

Quantitative and Qualitative Information

Information and data can be thought of as evidence that a phenomenon that is of interest to the researcher is actually occurring. That information will have one of two basic natures: *quantitative* or *qualitative*. Quantitative data indicate numerically measurable quantities about that base phenomenon, such as age, time, temperature, or number of items, whereas qualitative data focus on the more descriptive qualities that explain the underlying phenomenon, such as documents, images, and categorizations.

Quantitative Information

Quantitative information can always be measured and analyzed using statistical techniques such as descriptive statistics (average, median, standard deviation), correlation, and regression analysis. It is most often used in deductive reasoning situations for which conclusions about the base phenomenon can be directly drawn from the data.

Types of Quantitative Data

Data values can generally be categorized as being in one of three basic types. Each of these types lends itself to different ways of analysis and representation.

1. *Nominal* data values (think *named*) represent membership in a particular value or category. Nominal data can be counted and analysis done on the numbers of members of a particular member value. For example, gender is a nominal data type with two possible basic values: *male* and *female*. Males/females could be encoded as M/F, male/ female, 0/1, and X/Y. Even though it might be possible to add up all the 0's or 1's in that style of encoding, the only meaningful analysis can be gleaned from counting the frequency of their occurrence. Nominal data are often used in combination with another data element as a filtering criterion, such as "all the *men* over 40."

2. *Ordinal* data values (think *ordered*) follow a ranking order for which the members represent membership into category in a similar fashion as nominal data types, but the category itself represents order. An example of an ordinal scale would be height and could be represented as words (i.e., short, medium, tall), or numbers such as 0, 1, and 2.

3. *Quantitative* data values (think *quantity*) are the most amenable to quantitative data analysis techniques because they represent the value being measured directly and can have a host of statistical techniques applied to it. If height is represented as a quantitative value, short, medium, or tall people would be represented by their height in inches, something like 60, 66, or 74.

Qualitative Information

Qualitative information can be more difficult to visualize but is able to reflect a more nuanced and complex human-based phenomenon. It is observational and often requires subjective human interpretation to extract meaning through rich media types such as historic documents, letters, photographs, oral histories, and videos. Qualitative data tend to rely on inductive reasoning, where the information suggests the underlying truth of the base phenomenon, but the connection between the two is not necessarily conclusive.

Qualitative research has a long and extensive tradition, with very effective methodologies for looking at these information-rich but often typically unstructured sources and distilling data and insight. The role of the researcher as a participant in this process is an important element to be aware of because qualitative analysis requires subjective judgment in order to make sense of the data.

Using Qualitative and Quantitative Data Together

The most effective arguments make use of both quantitative and qualitative types of information, with each providing support as appropriate to the base phenomenon and the data that purport to represent it. Qualitative data can be quantified by identifying a collection of salient traits embedded within and coding the resource to see if those characteristics are present and to what degree. This coding process can also be done from the resource first, and a list of traits generated by close scrutiny. This coding in effect quantifies the traditionally "fuzzy" qualitative data and makes it available for more traditional visualization tools such as charts, graphs, and concept and network maps.

For example, this visualization[1] plots a thematic analysis of the autobiography of Shabkar, the eighteenth-century Tibetan yogi. In a large undergraduate lecture class on Tibetan Buddhism at the University of Virginia, 180 students analyzed the chapters of the book for mentions of nine specific themes. Each student determined a number that reflected its presence in every one of the 15 chapters. The students entered their ratings on a shared Google *Docs* spreadsheet that the VisualEyes visualization automatically drew from (figure 4.2). Controls offered options to view a single student's response, a section of students, or the entire class.

Data-Structuring Tools

It is certainly possible to structure data in word-processing programs with the creative use of the *Find and Replace* feature in applications such as Microsoft *Word* and Google *Docs*, but using more structured tools such as spreadsheets and dedicated programs

1. To view the live visualization: www.viseyes.org/show?id=62228.

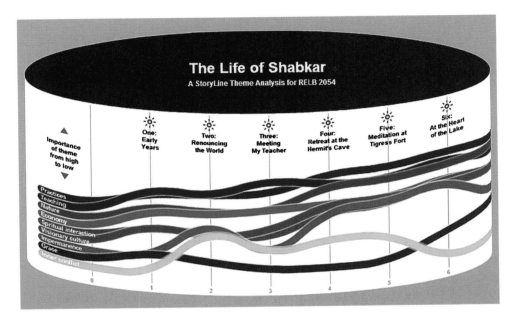

Figure 4.2
Visualization of the life of Shabkar.

will not only speed up this time-consuming and tedious task but improve the data's accuracy. Programs are available that are dedicated to data structuring, while others are designed for *data cleansing,* which is the process of detecting, correcting, or removing inaccurate records from a set of data by eliminating duplicate entries and correcting incorrect ones.

Spreadsheets as an Exploring and Structuring Tool

Spreadsheet applications such as Microsoft's *Excel* and Google *Docs* Spreadsheet are excellent tools to explore and structure datasets into useful configurations for visualizations. They contain rudimentary statistical and graphics functions that are much more accessible than packages such as SPSS and R and make it easy to explore the data in great detail. The ability to transform data using simple formulas embedded in cells offers powerful methods to restructure, group, and scale data items into useful forms. See chapter 11 for more information on using common spreadsheet applications. Spreadsheets can be used for:

• *Exploratory charts and graphs*   Being able to quickly graph parts of the dataset is one easy way to see if there are any relationships in the data that can be further explored.
• *Sorting*   Quickly sorting the data by fields will help give you a good sense of the range of the data and possible outliers.

• *Transforming data*   Data are often not in comparable ranges, so the ability to easily scale or add a numeric offset to a column can be useful in trying to get out the underlying relationships between the data fields.

• *Swapping columns and rows*   Spreadsheets can easily change the manner in which the data are organized from column-based to row-based material.

• *Filtering rows*   *Excel* has some powerful tools to include or filter out rows by establishing various criteria for inclusion and exclusion.

• *Capturing online data*   Spreadsheets make it easy to capture data from tables in web pages. Simply "pasting" a table of data "copied" from a web page will convert it to a simple table containing only the desired values.

• *Exploratory statistics*   Most spreadsheets, *Excel* in particular, have features for providing both descriptive statistics as well as access to powerful inferential techniques such as correlation, regression, *t*-test, and ANOVA.

Data Cleansing

Datasets often contain missing elements, or some of the elements can be clearly seen as being erroneous. Particularly when the dataset is small, it is important to *cleanse* the dataset of these values, as they will inaccurately influence any further analysis. It is imperative that this process be done in a thoughtful, objective, empirical, and transparent manner to eliminate potential biases that this cleaning might produce and that the rational and methodology for the choices taken be made explicit. There are a number of common techniques for dealing with missing and/or erroneous data:

• The offending data can be flagged in some way, so users understand it is of questionable reliability. The flagged data can then be selectively omitted or included in further analysis at the user's discretion.

• An average value of the entire dataset can be included in the missing or clearly erroneous element's place.

• Removing the element from the dataset is effective, assuming there are enough remaining elements and the reason that the data removal is not the result of some other issue, such as racial prejudice.

Dedicated Data-Structuring/Cleansing Tools

Dedicated data-cleansing and restructuring tools can potentially save large amounts of time and tedium by cleaning up "dirty data" (data that contain misspelling, formatting errors, and duplicated fields), restructuring the fields, and effortlessly converting data from one format to another. There have long been a number of commercial desktop software applications such as *WinPure*[2] and others, but a new generation of

2. http://www.winpure.com.

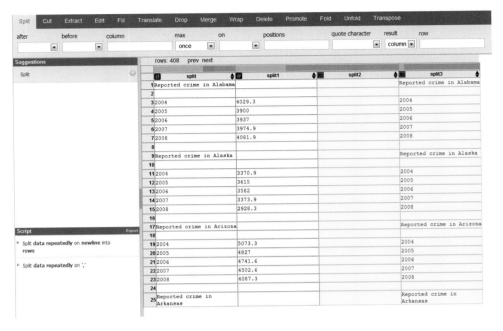

Figure 4.3
Wrangler data cleaning app by the Stanford Visualization Group.

freely available online applications such as Google *Refine*[3] and Stanford's *DataWrangler*[4] (figure 4.3) promise to help clean up datasets, convert formats, and reassign fields using easy-to-use Web-based tools.

Linked Data and the Semantic Web

There are other ways to structure information than using tables. One of the most promising techniques on the horizon is called *linked data,* often associated with the *semantic web* efforts promoted by the World Wide Web's inventor, Tim Berners-Lee. The Semantic Web project is aimed at developing a set of tools that will aid in making the Internet self-descriptive (Berners-Lee, Lassila, & Hendler, 2001). Instead of coaxing meaning from simple word associations the way Google does when searching, linked data promises to expose the semantic relationships from the ontology encoded in individual and independent elements through *Bayesian* networks. These networks provide a way to make inferences from a disparate collection of data based on their combined probabilities of occurring and offer a way to make some sense of incomplete data (figure 4.4).[5]

3. http://code.google.com/p/google-refine.
4. http://vis.stanford.edu/wrangler.
5. Image courtesy of linkeddata.org.

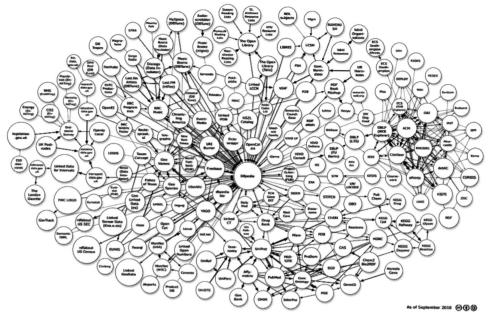

Figure 4.4
Linking Open Data cloud diagram (image courtesy Richard Cyganiak and Anja Jentzsch. http://
lod-cloud.net).

The goal of linked data projects is to create a wealth of interlinked data available for a growing collection of Web-based tools, such as SPARQL[6] (pronounced *sparkle*), which can query that data using the rich interconnections provided by the relation-ship information and generate more meaningful results than are possible with tradi-tional data searches.

Rather than rigidly constructing tables that sort items of data into collections of like-coded lists from the top down, linked data organize information from the bottom up and try to define items in terms of their relationship to other pieces of data. This directionality is important because instead of a centralized arbiter choosing what data will be classified into which field, the data can be categorized by any number of sources independently from one another, making the potential size of structured data available significantly larger than a single data creator.

How Linked Data Works

Each piece of information is given a unique name, called a *uniform resource identifier* (URI), which resembles a traditional web URL. Linked data depend on two URI-named

6. www.sparql.org.

pieces of information, the *subject* and the *object*, connected together by the *predicate* relationship between them. This *subject → predicate → object triplet* creates the basic building block of linked data and the semantic web.

The *predicates* represent our understanding of the part of the world we are trying to describe. For example, the triple *a lion is part of the mammal class, mammals are described by being warm-blooded,* and *lions have four legs,* uses the predicates *is part of, are described by,* and *have* to connect the subjects to the objects and in the process provides us valuable information about the world of lions.

Ontologies

These relationships build what is called an *ontology,* or network map of how the parts of the world relate to one another. They contain a list of classes, which are higher-level constructs that describe things (i.e., animals, mammals, and primates) and the predicates or relationships that connect them into a system (primates are *part of* mammals, which are *part of* animals, etc.). A number of useful ontologies have emerged, including *friend of a friend* (FOAF)[7] and the OWL ontology tools.

DBpedia

DBpedia[8] is an enterprising open source effort to extract structured information from the popular online encyclopedia Wikipedia. It does this by harvesting the information Wikipedia contributors created when filling out the information boxes and other structures in the wiki pages. The result is over 700 million subject-predicate-object RDF triplets and a robust ontology that can be queried using tools that go well beyond the simple word-matched results that Google and other search engines deliver.

RDF and RDFa

Just as the Hypertext Markup Language (HTML) is the native language of the traditional web, the *Resource Description Framework* (RDF) format is used to describe the *subject-predicate-object* triplets that form the basis of the semantic web. RDF has proven difficult for the general public to use, so a variant called *RDFa* was developed that can be easily coded into web pages along with traditional HTML. RDFa is gaining more acceptance and adoption from companies including Google, Yahoo!, Facebook, Newsweek, and Best Buy.

Some Caveats

The linked data and semantic web projects are exceedingly promising new ways to make the web of information accessible and computable by man and machine alike, but as

7. www.foaf-project.org.
8. www.dbpedia.org.

with many new technologies, the enthusiasm is high, but the adoption has been slow. The inability or unwillingness for people to adopt common ontologies will make it difficult to achieve the goal of universally indexed machine-readable Internet.

Summary

The chapter explores the importance of structuring the data that drive an interactive visualization. *Structured data* is information organized into categories that may provide meaningful insights when subsequently analyzed. The most common form of structure is the *data table*, where data are laid out in a rectangular matrix, with columns representing the categories and rows representing the items.

Information is initially defined in terms representing the environment in which it was originally collected. Often the data must be *translated* from the domain space to a more abstracted space so they can be more easily compared with other datasets and are closer to the idealization of the phenomenon under examination.

It is not always possible or desirable to use all of the available data collected for a project. It is important to be systematic when *culling the dataset* to a manageable size so that the new sample accurately reflects the population it was extracted from.

The iconoclastic data architect Richard Saul Wurman claims that in the 30 years he has been developing data-driven projects, all his methodologies for organizing data fall into five categories with the catchy acronym LATCH: *location, alphabet, time, category*, and *hierarchy*.

Data fall into two basic forms. *Qualitative information* can be more difficult to visualize but is able to reflect a more nuanced and complex human-based phenomenon. It is observational and often requires subjective human interpretation to extract meaning. *Quantitative information* can always be measured and analyzed using statistical techniques such as descriptive statistics. Very effective visualizations use both types of data to answer questions.

Spreadsheet applications such as Microsoft's *Excel* and Google *Docs* are excellent tools to explore and structure datasets into useful configurations for visualizations. There are a number of dedicated tools for cleaning and structuring data, some commercial and others freely available.

Finally, Tim Berners-Lee's dream of extending the structured data concept to the Internet is emerging in the *Linked Data and Semantic Web* projects. Freely available tools such as SPARQL, FOAF, DBpedia, and OWL are making the development of subject-predicate-object–linked data easier to create.

The chapter that follows discusses ways to look at the newly structured data and envisions ways that it might be analyzed and represented so that the data can answer the questions posed and tell their own story.

5 Envision the Answer

To have a great idea, have a lot of them.
—Thomas Edison

Envisioning is an exploratory process to develop ways of revealing answers to the questions identified, using the data found and structured in the earlier design phases. Envisioning involves looking at the relationship of the data to the research question as well as relationships within parts of the data. Like other phases in the ASSERT model, this will often lead to other sources of data that may be useful in answering the questions and suggest new questions and areas that can be explored.

The emphasis at this stage is on finding what might be useful ideas but not necessarily on determining the practicality in further developing these ideas or even implementing them. The goal of envisioning is to collect as many ideas that *could* be valuable without any critical judgment. The *Representation* stage will evaluate whether actually including the idea envisioned should be pursued in the final visualization.

To generate ideas at this phase, it can be useful to look at books, Web sites, and other sources of visualizations for inspiration on how other designers have solved similar problems. The following link contains a collection of bookmarks to visualization Web sites that may suggest some ideas: delicious.com/bferster/visualization.

The first step in envisioning ideas for a visualization begins by looking closely at the data collected. With the overarching context provided by the research questions, look carefully at the sources to see how they may provide direct evidence for answering those questions.

This chapter examines a number of methodologies and techniques for envisioning the design of an effective communication that provides answers to data-driven research questions:

- Design synthesis
- Tufte's principles of analytic design
- Quantitative analysis

- Qualitative analysis
- Factor matrix analysis

Design Synthesis

The industrial and interactive design community has been deconstructing the methodology used in arriving at innovation and design decisions to help demystify the creative process. *Design synthesis* is the application of abductive reasoning[1] to a problem by finding relationships and patterns among the data elements and *externalizing* those relationships by identifying them by name, ranking them in importance, and linking them to various perspectives (Kolko, 2010).

Abduction can be thought of as conditional insight into the discovery of possible causal relationships. Because many of the relationships identified using this technique are likely to be incorrect, it is important to test these ideas using new data to see if they lead to similar relationships, which would confirm if the initial insights are correct. That said, much of the historical data used in visualizations may be incomplete or inaccurate, and the abductive process can provide clues to actual relationships that would not be obvious through more empirical methods. Kolko (2010) has outlined an action framework for applying design synthesis to industrial and interactive projects. These methods are equally applicable to the problems encountered in envisioning interactive visualizations:

- *Prioritizing*   This involves collecting as much data as possible that might answer the research question. Using as rational a process as possible, rank the data as to its importance in answering the research question at hand.
- *Judging*   This is deciding which portions of the available data are ultimately relevant to the question being answered. Some information will be excluded if not immediately germane to the research question.
- *Forging of connections*   This comes from focusing not on the discrete elements themselves but on the relationships among them. Identify possible relationships between data elements and try to develop a causal reason for each connection using abductive reasoning techniques.
- *Reframing*   This involves thinking about the research question differently and casting it in a new perspective by explicitly identifying the current perspective and frame and then expanding that perspective along different dimensions in order to see the problem from multiple points of view.
- *Insight combination*   *Design patterns* are schemas for understanding or interpreting data patterns and relationships in the framework of patterns that were previously

1. Abductive reasoning is used where the data suggest possible causation not directly found in the data rather than deducing a theory from the data only.

recognized. It is helpful to make a list of design patterns that may be useful in the problem domain. *Insight combination* is the pairing of insights from the data with potential design patterns to suggest ways of envisioning the data.

The design synthesis discourse is rooted in a cognitive psychology concept called *sensemaking.* This has been defined as *"a motivated, continuous effort to understand connections (which can be among people, places, and events) in order to anticipate their trajectories and act effectively."* Sensemaking is the process we use to understand the world around us, where we let the information we have collected suggest a possible causal explanation (a *frame*) and then test that frame with new data. As new data emerge, the frame is modified in an iterative fashion (*reframing*) until we are satisfied with its explanatory power (Klein, Moon, & Hoffman, 2006).

The Spectrum of Understanding

Data are the raw material for a visualization and the result of archival research, direct experimentation, aggregation, synthesis, and discovery. They are necessary, but not sufficient, and not meant for direct consumption by a user. The data are transformed using organization and presentation techniques into *information* capable of communicating a message to the user and providing context for understanding. *Knowledge* is the process of integrating that information using narrative into a cohesive story, and finally, *wisdom* can be attained when the user reflects, interprets, and evaluates the knowledge provided on a personal and individual basis (figure 5.1) (Shedroff, 1999).

Shedroff (1999) insists that "Successful communications do not present data." Although data are a critical component, there is a *spectrum of understanding:* from raw *data* to *information,* where potential patterns and relationships between the data elements start to emerge, to *knowledge,* a participatory understanding that is ultimately communicated, and finally, the personal realization of *wisdom* as a result of the communication.

The London-based designer Mark Johnstone's *Data Cake* (figure 5.2) is a somewhat more humorous but equally insightful illustration of the spectrum of understanding as it might relate to visualization.

Tufte's Six Fundamental Principles of Analytic Design

Edward Tufte, a Yale University professor of political science, statistics, and computer science and the author of a number of excellent books on data and design, has identified six principles of analytic design that exemplify excellent data-driven visualizations. These principles are derived from the tenets of analytic thinking and have been defining in the production and consumption of data-driven visual representations from cuneiform tablets to interactive computer-based displays. Tufte's principles are

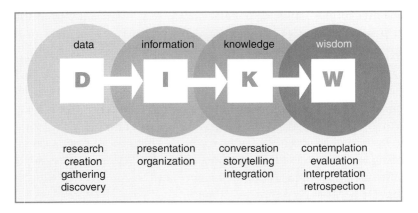

Figure 5.1
The spectrum of understanding (adapted from Shedroff, 1999).

Figure 5.2
A humorous take on the spectrum of understanding (courtesy Mark Johnstone: http://epicgraphic.com/data-cake).

underscored by a symmetrical relationship between the producer and the consumer: *"at a good evidence presentation, we're all in it together"* (Tufte, 2006).

1. *Show comparisons, contrasts, differences* Answering the "compared to what" question is the fundamental role of statistical reasoning in making comparisons that graphically show contrasts and differences between sets of data. The degree of difference should be significant; as Gregory Bateson (2000) said, *"a difference which makes a difference."*

2. *Show causality, mechanism, explanation, systematic structure* Providing visual evidence to suggest causality through the use of explanation, commentary, showing process, and internal structure will help communication.

3. *Show multivariate data* Providing multiple datasets that allow the viewer to graphically see the relationships between two or more factors will help support comparisons and suggest causality. A richer and more understandable explanation will result from using multiple datasets because the real world the data are attempting to represent is also the confluence of many factors.

4. *Completely integrate words, numbers, images, diagrams* Providing a holistic experience in which parallel data representations are completely integrated with one another and with the supporting words, numbers, and images will greatly improve understanding.

5. *Documentation* Basing arguments on data depends on understanding the origins and original intentions of those data. Show the provenance of any data used, including the sources, the person or organization collecting the data and their role, the date collected or drawn, the location, any known assumptions, and publication information.

6. *Content counts most of all* Because data-driven visualizations derive their effectiveness and persuasive power directly from representations of the data, *"Analytic presentations ultimately stand or fall depending on the quality, relevance, and integrity of their content"* (Tufte, 2006).

Quantitative Analysis

Qualitative data offer the opportunity to employ a wide range of techniques from informatics and statistics to help evaluate a given data source. This is possible when one or more dimensions of the underlying phenomenon the dataset is representing have been translated into numbers that can be counted or compared in the same manner.

Evaluating Data Quantitatively
The methods of statistics can help illuminate how those numbers might provide evidence in answering the research questions. It is important to look at quantitative analysis problems from a broader perspective before employing any of the many

specific techniques, particularly the more complex tests, and look at some basic ways to frame the problem.

Relationships

Carefully looking at the *relationships* between sources can be valuable in uncovering causal associations between them. Tools such as network maps and concept maps can be used to visually represent those latent relationships along various factors, such as density, apparent wealth or happiness, and others with factors such as ages, numbers of people, and so on.

Even traditionally textual sources of data can be analyzed with a number of sophisticated, freely available text-mining tools to uncover latent trends within and between sources that may provide evidence in answering questions. Google's *Ngram Viewer*[2] Web site provides easy access to visually display graphs of words or phrases found in the full text of the millions of books they have digitized. The following section discusses in more detail some of the ways text can be critically analyzed.

Compare and Contrast

Comparing sets of data from two or more locations can provide support for some kinds of questions through the process of *compare and contrast*. All other things being equal, if there is a change in the data values between the sets, there is evidence to suggest that the location may be responsible for those changes. Statistical methods provide ways to empirically make those comparisons and try to compensate for times when all other things are *not* equal.

Change over Time

Changes over time in a dataset can often help to reveal and provide insight into the cause-and-effect questions. As with compare and contrast, one must be careful that all other factors are equal, but analyzing the effects of change over time by looking at the data from the temporal perspective can offer insight why one particular phenomenon is occurring by observing other events occurring around the same time.

Statistical Concepts for Preliminary Analysis

The first step in any quantitative analysis is to obtain the *descriptive statistics* about the dataset. Some very simple statistical tests that can be done in a spreadsheet to get an overview of the basic features of the data include the range of the numbers, the average value, and the degree of variation in the dataset. See the section on basic statistics in chapter 10 for more information. From a preliminary analysis perspective, the following statistical concepts may be useful in evaluating a dataset:

2. http://books.google.com/ngrams/

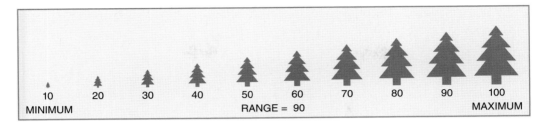

Figure 5.3
Data range.

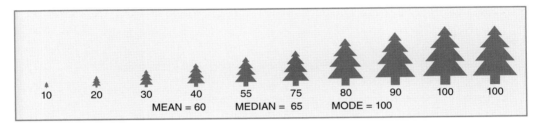

Figure 5.4
Mean, median, and mode.

• *Data range*   Looking at the range (the lowest and highest values) in relation to individual members of a group can offer information about the scale of the data. For example, if we had a dataset of pine trees offered for use as the national Christmas tree in Washington, DC (figure 5.3), one might expect a range from 20 to 40 feet. If the range were 10 to 100 feet, we might wonder why a small 10-foot tree was offered and if the 100-foot tree was a data-entry error.

• *Mean, median, and mode*   These are basic statistics that take a group of values and offer a single number that represents the group. The *mean* will say what the average data values are, the *median* is the middlemost value by quantity, and the *mode* is the value that occurs the most (figure 5.4). Looking at the three together can offer clues about the nature of the dataset. If the mean and median are close, that suggests a *normal* distribution of values in the set.

• *Variability*   The variation (measured by the *standard deviation*) is how much any given data value varies from the average curve of what we usually would expect (figure 5.5). Values may be clustered around a certain level, suggesting that something is behind the grouping (i.e., number of pimples at age 15). Value may be evenly distributed along a bell curve, suggesting the data represent the normal range of naturally occurring phenomena, or be erratic, suggesting no underlying factors behind the values.

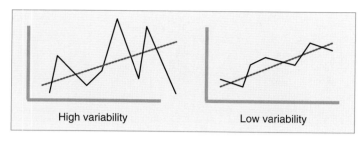

Figure 5.5
Variability of data.

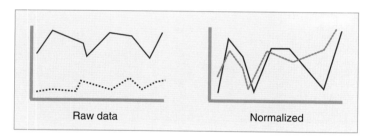

Figure 5.6
Normalization of data.

• *Normalization* When two or more datasets are compared, the scale of the numbers can mask or overemphasize the underlying pattern, so it is useful to normalize (scale the set to a common range, say 0–100) to see the variation apart from the range. For example, the Chinese birthrates graphed by month would dwarf the Swedish monthly births, making a comparison very difficult. But if the numbers were expressed on the same scale, relative differences would become evident (figure 5.6).
• *Controlling for factors* Similar to normalization, the scale of the numbers can distort the underlying pattern because they need to be considered relative to some other factor. For example, China has the largest number of soldiers in the world (2.3 million) and North Korea only 0.7 million, but if we take China's massive population relative to North Korea, the places are reversed, painting a much different picture of the relative importance of their respective militaries (figure 5.7).

Time-Series Data
Datasets that involve the concept of time present some additional possibilities for exploration beyond looking at simple statistics. Known as *time-series* data, the values represent ever-increasing points in time and are the most common form of analytics

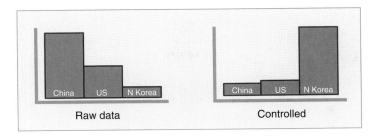

Figure 5.7
Controlling for factors.

Figure 5.8
Trends of data.

used. Time-series data are most easily analyzed by creating simple line graphs in a spreadsheet, with the time component on the *x*-axis plotted against the values. Using the time-tested technique of "interocular analysis" (i.e., looking at it with your eyes), the data can be examined along the following dimensions:

• *Trends*   A line graph will show that the data tend to increase, decrease, or stay the same by imagining a line through the data averaging their highs and lows, called a *trend line*. Spreadsheet applications can easily visually add this to graphs and also provide a numeric indication of the line's slope. An uphill line is a *positive trend* and means the values increase over time; a downhill line is a negative trend and means whatever phenomena the values reflect are waning; and a flat line is *no trend* and indicates stability over time (figure 5.8).

• *Variation*   Real data are "messy" and rarely conform to a perfect line. The degree to which the data vary from the trend line is their *variability* and offers clues on how to evaluate changes. If the line were erose or erratic, one would not be surprised if a value or group of values varies from the trend line; however, if variability were low, that might suggest some phenomena to further explore (figure 5.9).

• *Rate of change*   The slope of the trend line gives clues to the speed at which the values are changing. This is especially useful when one is comparing the rate of change

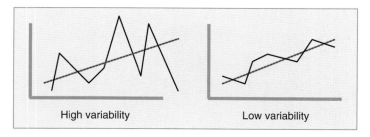

Figure 5.9
Variability of data.

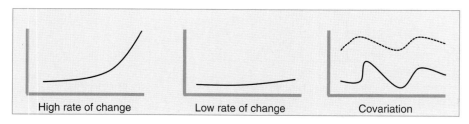

Figure 5.10
Rate of change.

in two lines, seeing how the rates compare, or if they vary together (called *covariation*; figure 5.10), suggesting some relationship or common factor between them that may be causing the covariation.

• *Patterns and cycles*   Patterns and cycles within the data might suggest some temporal influence on the data. For example, we would expect a dataset of 8 years of temperature measurements (figure 5.11) to show a wavy pattern suggesting seasonal influence and a flat section perhaps to indicate an ice age.

• *Outliers*   Outliers are the "exception to the rule"; they have values that are not in the range of other values in the dataset (figure 5.12). They can reveal anomalies that occur rarely but naturally (an 8-foot man), interesting case studies to explore (basketball player Manute Bol), or simply indicate mistakes in the data-entry process that should be corrected or omitted.

Qualitative Analysis

Qualitative information is typically rich in depth and the potential for powerful insights into the complex motivations and behavior of human activity, but it is often difficult to make use of in an interactive visualization. This is because of its observa-

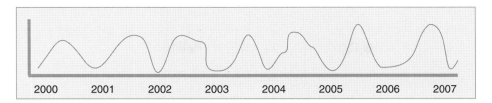

Figure 5.11
Patterns and cycles in data.

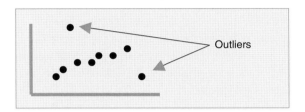

Figure 5.12
Outliers.

tional nature, which requires subjective human interpretation to extract meaning. Through rich media types such as historic documents, letters, photographs, oral histories, and videos, qualitative analysis relies on inductive reasoning to suggest the underlying truth of the base phenomenon.

Qualitative information is typically more abstract and lends itself to narratives rather than charts and graphs. Process diagrams and timelines can be useful methods for visualizing qualitative information, and there are a number of techniques for quantifying qualitative data. These include *coding*, where a person decides that a particular feature belongs in a particular category, and *text analysis*, sometimes referred to as text mining, where a single text or a collection of volumes is analyzed.

Coding Features

Coding is the process of assigning labels called *codes* to identify particular features found in a close reading or examination of the data resource. The codes can represent ideas, concepts, topics, themes, and descriptors that are found within the data. The code is given a meaningful name to uniquely identify the presence of that feature. This is an inherently subjective methodology, relying on one or more people's ability to be consistent in their feature identification and classification. A good guide to coding can be found onlined here.[3] Once features are coded, their frequencies can be

3. onlineqda.hud.ac.uk/Intro_QDA/how_what_to_code.php.

counted, and the more traditional statistical and presentation techniques can be applied to the code counts in order to gain insight from the frequency of their occurrences and their proximity to other codes (Taylor & Gibbs, 2010).

Text Analysis

A large majority of the historic artifacts available for analysis are textual in nature: books, letters, diaries, and official records. Text analysis has become increasingly popular. As more and more text-based historical records are transcribed and digitized, storage costs have dramatically fallen, and computation power has increased, new research in text- and data-mining techniques has been refined. These new technologies promise to unlock the meaning that is so evident to human readers but was previously opaque to computers on any meaningful level. Texts are analyzed in a five primary: by counting the frequency of words, mapping the differences in texts, parsing the sentence structure, finding where words cluster, and, ultimately, using software that can decipher the semantic meanings of words in a text.

Word Frequency Analysis

The number of times a given word is mentioned in a text or collection of texts is a useful piece of information regarding the importance of that word relative to others. Google has leveraged its digitization of millions of volumes by its *Ngram Viewer*, which allows people to search for words or phrases among the books. The *Ngram Viewer* will produce a graph showing the frequency of one or more terms over time in a line graph (figure 5.13).

Word clouds are a popular visualization technique used to communicate the frequency of words used in a particular text. The more often a word appears, the larger it is drawn. The word cloud shown in figure 5.14 was created using all of the words in this chapter by the *Wordle*[4] word cloud generator. Not surprisingly, *data* is the single most often-occurring word, followed by *values, relationships, information,* and *analysis*.

Sentence Structure Analysis

Text is largely unstructured, in contrast to more conventional quantitative data, for which items can be easily arranged into specific categories; however, that does not mean the text does not have structure that can be analyzed. Creating word trees using freely available tools such as ManyEyes[5] can parse texts into tree structures with branches that diverge based on certain words specified by the visualization designer.

4. www.wordle.net.
5. www-958.ibm.com/software/data/cognos/manyeyes.

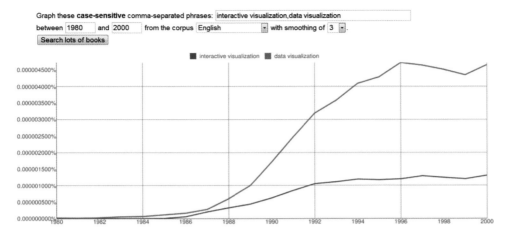

Figure 5.13
Word frequency analysis using Google's *Ngram Viewer*.

Figure 5.14
Word cloud of the text in this chapter using *Wordle*.

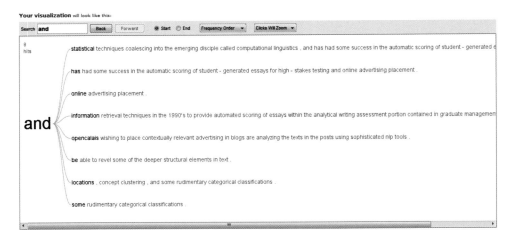

Figure 5.15
Word tree using ManyEyes' *WordTree* (courtesy of International Business Machines Corp, ©IBM).

Such branches might include parts of speech, locations, proper names, or transitive terms such as "encourages," "won't," "will," and others. The resulting tree structure can potentially reveal relationships between branches and highlight recurrent themes.

Along the same lines, ManyEyes also has an exploration/visualization tool called Phrase Net, which diagrams the relationships between words. In this example, "the" is connected to other words by thicker arrows. Users typically want to hide such common words, but if done, "smarter" appears to be a central word, resulting in a more interesting view of the concepts in the text (figures 5.15 and 5.16).

Differences Analysis
Literary scholars frequently want to compare the text from various editions or versions (called witnesses) of a single textual work. Tools such as *Juxta*[6] can present multiple witnesses and allow annotation and graphical comparison between them and provide quantitative tools such as histograms and heat maps to understand the relationships between and among passages (figure 5.17).

Visualization author and designer Ben Fry produced an interesting visualization that illustrates the value of highlighting textual difference. *Preservation of Favored Traces*[7] graphically maps textual changes between versions of Charles Darwin's *On the Origin of Species* to show the evolution of the book in its six editions on a page-by-page basis (figure 5.18). This allows viewers to get a sense of Darwin's thinking over the 14 years between the first edition in 1859 and the sixth edition published in 1872.

6. www.juxtasoftware.org.
7. http://benfry.com/traces.

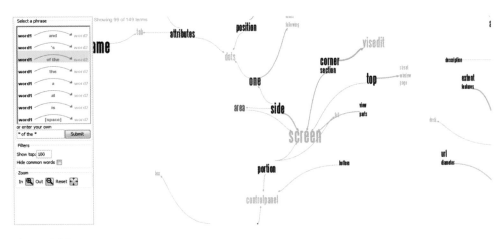

Figure 5.16
Phase mapping using ManyEyes' *Phrase Net* (courtesy of International Business Machines Corp, ©IBM).

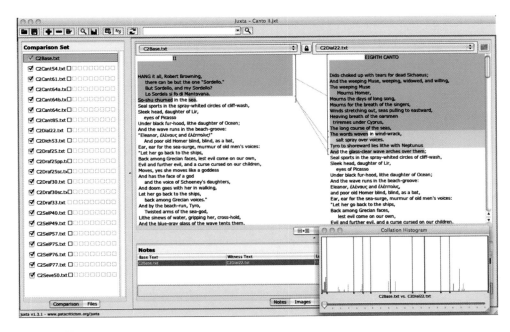

Figure 5.17
Juxta text difference analysis tool.

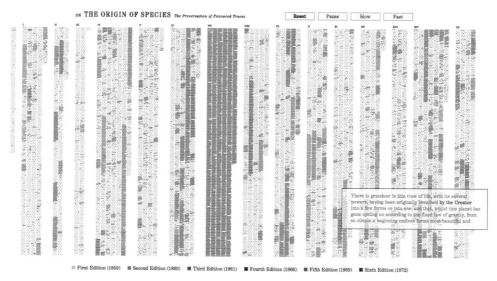

Figure 5.18
Differences in editions of Darwin's *On the Origin of Species*.

Cluster Analysis

Cluster analysis is a powerful data-mining technique for exposing potential relationships between words in a document or group of documents and can graphically reveal new insights into the underlying phenomenon previously possible only by time-consuming close reading. A number of methods can be used to achieve this kind of analysis, but the following is a description of how Jonathan Stray from the Associated Press used cluster analysis to reveal patterns in the WikiLeaks Iraqi war[8] documents. The process was able to automatically generate clustered categories from them and reveal some interesting observations.

The text from the document is first converted into a *"bag of words,"* meaning the word's order in the sentence is ignored. The words are then *stemmed*, so that they are reduced to their root forms (i.e., *looks, looked,* and *looking* become *look*). The stemmed words are then counted and given a *TF-IDF score*[9] based on their importance, which also gets rid of stop words, such as *a, the,* and *of*. These make up the dots or *nodes* in the graph, and they were colored according to the military's original coding of the document. Each individual document was analyzed for its similarity to each other document using a technique called *cosine similarity*, and the nodes were

8. WikiLeaks refers to a set of stolen government documents released to the press.
9. This is a proportion of the word's frequency in the document compared to the full corpus.

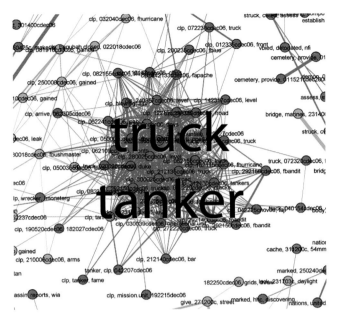

Figure 5.19
Cluster analysis of WikiLeaks documents (image courtesy Jonathan Stray/Associated Press).

placed according to their degree of similarity, with a line or *edge* connecting each similar node.

What emerges is a network map of the words, spatially arranged by the similarities of the documents they appear in. For example, the multiple reports of tanker trucks appearing in documents coded in red as "explosive hazard" cluster together around the words "truck" and "tanker," suggesting that fuel trucks were being used as explosive weapons (figure 5.19) (Grimmer & King, 2009; Stray, 2011).

Semantic Analysis

There has been tremendous progress in the ability of computers to understand what words actually mean called *natural language processing* (NLP). This is done through the use of artificial intelligence, computer science, and probabilistic and statistical techniques coalescing into the emerging discipline called *computational linguistics* and has had some success in the automatic scoring of student-generated essays for high-stakes testing and online advertising placement.

The Educational Testing Service began experimenting with NLP and information retrieval techniques in the 1990s to provide automated scoring of essays within the Analytical Writing Assessment portion contained in the Graduate Management Admissions Test used for business school entrance (Wang & Brown, 2007). More recently, firms such as OpenAmplify[10] and OpenCalais[11] wishing to place contextually relevant advertising in blogs are analyzing the texts in the posts using sophisticated NLP tools.

Semantic analysis presents promise for visualizations of textual material to move beyond simple counting and be able to reveal some of the deeper structural elements in text. NLP tools can accurately classify words as their parts of speech (i.e., nouns, verbs, etc.), identify proper names and locations, concept clustering, and some rudimentary categorical classifications. The tools are currently mainly the domain of computation linguists, but there is rapid progress in providing usable capabilities for digital humanists (Oard, 2009).

Factor Matrix Analysis

One of the advantages of having multivariate data that consist of multiple factors is the ability to make connections between elements that may not have been apparent at the time the data had initially been collected or structured. It can be useful to construct a matrix of the categories and systematically look at pairs of factors to evaluate whether exploring the interaction between them might yield any useful understandings.

A *factor matrix* lists the factors to explore in a table, with both the column and row headers populated with their field names (figure 5.20). Obviously, comparing identical fields is not valuable, but systematically comparing each field with every other may suggest one or more possibilities to explore that may not have been obvious. These relationships can be bidirectional so that alternative perspectives about causation can

factors	Height	Weight	Sweet-toothiness
Height	x	Do tall people weigh more than short?	Does sugar stunt growth?
Weight	Are obese people taller than skinny?	x	Does eating sugar make you obese?
Sweet-toothiness	Do tall people like to eat sugar more than short?	Do obese people eat sugar because they're obese?	X

Figure 5.20
Factor matrix analysis (thanks to Kurtis Schaeffer).

10. www.openamplify.com.
11. www.opencalais.com.

be easily explored as possible research questions. The pairs of factors can be contrasted and compared with one another and graphically plotted against each other to see correlations.

Summary

This chapter discusses many ways to look at the newly structured data and envision strategies through which data can be *analyzed* and *represented* so that the data can answer the questions posed. The emerging field of design synthesis is a useful framework for demystifying and making explicit the creative design process using abductive reasoning techniques. Rooted in sensemaking theories, design synthesis develops design patterns by judging what data are relevant, making connections between elements, and reframing perspectives.

Nathan Shedroff's *spectrum of understanding* defines a useful way to look at the different elements from the raw data to the information where potential patterns and relationships between the data elements start to emerge and to knowledge, for which a participatory understanding is ultimately communicated, and finally, to the personal realization of wisdom that is a result of the communication.

Edward Tufte's *principles of analytic design* can provide guidance in creating evidence-based presentations that put producers and consumers in reflexive harmony. His six principles—offer comparisons, show causality, show multivariate data, integrate words and images, document the provenance, and have good content—provide a practical guide to getting insight from data.

Statistics and *informatics* provide powerful tools for an analysis of quantitative data. Looking at relationships among elements, trends, contrasts, change over time, and preliminary statistical analyses can be useful ways to understand the dataset and make decisions on how best to represent it.

Qualitative information is typically rich in depth and has the potential for powerful insights into the complex motivations and behavior of human activity. *Qualitative analysis* has its own set of powerful tools for making sense of qualitative data. *Coding* is the process of assigning labels to identify particular features found in a close reading or examination of the data resource. A rising number of powerful and freely available text programs are available for analysis and text mining through word-frequency, sentence-structure, differences, and semantic analyses.

It can be useful to construct a matrix of the categories and systematically look at pairs of factors to evaluate whether exploring the interaction between them might yield any useful understandings. A *factor matrix* lists the factors to explore in a table, with both the column and row headers populated with their field names.

The next chapter looks at how visualizations are structurally, dynamically, and graphically represented for users to interact with.

6   Represent the Visualization

The way to get started is to quit talking and begin doing.
—Walt Disney

Creating a successful visualization involves the marshaling of effective data sources to answer meaningful questions using interactive methods that exhibit appealing aesthetic design and strong usability. The visible product of the entire visualization process is its *representation*, which is where users will interact with the information presented. Creating that representation is a careful blend of *science*, *art*, and *display technology*, and this chapter examines all three elements in detail.

The *science* component of a visualization's representation addresses the current thinking on how people perceive and interpret the world around them. Because of biology and evolution, human beings have both advantages and limitations in the way they interpret information presented through the senses. Effective representations should be aware of those bounds to exploit natural abilities while they avoid taxing the limits using the research in interaction, perception, cognition, usability, and even fun as a guide.

Interactive visualizations are visual expressions of data. The aesthetic issues of the *art* segment are important in how effective the visualization will be viewed by the user. According to research cited by cognitive scientist Don Norman (2004), *"attractive things work better."* Because visualizations are often instruments of persuasion, the art is not limited to the skills offered by visual design, but need to include the crafts of storytelling and rhetoric.

Finally, the *display technology* provides the ultimate embodiment of the visualization in the eyes of the user. Recent advances in computer and Internet technologies have opened up a wealth of possibilities for visualization designers that are just now being explored as new software tools are developed and made available. These advanced capabilities have led to many innovative and useful techniques for representing information in ways that encourage discovery and understanding.

- The science of interaction, perception, cognition, and fun
- Art of aesthetics, color, space, and persuasion
- The display of charts, images, networks, and time
- The display of location, dimension, animation, and media
- Tools for building visualizations

The Science Component of Visualization

The *science* component of a visualization's representation requires a good understanding of the current research that helps explain how people perceive and understand the world that surrounds them. Human beings have both advantages and limitations in the way they interpret information presented through the senses, and effective representations should be aware of these boundaries and rely on the research in *interaction, perception, cognition, usability*, and even *fun*.

The Science of Interaction

Interaction describes how the user dynamically manipulates the visualization to change the nature of the information being represented. Interaction is what separates a traditional *information visualization* from *interactive visualization*. An interactive visualization provides an opportunity for the user to be in a virtual dialogue with the visualization in which the user manipulates elements that the visualization should rapidly respond to, optimally within 1/10 second (Williamson & Shneiderman, 1992).

Affordances and Constraints

In interactive visualizations, *affordances* can be traditional user-interface controls such as sliders, radio buttons, checkboxes, and text-entry fields. These are obvious potential manipulatives, but directions provided as explanatory text can point out less apparent control opportunities, such as prompting the user to drag elements to rearrange them or reveal other spaces within. The goal of an affordance in an interactive visualization should be to make these affordances visible and relevant to the visualization's desired goals and user experience.

Constraints form the counterpoint of affordances. Constraints restrict the range of action possible by the user and guide the user toward a more productive relationship with the visualization. Constraints can be effected in a visualization by graying out or hiding information and interactive options that are not germane or by limiting the range of options available. It is that balanced interplay between affordances and constraints that successfully guides the user toward a rewarding interactive experience.

The Action Cycle

Interacting with a problem can be broken down into a series of discrete goal-directed steps taken by the user when trying to achieve that goal. These steps can be instructive

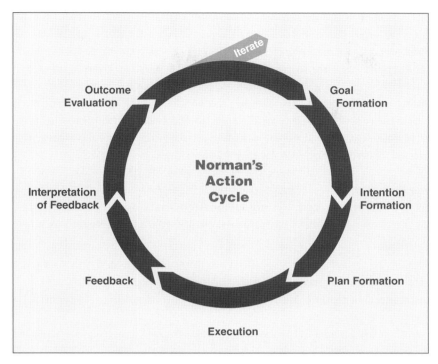

Figure 6.1
Donald Norman's action cycle (adapted from a drawing by Pete Kinser).

in designing interactive visualizations. Norman (1988) described this as an *action cycle* with seven sequential and iterative steps toward achieving a given goal (figure 6.1):

1. *Goal formation* Setting a goal that can be planned out, opportunistic, or the end result of a previous action cycle iteration. The goal represents the desired outcome of the process: *The room is dark, and I need more light to read my book.*
2. *Intention formation* Making a commitment to reach the goal: *Turning on the nearby light would help me read.*
3. *Plan formation* Determining the specific actions required to reach the goal: *I need to turn on the light switch.*
4. *Execution* The actual action: *Turning on the light.*
5. *Feedback* Perceiving the state of the world: *Seeing that the light turned on.*
6. *Interpretation of feedback* Determining the effect of the action: *Is there enough light now so that I can now read my book?*
7. *Evaluation of outcome* Determining if the goal has been reached: *If I can read my book, nothing more needs to be done. If I cannot, I need to repeat the action cycle or choose a new goal, such as move the lamp closer to me.*

Within this action cycle are two chasms or roadblocks that may prevent a user from reaching his or her goal. These are sometimes referred to as the *gulf of execution* and the *gulf of evaluation*. The former refers to a situation when the system does not provide affordances that enable the user to attain the desired goal (i.e., the lamp has a switch that is hard to turn on). The gulf of evaluation occurs when the user cannot assess the current status of the system to see whether the action had the desired effect, such as the lamp that turns on very slowly in response to the switch. The idea is to minimize the size of these two gulfs, and the action cycle provides a systematic means to investigate the process (Norman, 1988).

The Interaction Dance

Meadows (2003) identified interaction through four steps that form an iterative process that encourages the user to "dance" with the visualization in a reflexive and recursive manner:

1. The user makes an *assessment* of the initial environment provided and sees what affordances for manipulation have been provided by the visualization.
2. The user starts to *explore* some of those affordances and experiment with the ways they can be manipulated.
3. The visualization will *respond* to the user's manipulation, and much as when a driver turns the steering wheel and observes a change in the car's direction, the user begins to understand how to control the visualization's response.
4. The previous steps may encourage *reciprocal change* in which the user and visualization continue to react to one another. The visualization reacts to changes from the user, and, in response, the user will reframe the manipulation to seek new information. The process may repeat itself endlessly.

A Taxonomy of Interaction

There have been a number of attempts to create a taxonomy of the kinds of interactive elements used in interactive visualizations, but the most comprehensive list was compiled by a group of Georgia Tech researchers. Coming from a user-centered perspective of *user intent*, they reviewed over 100 existing information visualizations and papers and found 311 individual interaction techniques that they categorized into the following themes (Yi, Kang, Stasko, & Jacko, 2007):

• *Select*   The act of marking some element of the dataset as interesting in some way to keep track of, analyze, or represent it in a visually distinctive manner; this is usually coupled to other categories of interactive elements.

• *Explore*   The ability of users to select a different subset of the dataset using techniques such as panning through the data via scrollbars and drilling down to different subsets by clicking on them.

• *Reconfigure* To show a different arrangement or organization of the dataset, for example, by time or some other facet, or simple changes to the display rendering. This can uncover patterns when data are occluded by other data.

• *Encode* To change the graphical encoding of the representation to better communicate the underlying phenomenon. This can be done by changing the display techniques, such as changing from a line chart to a scattergram, or by changing the color coding.

• *Abstract/elaborate* Changing the level of detail provided can help users see overarching issues and spot outliers, supporting Shneiderman's *details on demand*.

• *Filter* Allowing the user to dynamically change the selection criteria can highlight internal dynamics present in the dataset. The filtering can be done by eliminating items based on volume or any of the data's structured dimensions.

• *Connect* Provides techniques that highlight the interconnections between different data elements, such as those found in social networks.

The Science of Perception

People make sense of visual representations by using a combination of their eyes and their brain. The interplay between the two creates an interpreted internal representation that may not precisely follow what is actually being displayed. A given person's visual system has many features and limitations that mold that individual's perception before information is presented to the brain for higher-level interpretation. Eyes, for example, are sensitive to changes in color, line, shape, and luminance that are not linear. For some, a 50 percent reduction in light intensity may not result in perception of the light being half as bright.

That raw visual input is then interpreted by various parts of the brain, some that specialize in detecting patterns and motion and others trained by life to respond with expectations and assumptions. An understanding of how perceptual issues factor into understanding is useful in designing and representing data visually. Stephen Few (2009) makes three observations about how people collect and process visual information:

1. *Visual perception is selective* To keep from being visually overwhelmed, we do not pay attention to everything we see. Capturing our attention is a precious commodity. We are sensitive to contrast and change.

2. *We see what we know* Our attention and perception are drawn toward familiar and previously seen objects. Visualizations will work best when composed of familiar and easy-to-recognize patterns.

3. *Memory is limited* The relatively small capacity of our short-term visual memory plays a big role in limiting the amount of information that we are actually able to perceive from looking at an image at a given moment.

Figure 6.2
Some common preattentive visual attributes (adapted from Few, 2009).

Preattentive Perceptions

Some perceptions appear to target a more primal reaction than others, probably because of evolutionary advantages at some point in our history as a species. These perceptions are called *preattentive attributes* because they are processed at a more automatic, associative level and require less specific focus by the conscious mind (Treisman & Gormicon, 1988). This is a useful evolutionary artifact to exploit when one is designing effective visualizations.

When looking to contrast two or more visual elements, it is important that viewers can easily distinguish between them with a minimum amount of effort. An unlimited number of techniques can be used to visually differentiate sets of data, but some are inherently preattentive and thus provide the most contrast. These techniques include changing the hue, brightness, size, shape, length, enclosure, orientation, or spatial grouping as demonstrated in figure 6.2 (Few, 2009).

Preattentive perceptions are typically processed rapidly, usually within ¼ second and take advantage of the brain's largely subconscious parallel processing capabilities to render cognition with very little conscious effort. This capability can be harnessed to direct viewers to the most important elements in a visualization and ensure that particular contrasts are readily apparent (Healey, 2007).

Postattentive Perception

Postattentive processing is slower than preattentive processing and involves more directed and conscious activity by the cerebral cortex. Postattentive processing occurs when the user is forced to search for patterns that were not made obvious through preattentive perception because the differences were initially hard to discern or required high-level thought to mentally combine or interpret visual features (Healey, 2007).

Activities that involve a mental lookup or require a user to do some calculation in order to interpret the relevance of a perception will be processed postattentively. This can occur in an interface that uses arbitrary icons or colors that require the user to consult a legend or force the user to compute the percentage of some values to a whole in order to understand the underlying phenomenon displayed.

The Gestalt Laws

The Gestalt school of psychology, founded in 1912 by group a German psychologists, investigated how people recognized patterns (the German word *Gestalt* means pattern). The Gestalt school of psychology came up with eight *Gestalt Laws* of pattern recognition.

1. *Proximity* Objects near each another will be perceived as being connected with one another.
2. *Similarity* Objects that look alike will be perceived as being part of the same group. The similarity can be achieved by color, shape, size, texture, or orientation.
3. *Connectedness* When objects are physically connected, they are perceived as group members. This law can override other laws such as proximity or similarity.
4. *Continuity* Intersecting lines and shapes are perceived as continuous objects and shapes rather than as the sum of their intersections.
5. *Symmetry* Symmetrical objects are perceived to be part of the same group.
6. *Closure* Objects whose paths are occluded by other objects are perceived with the missing gaps included.
7. *Relative size* The smaller components of a pattern tend to be perceived as objects, with the larger components perceived as the background.
8. *Figure and ground* The preceding seven laws contribute to the pattern perception, but they are dependent on what is considered foreground or background.

Gestalt Laws provide a useful way to design groups of objects so that people can make sense of their intended organization (Ware, 2004).

Color/Shape Perception

Perception can be controlled by providing elements with enough contrast so they are perceived as separate entities. Color can be contrasted by three primary attributes: its chrominance (hue), luminance (brightness), and the background the color is drawn on. The perceived contrast will be greater when the chromatic or luminance difference is larger, when a limited number of other colors are competing for attention, or when the color's chrominance or luminance is different from that of the background (Ware, 2008). Some attributes such as size, brightness, and color are relative to their surroundings. This is important to be aware of when these attributes are used to indicate relative quantities; otherwise, as in examples given below, they may not accurately reflect the true values they are employed to represent:

The colors of the two X's in figure 6.3 are identical, but their appearance varies depending on the color of the background.

The two arrows in figure 6.4 are exactly the same length, but the arrows encourage the perception that the lower line is longer.

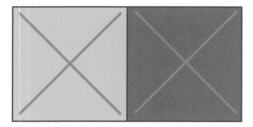

Figure 6.3
Color is dependent on background luminance.

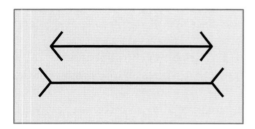

Figure 6.4
Shape can affect length perception.

The six boxes in figure 6.5 are exactly the same color but appear to be different intensities based on which part of the grayscale they are positioned over.

The pairs of boxes in figure 6.6 are identical, but their luminance appears different depending on the background (adapted from Fairchild, 1999).

The grayscales in figure 6.7 are identical, but their ranges appear different depending on the background (adapted from Fairchild, 1999).

The Science of Cognition

As complicated as the recent brain research can be to understand, there is one "big idea" that impacts the representation of visualization, and that is the limitation of the number of separate items we can hold in our *short-term working memory*. It is able to hold only seven items, plus or minus two, at one time (figure 6.8) and, equally important, able to contrast, combine, or manipulate only two to four elements (Miller, 1956). In addition, all of the contents of working memory are lost within 20 seconds without internal exposure to the information. Although it is possible to extend that number using techniques such as "chunking" (i.e., putting things in groups, like area codes), this fundamental limitation needs to be respected for effective visualizations.

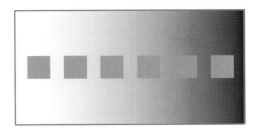

Figure 6.5
Perception of luminance is dependent on background.

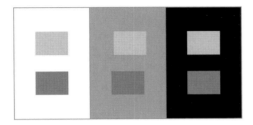

Figure 6.6
Perception of luminance is dependent on background.

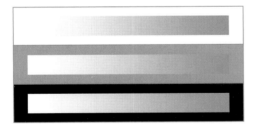

Figure 6.7
Perception of luminance is dependent on background.

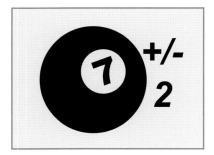

Figure 6.8
The magic number 7 ± 2.

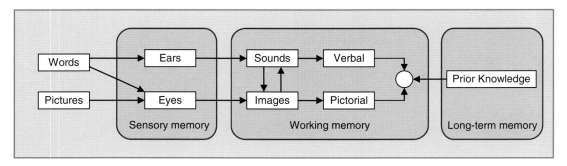

Figure 6.9
Cross-encoding of information (adapted from Mayer, 2005).

Later research has suggested that there are actually two separate stores of short-term memory: a visual/spatial memory that stores perception of two- and three-dimensional objects and a phonological loop that stores audio perceptions (Baddeley, 1992). The two channels operate relatively independently, and certain kinds of information can be cross-encoded. For example, on-screen text is presented and processed visually, but it is encoded both verbally and pictorially (figure 6.9).

Implications for Interactive Visualizations
The implications of these cognitive issues for design are critical in interactive visualizations. Communication, understanding, and persuasion can be increased by designing with our uniquely human limitations in mind:

• Projects should be designed to limit the number of items a user needs to keep in his or her head at any given time using chunking, aggregation, and redundant displays of key information.

• Visualizations should not depend on the user needing to compare more than two or three independent elements at a time to encourage maximum understanding.

• Information can be cross-encoded. Even though text is perceived visually, it is stored phonologically and thereby can be used to help users consider more options simultaneously.

• Visualizations can reduce the need for working memory by making identifications explicit. For example, representing a concept indirectly so that the user needs to look up something in a legend or table should be avoided.

• Provide representational opportunities that encourage thinking to become a joint activity working with knowledge both "in the head" and "in the world."

The Science of Usability

The representation of interactive visualizations is a dialogue between the designer of the project and those who interact with it, and it is important to make that experience a productive one. There is a vibrant research community focused on recognizing the central role the "user" (an unfortunate choice of word) plays in that exchange, called *user-centered design* (Shneiderman & Plaisant, 2010). Cognitive psychologist Donald Norman is the most visible proponent of improving the usability of things we interact with. The usability of most projects can be dramatically improved if we pay attention to just a few factors (Norman, 1988):

• *Provide consistent models*   When a visualization designer develops a project, there is an underlying organization to the project's design. But this is just one of three possible understandings of that organization once the project is completed. Equally important are the way the designer's model is actually represented in the visualization itself and, finally, the user's own understanding of it. The visualization is the intermediary the designer uses to interact with the user, and in a perfect world, all three perspectives should be precisely aligned.

• *Make things visible*   Making features obvious to users helps them see what elements can be interacted with. The designer chooses what features to make visible (*affordances*) and which ones are hidden or unavailable (*constraints*) at any given time. This interplay of affordances and constraints provides an opportunity to guide the user to explore potentially useful features while ignoring superfluous ones. Too many options can be as stifling as too few; so a thoughtful and dynamic balance will improve a project's usability.

• *Provide good mappings*   The actions the user is prompted to perform or to represent an activity should mirror that activity's nature. For example, a left-to-right slider is more appropriate for setting the width of an object than its height.

• *Offer good feedback*   If a user performs an action, the visualization should acknowledge that action by providing immediate feedback to indicate what changes were

made. If the state of the visualization has changed based on user interaction, make that new state readily apparent to the user. Feedback can be visual and/or auditory to provide information about the internal state of the model. Feedback is more effective when repeated, immediate, and consistent. The subtle use of color, font, shape, cursor shape, and so forth, can help reinforce cues about its internal state.
• *Design for humanity*   To err is human. Users will consistently do things the designer did not expect them to do. A good visualization will try to anticipate as many of these situations and deal with them proactively. Designers should try to make all appropriate actions reversible, so if unforeseen actions occur (and they will), they can be undone with a minimum of effort on the user's behalf. It is also important to be aware of the limits human beings have in terms of short-term memory and perception and not expect them to do things that breach those limits.

The Science of Fun
A well-designed visualization should be fun and pleasurable to use. The potential benefit is that users will be willing to spend more time interacting with the visualization, get more out of the experience, and be more likely to recommend it to others.

Pleasure
Usability researcher Patrick Jordan (2000 sees the role of usability as a necessary but insufficient requirement for creating products that are pleasurable to use. He identified four ways that products can be perceived as pleasurable based on the work of Canadian anthropologist Lionel Tiger. These factors provide a framework to look at a visualization's potential to deliver a pleasurable or fun experience:

1. *Physio-pleasure*   Refers to pleasure derived from the various senses. Visualizations typically cannot facilitate this kind of pleasure, but a coffee maker does this by providing an enticing aroma.
2. *Socio-pleasure*   The enjoyment from the collegiality shared with other people through facilitating social gathering, such as the coffee maker's role in attracting colleagues, associations, and a visualization's ability to promote comments by others.
3. *Psycho-pleasure*   The delight received from emotional reactions to the product. The coffee maker lacks the sophistication to provide many emotional cues, but visualizations can evoke psycho-pleasure by instilling a sense of mastery of manipulating a complex inquiry or making a new connection to disparate pieces of data.
4. *Ideo-pleasure*   The pleasure of identifying with personal tastes, aspirations, values, and value positions that resonate with the user. An espresso maker may appeal to the user's sense of urban sophistication, and a visualization may provide confirmation of beliefs based on the data presented.

These four elements provide a useful framework to view the way human beings feel pleasure: *physiologically, emotionally, sociologically*, and *ideologically*. Applying this anthropological concept to design can be valuable by providing a structured approach to a topic that is often difficult to quantify.

Flow

The concept of flow was identified by psychologist Mihaly Csikszentmihaly (1991) to describe the state of mind achieved when a person is completely engrossed in the activity he or she is performing and experiencing pleasure at that immersion. People experience flow when engaged in games, sports, and even many work situations. When in a *flow state*, people's sense of time is compressed, and they tend to perform the task better.

Visualizations can encourage this flow state by:

- Making clear the structure and goals of the project
- Making the visualization intrinsically rewarding
- Providing a good sense of control over the process
- Striking a good balance between the user's being capable of achieving and the goal still representing a challenge
- Providing clear and immediate feedback as to the progress in achieving those goals, so that the user can modulate his or her performance to meet them.

How Video Games Can Inform Visualization

Video games have long been envied by educators for the degree of engagement they elicit from their students compared to students' levels of classroom engagement. Games have received a large amount of critical attention from authors such as literary studies professor James Paul Gee and game designer Marc Prensky. Gee used games as a means to understand the educational process and to develop some principles for the K–12 classroom. He identified 36 learning principles that can be employed beyond gaming and grouped them under three main ideas: empowering learners, problem solving, and understanding (Gee, 2003).

Video games rely on a sense of the immersion to provide a high degree of pleasurable involvement with the game (Brown & Cairns, 2004). The first phase of immersion is *engagement*, where the player interacts with the game with an ever-increasing degree of time, effort, and attention. The second phase is *engrossment*, in which the player becomes emotionally connected to the play activity, and attention to thoughts and events external to the game become less dominant. Finally, a state of *immersion* is achieved, very similar to Csikszentmihaly's state of flow. The total attention of the player is directed toward the game, the player's sense of time is altered, and a Zen-like focus on the present activity is achieved.

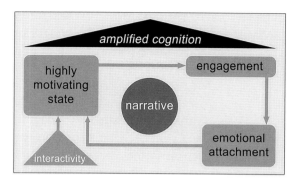

Figure 6.10
The narrative motor (adapted from Man, 2011).

New-media researcher Philip Man believes that video games can inform interactive visualization as well as education. Their narrative can act as a driving force to engage users to become emotionally attached and realize a highly motivated emotional state in an iterative loop that encourages the user to *"not only feel the data, but live it."* The narrative provides the context for understanding the data and a context in which to begin to develop questions to explore, and it provides the precursor necessary for immersion into the experience. The interactivity component provides the user empowerment to navigate this virtuous cycle (figure 6.10) (Man, 2011).

The Art Component of Visualization

Interactive visualizations are visual expressions of data, and the aesthetic issues of the *art* segment are important to how effective the visualization will be viewed by the user (Cawthon & Vande Moere, 2007). The innovative industrial designer Branko Lukić (2011) offered: *"The role of aesthetics is not to make things beautiful. It is to awaken the senses."* According to research cited by cognitive scientist Don Norman (2004), *"attractive things work better."* Because these visualizations are often instruments of persuasion, art is not limited to the skills offered by visual design but needs to include the crafts involved in storytelling and rhetoric.

The Art of Visual Aesthetics
The role of visual aesthetics cannot be overemphasized. The effective use of visual design principles will greatly improve the communicability and success of a visualization and encourage people to spend more time with it. Naturally, designers with more experience will tend to produce better designs, but these principles are much less subjective than they are generally assumed to be and are easily learned, providing an achievable baseline for success. A number of excellent guides to graphic design include

Nancy Duarte's (2008) *slide:ology* and Robin Williams' (2004) *The Non-Designer's Design Book,* which rapidly cover the fundamental concepts of presentation design.

The Role of Aesthetics in Visualization

A common criticism of some infographics and visualizations is that they sacrifice substance for style, resulting in what is sometimes called *eye candy* or *chart junk* (Tufte, 1983). This occurs when the design elements distract from the communicative message and should be avoided when the added graphics do not increase the communicative value.

Increasing the aesthetic quality in a visualization is not an act of vanity on the part of its designer. A number of studies have shown a strong positive correlation between the perceived aesthetic quality of the visualization and the willingness of users to take the time to interact with it, to understand its meaning, or to extract information from it. These were measured by the degree of task abandonment and the time it takes to recognize false information retrieval results (Crawthon & Vande Moere, 2007).

Some visualizations are designed to be purely artistic, such as the automated music visualizations within Apple's iTunes player (figure 6.11), whereas others, such as stock market displays (figure 6.12) forgo aesthetic qualities for more pragmatic communication.

Figure 6.11
Abstract visualizations of music.

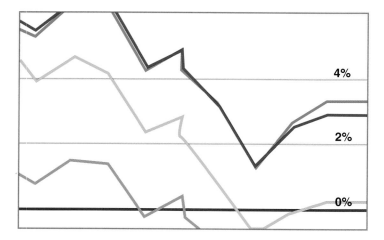

Figure 6.12
Stock market data.

Both are data-based visualizations: the music pattern from the sound file's data and the chart from market trades. They differ because the music data are not *readable*, meaning that while the shifting patterns dance with the music, it is not possible to connect the music data to a shape, in contrast to the stock chart, where the shape of the line directly conveys the underlying stock trading data (Kosara, 2007).

Aesthetics is, of course, closely associated with art and artistic endeavors, but one of an information visualization's primary goals is to provide an *exploratory* and/or *expository* experience that is based on data. Exploratory environments provide more objective renderings that offer opportunities to develop new hypotheses and understandings, such as census information. Expository visualizations leave less room to explore in favor of a more focused and subjective message (Wijk, 2005).

The Art of *Color*

The choice of color in visualizations is often a problem for designers. There are the competing goals of desiring an attractive rendition versus the need for clarity and communicative value, and overall ignorance of how color theory can be employed to resolve that conflict. A trained colorist can distinguish among a million or more colors, but the average person can detect only 20,000 and is able to definitively distinguish about 25 (Tufte, 1990).

A good visualization will typically have a core set of three to five colors (called a *palette*) plus one *neutral* and one *highlight* color to draw from. Neutral colors (such as shade of gray or beige) are typically used as the background and to divide spaces up.

The highlight color provides accent and creates emphasis for particular elements such as text (Duarte, 2008).

It is also important to keep in mind that approximately 8 percent of the world (mostly men) have some form of color blindness, where they are unable to distinguish between shades of certain colors, such as red and green. It is possible to compensate for this inability by making sure the contrast between elements is high, particularly when it is important to make that discrimination in the visualization. See the section on accessibility in chapter 13 for more information on these and other accessibility issues.

Color Systems

A given color can be described in a number of ways. Computers use the *Red Green Blue* (RGB) model to match the way the individual pixels are stored in system memory, where the final color is the combination of those three colors. This structure has dominated how web-based tools describe colors, but this is an extremely unintuitive way to think about color. A more useful model is the *Hue Luminance Saturation* (HLS) model, where *hue* refers to the shade of the color (e.g., red, yellow, cyan), *luminance* is how light or dark the color is, and *saturation* is how vibrant it is ranging from pastel to pure color.

The same color can be represented in any model; so a designer can envision a color in HLS and easily convert it to RGB (i.e., HLS 0,100,100 is the same color red as RGB 255,0,0) for use on a computer graphic device. RGB colors are usually expressed as a single hexadecimal 6-digit code like this for the color red: 0xff0000 or #ff0000.

Color Schemes

Sir Isaac Newton introduced the world to the concept of the color wheel in 1666, where the colors are arranged according to their hue (figure 6.13). It serves as a powerful visualization that graphically reveals the underlying structure behind color theory and provides a framework to construct useful relationships between colors (Itten, 1970).

Just as there is a structure in music that generates pleasing sounds based on the relationships to their base notes (i.e., thirds, fifths, sevenths), there is a foundational basis in choosing colors that work well with one another based on their place on the color wheel:

• *Monochromatic* These are colors that have the same hue component of a single color on the wheel (figure 6.14), which makes them ideal to represent continua of values within a single category, such as coloring features of maps to represent populations and other kinds of ordered data.

• *Neutral* A variant of the monochromatic color scheme, neutral colors have little or no color saturation component. They can be grayscales or other low saturated colors

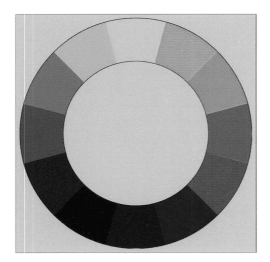

Figure 6.13
The color wheel.

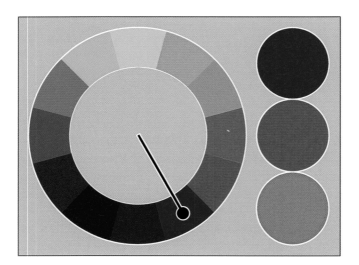

Figure 6.14
Monochromatic color scheme.

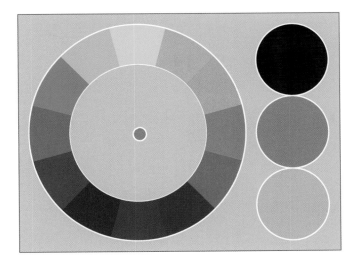

Figure 6.15
Neutral color scheme.

such as brown or beige (figure 6.15). Like monochromatic schemes, neutrals are useful with ordered data.

• *Analogous*   These are colors that are adjacent to one another on the color wheel (figure 6.16); they promote a sense of harmony while still providing some hue-based discrimination. Analogous color schemes need to have enough contrast if being used to identify datasets.

• *Complementary*   These are colors on opposite sides of the color wheel, such as red/green or blue/yellow (figure 6.17), and create a sense of vibrancy when highly saturated. This is particularly useful when one is trying to highlight items and make them stand out.

• *Split-complementary*   Using the base color and the two adjacent colors provides good contrast with less stress than the straight complementary scheme (figure 6.18). This scheme is a favorite of beginners, as it generally looks satisfying regardless of the colors chosen.

• *Triad*   Like a musical chord, the triad (figure 6.19) provides a harmonious color combination that is vibrant. It is made by choosing three colors evenly spaced around the color wheel. One color is the dominant color, and the other two are used as accents.

• *Tetrad*   This scheme is similar to the triad, but four colors are evenly spaced around the color wheel (figure 6.20), arranged around two pairs of complementary colors but offering more variety.

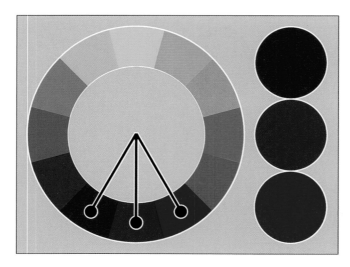

Figure 6.16
Analogous color scheme.

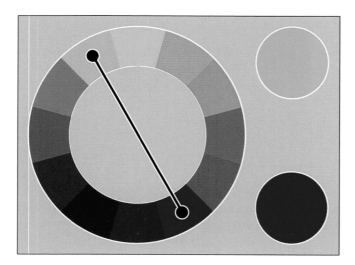

Figure 6.17
Complementary color scheme.

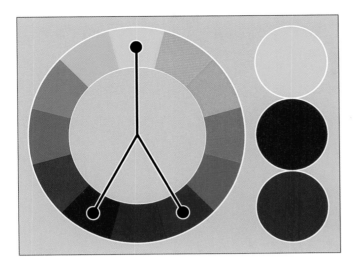

Figure 6.18
Split-complementary color scheme.

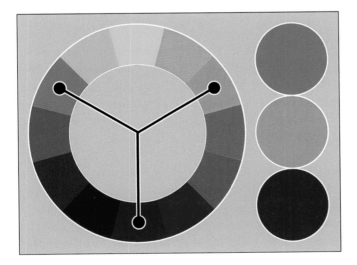

Figure 6.19
Triadic color scheme.

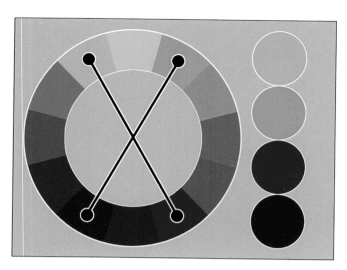

Figure 6.20
Tetradic color scheme.

Color Design Tools

A number of excellent online tools can help you select colors by interactively harnessing color theory and the color wheel to make selection by the schemes outlined above very easy. *Color Scheme Designer*[1] and Adobe's *Kuler*[2] are free web sites that enable rapid creation of color schemes from any color. Kuler (figure 6.21) allows you to browse a large collection of palettes created by others and use them as a starting point and is built into all of Adobe's image-editing tools such as *Photoshop*, *Flash*, and *Illustrator*.

The Art of Spatial Arrangement

The arrangement of the individual graphical elements displayed on the screen at any given time provides an opportunity to communicate the message with more clarity. How the elements visually interact with one another provides a number of tools for creating a more effective message, and the order in which they occur or are perceived will alter that message. The following dimensions offer ways to use arrangement to full advantage (Duarte, 2008):

• *Contrast* The ability to differentiate one element from another provides a powerful communicative tool and allows the viewer to rapidly identify the main point. Contrast can be achieved by differentiating size, color, texture, and orientation. The degree of contrast need not be overwhelming but just enough to make a clear difference.

1. http://colorschemedesigner.com.
2. http://kuler.adobe.com.

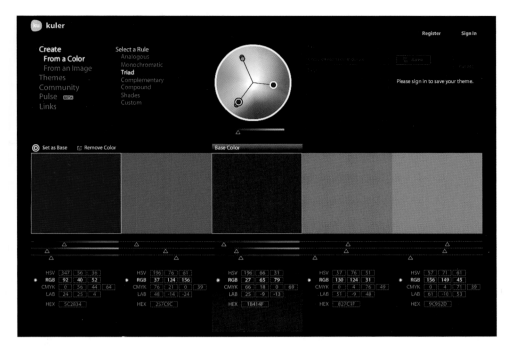

Figure 6.21
Kuler color software (screenshot reprinted with permission from Adobe Systems Inc.).

• *Flow*   Western readers naturally scan the screen from left to right, but that flow can be redirected by progressively sized or colored elements, arrows, and other highlighting techniques to call attention to particular elements and tell a story using the sequencing of the elements in the viewer's eye.

• *Hierarchy*   People have a natural affinity to sense the relationships between elements, and those relationships can be important communications of meaning. A purposeful use of that tendency can be to reinforce how the data are structured and increase their understanding. For example, small elements clustered around a larger central element might suggest a *parent-child* relationship between them.

• *Unity*   Using overarching frameworks, such as a grid, unified color palette, or graphical template can help organize the composition and provide viewers a fast way to navigate the visualization. As with flow and hierarchy, unity can also provide the viewer with valuable visual cues as to the information's internal structuring.

• *Proximity*   The proximity of elements to one another can convey information about their relationships. The arrangement can convey order/chaos, equality, sequence, and other relationships.

• *White space*   The scarcity of screen real estate often discourages opening up the visualization to "breathe," but empty spaces increase the communicative effectiveness, and the need for screen space can be solved by using fourth-dimension space-sharing techniques described below.

The Art of the Fourth Dimension

A visualization typically consists of a number of graphical elements: some always present, some appear on demand, and some make multiple uses of the limited space the screen can show at any one time. Management of this scarce resource (sometimes called its *real estate*) is one of the most important tasks in representing an interactive visualization and adds a *fourth visual dimension* to the problem, which can be thought of as time or layers or some combination of both. Fourth-dimensional solutions include techniques such as shared spaces, layers, pop-ups, tabbed spaces, timelines, zooming, and progressive disclosure techniques (Mok, 1996).

Shared Spaces

The ability to use the same screen area for different visuals is an extremely useful technique in interactive visualizations. This provides users with a consistent area in which to expect information to appear while it provides the opportunity to display new information when contextually appropriate. The area can be the entire screen (such as navigating to a new web page), scrollable areas of images or text (such as a product shelf, or grid), inspector and property boxes that show attributes of an item in focus, and more unique views such as "cover flows" album views in Apple's iTunes music player. Typically a control such as a menu bar, pull-down menu, or radio button dictates what information is displayed when, or the area can dynamically respond to internal states or mouse clicks to other areas (figures 6.22–6.24).

Layers

Layers are one or more overlays atop a base image, which can be a graphic or map that augments that image by adding information that relates to features within it (figure 6.25). This technique is common in geography-based (GIS) systems, which add or remove layers from a base map to change the amount of information shown at any given time through the use of check boxes and other controls.

Figure 6.22
Image shelf.

Figure 6.23
A grid display of image thumbnails.

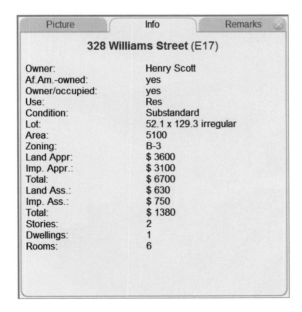

Figure 6.24
A property box dialog.

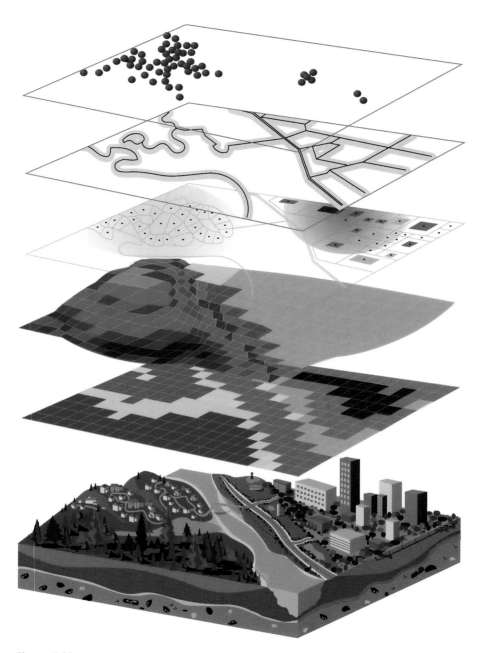

Figure 6.25
Map with multiple layers (©ESRI—All rights reserved. Used by permission: www.esri.com).

These layers can be considered slices of different aspects of the same basic view, all registering to the same underlying shape or geography. Each layer represents some aspect of the visualization that can be considered separately or in combination with other layers. It is this ability for the user to control which layers can be viewed with others that provides an opportunity for inquiry.

For example, a map of the United States could have multiple layers—some geographic, such as the county lines, terrain and elevation, and presence of waterways, and some informational, where the counties could be colored by population, income, and racial makeup. By turning on various layers, it is easy to visually explore the relationships among factors, such as population and access to water, or income and the presence of mountains.

It is often useful to be able to blend layers together, so the top layer has some degree of transparency (called its *alpha*) that controls how much of the underlying layer can be seen. The amount of alpha can be easily controlled in real time using a control such as a slider, making it easy to quickly switch between the foreground and background images in whatever degree is useful.

It can sometimes be tricky to present multiple layers simultaneously because the individual layers will often mask the effects of the others. For example, if the income in counties is being compared with voting patterns, it will be difficult to use color as a differentiator for both, so the color of a county must be combined with another display method, such as alteration of the county's interior texture or its edge color.

One variation on turning on and off layers is to use a graphical technique that allows the user to drag a bar that performs a "wipe" from one image to another. This was used with great effect by the *New York Times* to highlight the devastation of the 2010 earthquake in Haiti. Dragging the bar shows a satellite image from after the quake to the left of the bar, compared with one taken in 2008 to the right of the bar to display a visceral sense of the damage.

UCLA and USC's Hypercities project[3] makes great use of layers as an exploration mechanism in urban environments. The geographic layer provided by Google Maps and Google Earth is overlaid with multiple historical layers that make it easy to navigate through time to explore city spaces in a fluid hyperlinked manner (figure 6.26).

A menu provides buttons that turn on and off layers to highlight particular information for any given time frame. Other controls dynamically query data to display data such as media, images, and 3D reconstructions that are linked to the geography.

Zooming

Also common in geographic displays is the ability to move through a large virtual two- or three-dimensional space through the use of zoom and pan controls, scrollbars,

3. http://hypercities.com.

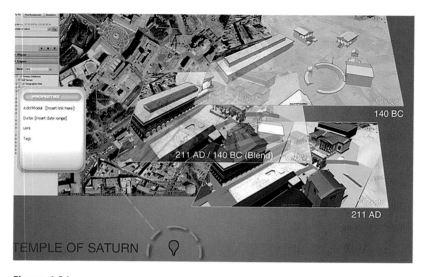

Figure 6.26
Hypercities map with historical temporal layers (image courtesy http://hypercities.com).

magnifiers, and rotation controls to navigate a virtual window within a larger space. Google Maps and Google Earth are good examples of applications that use these techniques (figure 6.27).

Some online presentation software applications[4] provide a large virtual canvas containing areas that the presenter zooms into and pans around to get a detailed close-up while maintaining a sense of context to the whole presentation (figure 6.28). Stanford's Republic of Letters project[5] uses this large canvas technique as the main page for their web site. Instead of dividing the site's content into individual pages as most traditional web sites do, they present a very large virtual canvas containing all the pages, and provide controls that help the user smoothly navigate to the desired page.

Pop-ups

Some information such as word definitions or data details are relevant only when a user wants more information and then should be quickly dismissed from view once the information has been provided. Common ways to present this information are *tooltips* (figures 6.29 and 6.30), which present small amounts of information as the user's mouse is over them and disappear when the mouse leaves the area, and *dialog boxes* (figure 6.31), which appear when one clicks on an area to allow for larger

4. www.prezi.com.
5. https://republicofletters.stanford.edu

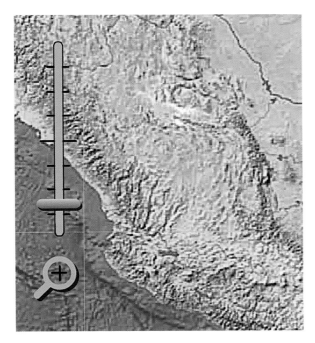

Figure 6.27
Zoom control for changing a map's magnification.

amounts of information to be displayed and even interacted with before being dismissed with a click. Pop-ups do not always need a graphical container such as a dialog box to present text, and the text can appear contextually within another element of the visualization.

Tabbed Spaces

Tabbed spaces, which are shared areas of the screen that are displayed by selecting tabs, are a common space fourth-dimensional solution (figure 6.32). Clicking on a tab quickly replaces the contents of the window beneath it. An interesting variant is the accordion control, where content is replaced within a list of possible options.

Timelines

Timelines are controls that facilitate the display of temporal information in a scrolling space that shows some portion of the overall time span at a time (figure 6.33). Timeline widgets like MIT's *Simile* and VisualEyes's *TimeView* make it easy to show multiple timescales in separate bands (like a 1930s-era radio with a coarse- and fine-tuning dial).

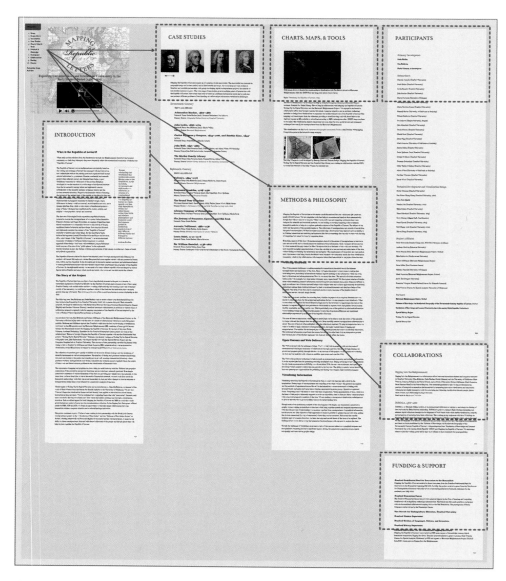

Figure 6.28
A virtual canvas navigational technique (image adapted from Mapping the Republic of Letters).

Figure 6.29
A tooltip popup display.

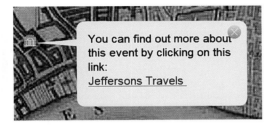

Figure 6.30
A popup dialog display.

Figure 6.31
A popup dialog display without a graphical container.

Figure 6.32
Tabs controlling display of a central area.

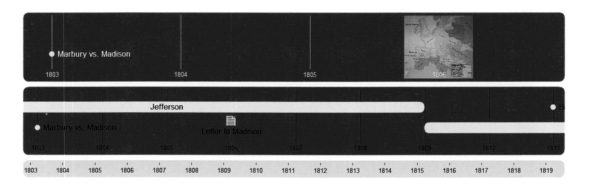

Figure 6.33
A scrolling timeline display.

Progressive Disclosure

Using time or some other factor to cause the progressive revealing of information can be quite useful in showing process. As the factor increases, more of the image is exposed. An example of this is a line showing the progress along a path, in this case Jefferson's travels to England in 1789 (figure 6.34). As the timeline is moved, the line draws, revealing his path and stops along the way, offering the user opportunity to click on them and get more detailed information.

The Art of *Persuasion*

An important goal of interactive visualization is to effectively communicate information to the user in an understandable and persuasive manner. This persuasion should not be ideological, political, or self-serving (e.g., advertising) but an opportunity to effectively communicate a story using data to provide the evidence.

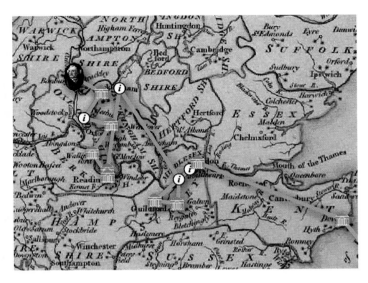

Figure 6.34
Progressive disclosure of Thomas Jefferson's travels to England.

Wurman's Five Rules of Information Communication

Richard Saul Wurman, the founder of the popular Technology Entertainment and Design (TED) conference, consummate information architect, and author of nearly 100 books that exhibit a high degree of design excellence, offers five rules for more effectively communicating information (Frischetti, 1997; Wurman, 1996):

1. *Understanding is relative*   People are only able to learn new things in relation to what they already know. This observation is echoed in the recent cognitive science literature on learning. *"For most things in everyday life, scale is best understood if it's based on a relationship to a human being,"* according to Wurman. *"Scale always relates to us."*

2. *LATCH: There are only five ways to organize information*   As mentioned earlier, there are only five basic ways to organize information: location, alphabet, time, category, or hierarchy. *"I've tried a thousand times to find other ways to organize,"* Wurman says, *"but I always end up using one of these five."*

3. *Do not beautify, clarify*   In resonance with Edward Tufte's design ideals, the goal of information design is to facilitate communication by avoiding the addition of extraneous graphics. *"The goal is to clarify—make it easy to understand."*

4. *Focus on what you really want to know*   Figure out what you really want to know about the topic and focus in on that by asking questions. *"We're taught when we're young that we're not supposed to look stupid. So we don't ask questions. Well, you'd better ask questions, and you'd better ask about things you really want to know. That way you'll convey your fascination and explain it in a way that other people will understand."*

5. *Get rid of useless information*   According to Wurman, most information is useless and will not improve the viewer's insight and understanding. People can only remember a half-dozen things in working memory at any given time. Get rid of the extraneous information to let the salient points have a chance to be absorbed. *"It's worthless to read something you're not interested in, because you won't remember it anyway."*

The Display Component of Visualization

The display technology delivers the ultimate embodiment of the visualization in the eyes of the user. The recent advances in computer and Internet technologies have opened up a wealth of possibilities that are just now being explored as new software tools are developed and made available to visualization designers. These advanced capabilities have led to many innovative and useful techniques for representing information in ways that encourage discovery and understanding.

It would be impossible to provide an exhaustive list of techniques used in interactive visualizations, but a number of common themes underpin many effective visualizations and can provide a starting point for design. Researching the wide array of innovative interactive visualizations on the Internet will provide inspiration that may spark ideas for your specific question and data. Manuel Lima's site (www.visualcomplexity .com) highlights hundreds of exemplary visualization examples, the author's visualization bookmark site (delicious.com/bferster/visualization), or simply a search in Google for "interactive visualization" will yield thousands of inspiring results.

The techniques and examples listed below are only a fraction of the possibilities available to visualization designers to represent their ideas. They are often effective when used in combination with one another, taking advantage of the ability to overlay them together in meaningful ways.

The Display of Charts

Graphs and charts are the obvious choice for graphically representing quantitative data. There are three broad categories of charts: those that compare *part to whole*, such as a pie or bar charts; those that *correlate* one or more datasets, usually represented using scatter charts; and trends and *time series* data, represented using line and area charts (figure 6.35). There is an infinite variety within those broad categories. Robert Harris's (1999) book, *Information Graphics*, provides an encyclopedic reference to thousands of charts, graphs, and other visual tools for graphically communicating quantitative information.

The Display of Images

Images from photographs, maps, drawings, and artwork are effective elements to support an argument directly or provide rich context to other representative forms.

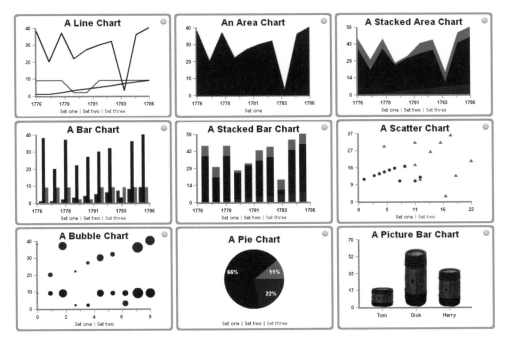

Figure 6.35
Various styles of data charts.

Images can be layered atop one another, with transparency revealing or hiding areas, and are able to be turned on and off at will using controls such as checkboxes. Time-sequence images can be animated in place to visually reveal transitions over time, or laid out individually as a series of smaller images (figure 6.36). Images can appear as backgrounds and icons for charts and other display elements or be called up at will in dialogs and pop-up boxes.

Raster and Vector Images

In computers, images are drawn in two basic ways. *Raster* images are made up of a series of dots (called *pixels*) in much the same way as the French Impressionist painter Georges Seurat's pointillist artwork, consisting of discrete color dots, creates the impression of a continuous image. The more pixels in the image, the better the resolution of the image is, and fewer *jaggies* will appear. But more is not always better: The bigger the picture, the more space it takes to store, and the longer it will take to load.

Vector images are typically drawings, and instead of storing the individual pixels, a series of end points define lines and curves to be drawn at any resolution defined. Images such as photos are best represented as raster images, and drawings are often best drawn as vector-based images. It is sometimes useful to display both raster- and

Figure 6.36
Irregular Athletes by Eadweard Muybridge (image courtesy the Library of Congress).

vector-format images together, such as the aerial photograph in figure 6.37 with a vector overlay transparently on top of it, delineating the area but still revealing the image below.

In the example in figure 6.38, the encircled area within the letter *R* is shown as it appears as a vector drawing in the top circle, with its endpoints drawn in red and perfectly smooth lines and curves connecting them. This letter can be infinitely scaled with no jagged edges appearing. In contrast, the lower circle shows the same area drawn as a lower-resolution raster- or pixel-based image, and as the image is enlarged, the jaggedness of individual pixels will become more and more apparent.

There is no practical limit on how images can be used in interactive visualizations. The web site HistoryPin[6] encourages people to hand-hold historic photographs in front of the current-day view from the same perspective. For example, the image in figure 6.39, taken by historian Scot French, shows a 1920s image of an African-

6. www.historypin.com.

Figure 6.37
Vector overlay on raster image.

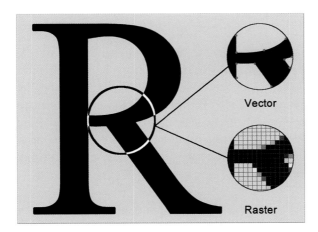

Figure 6.38
Raster and vector types of images.

Figure 6.39
Historic and present-day photos of Inge's store (image courtesy Scot French/Virginia Center for Digital History).

American–owned general store in Charlottesville, VA held in front of the building in 2010, which is now an upscale restaurant, showing a nice juxtaposition of old and new.

Image Storage Services
At the University of Virginia, we are big proponents of using online image storage sites such as Yahoo!'s *Flickr* and Google's *Picasa* because they provide easy, fast, distributed, and free or inexpensive access to digital images online. The fact that the images reside on external servers reduces the load on the visualization's own server. They also automatically provide versions of the images at various sizes, eliminating the time-consuming job of resizing them manually and making sites load faster because a size appropriate to the desired size can be used rather than a larger image that would take longer to load.

The Display of Networks
Network maps help show relationships among elements in the dataset. There are a wide number of ways to render networks depending on the data. The structure of network data is sometimes different from that of other types, such as time-series data, in that the data specify relationships among other members in the dataset, for example,

maps of social networks, organizational charts, and family trees. The whimsical illustration in figure 6.40 by French designer Manu Cornet shows a number of different organizational charts for popular technology companies, choosing topologies that fit the public perceptions of their corporate management.

Network Diagrams

Larger sets of data and the need to find patterns within them to make sense have prompted fertile research in techniques for meaningfully visualizing huge datasets and showing the relations between individual and groups of members. Going beyond traditional scatter plots, these network diagrams make explicit connections and attempt to show relationships between and among members (figure 6.41).

These network diagrams were made even more powerful by the ability to dynamically interact with the center of the network's focus, allowing users to drill down into individual elements (called *nodes*) to see the relationships in ever finer detail. An early example of this was the Visual Thesaurus,[7] which mapped the connections of over 150,000 English words and their interrelations.

Radial Maps

Radial network maps spin a circular array of nodes stemming from a central point (figure 6.42). Other network maps can show complex interrelations between random nodes and across many factors but tend to get confusing if there are too many nodes or lines (called *edges*) connecting them.

Tree Maps

Tree maps are a technique developed by Ben Shneiderman at the University of Maryland's Human Computer Interaction Lab to help users understand *the part-to-whole* distribution of data containing multiple factors. The space is hierarchically divided into sections based on one factor. That space is continually subdivided into blocks, with their relative size determined by some another factor, and the blocks are colored by yet another factor (figure 6.43).

Process Maps

Process maps use graphics to illustrate a process, procedure, or historical sequence, typically exposing multiple dimensions of data. These maps can be static or animated and use size, color, arrows, and other graphical devices to walk the viewer through understanding a complex process and its interrelations. Figure 6.44 shows a simplified view of how a color television operates, and the numbered areas would be annotated with textual descriptions.

7. www.visualthesaurus.com.

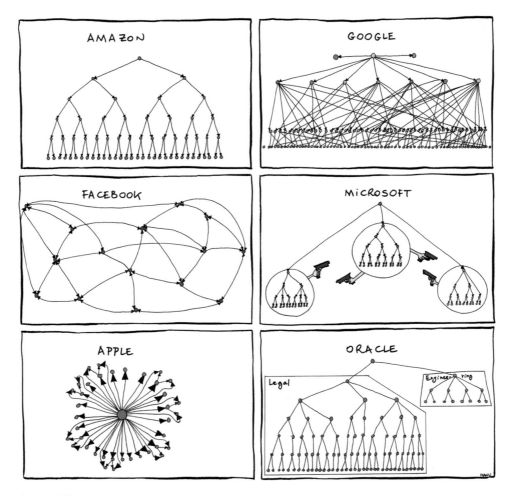

Figure 6.40

Organizational charts (courtesy Manu Cornet: www.bonkersworld.net).

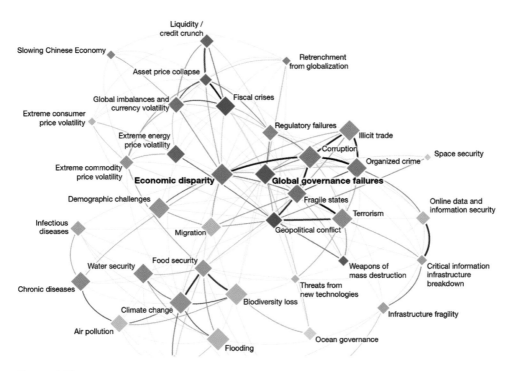

Figure 6.41
Network map (image courtesy Mortitz Stephaner).

One kind of process map is the *Sankey diagram*, named after the late-nineteenth-century English mechanical engineer Matthew Sankey, who developed a style of illustration that showed material energy flows where the arrows were proportional to the amount of energy flowing through the system (figure 6.45). The iconic visualization of Napolean's invasion of Russia created by Charles Minard in 1869 (see figure 3.2) is a good example of a Sankey-style diagram.

The Display of Time
Timelines help users control the temporal aspects of the visualization, typically by dragging left to right across the screen. Timelines can have scrolling areas associated with them that move based on the current date. Some timeline tools can represent multiple synchronized time scales, useful when combining events that occur over long and short time scales. The MIT *Simile* timeline in figure 6.46 shows the minute-by-minute events of the Kennedy assassination in the top band and a monthly perspective in the bottom band.

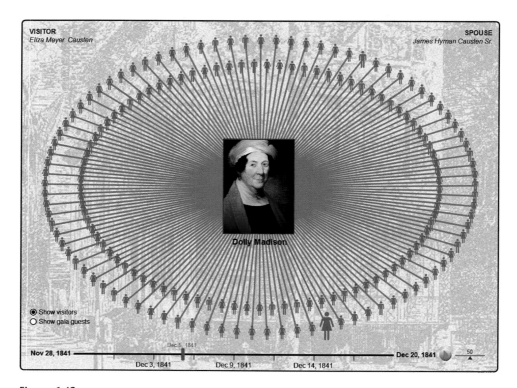

Figure 6.42
A radial network map of Dolly Madison's visitors in 1841.

Timelines can take many forms, as shown by the example in figure 6.47, where a traditional flat timeline is overlaid onto a cylindrical shape and can be spun by the user by dragging with the mouse.

Timelines can be used to convey much more than a simple chronology of events over time. The *Temporal Modeling Project*, developed at the University of Virginia by Bethany Nowviskie and Johanna Drucker, enables humanities scholars to create complex sequences that depict the flow of aspects such as dialogue, action, character viewpoints, and relationships. The flow can move backward and forward through time within a textual work such as a novel or a poem. A control called a *nowslider* can set the current time to view from, and the display will change from what the character knows or does not know at that point in the text (figure 6.48).

The Display of Maps
Maps are one of the most often used visual elements in interactive visualizations because location is a principal dimension for exploration. Just as with images, maps

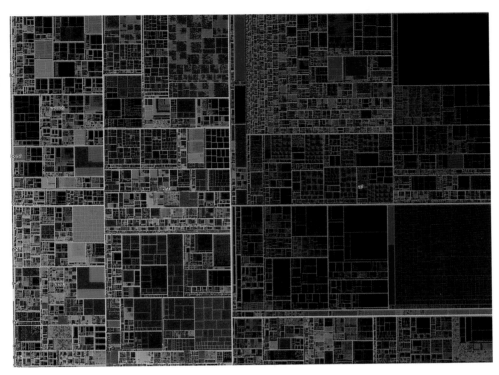

Figure 6.43
A tree map (used with permission of University of Maryland Human-Computer Interaction Lab).

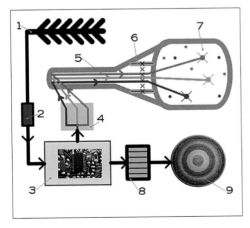

Figure 6.44
A process map (courtesy Chris Woodford: www.explainthatstuff.com).

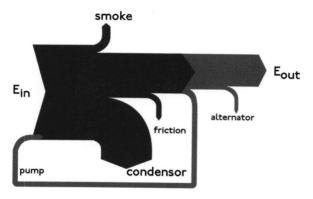

Figure 6.45
A Sankey map showing an energy process.

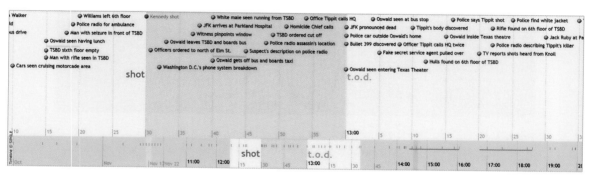

Figure 6.46
Screen shot from MIT's Simile timeline tool.

come in two basic varieties: *raster,* where the map is an image file made up of pixels like any other photograph; and *vector,* where the map is a collection of drawn lines and polygons. Raster maps, particularly historic ones tend to be richer in texture, but there are limits to how far they can be zoomed into before becoming pixilated. Vector maps, on the other hand are resolution independent because they are *dynamically drawn* and have much greater zooming limits. Because the map features are drawn, it is possible to use the areas on a vector map to dynamically convey information by coloring sections independently from others.

As an example, historian Andrew Torget used a raster base map of the Texas topography with a drawn vector map transparently overlaid (figure 6.49). The raster map adds an informative and attractive texture, and the vector layer clearly delineates each county, shaded differently to graphically show the 1841 enslaved population numbers.

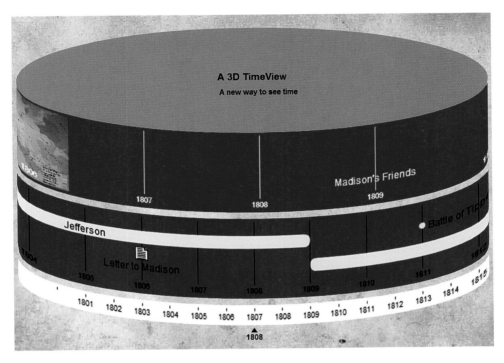

Figure 6.47
A scrolling timeline wrapped around a 3D cylinder.

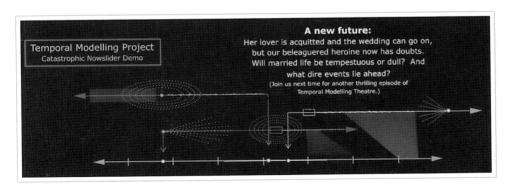

Figure 6.48
Timeline from Temporal Modeling Project.

Figure 6.49
Raster map with vector overlay (image courtesy Andrew Torget: www.texasslaveryproject.org).

Choropleths

The process of using different colors in a map (known to cartographers as a *choropleth*, from the Greek: *area* + *multiply*) to represent quantitative data is a valuable way to directly link data to location. The colors are typically arranged in a meaningful progression, such as a series of colors within the same hue but varying in luminance or saturation when representing only one dimension, to more complex schemes such as bipolar progressions, blended-hue progressions, and full-spectral color progressions (figure 6.50).

Heat Maps

An interesting variation on the choropleth is the *heat map*, where a blurred color overlay represents a continuum of data values by varying its transparency. Additional data dimensions can be represented by using a meaningful color progression as in choropleths (figure 6.51). Heat maps are useful when representing information that crosses hard boundaries, such as state and county lines, but still give a good indication of the existence of some phenomena of interest.

Interactive Maps

Rather than being a passive source of geographic information, maps often play a special role in interactive visualizations because they enable the user to actively engage

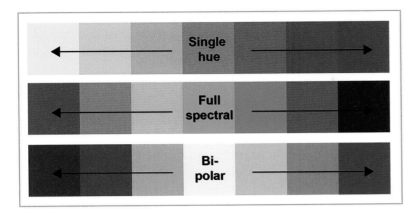

Figure 6.50
Color progressions used in choropleth maps.

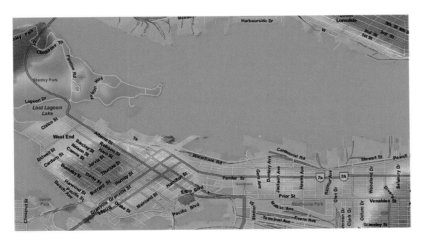

Figure 6.51
Heat map (courtesy Geotechnologies Inc.: www.web-demographics.com).

and control the map. That engagement can be as simple as quickly navigating through the geography, or as sophisticated as control of rendering techniques such as choroplethy and heat mapping, and involve tight integration with other kinds of data and display methods.

The Internet has made these features much easier to implement than before by providing simple interfaces to embed sophisticated tile-based[8] mapping into online projects. These are freely available from companies such as Google, Yahoo!, and Microsoft and can be created through simple form-based web pages. More control and functionality can be achieved using the application programming interfaces (APIs) they make available.

The *New Map of Empire* project[9] by the historian S. Max Edelson uses the Google Maps/Earth interface embedded in VisualEyes to visually browse and interact with hundreds of early-American historical maps. The 3D navigational controls make it easy both to see detail and to get a sense of overall context. One or more of the historic maps can be overlaid atop the Google map. The amount of transparency is controllable, so the historic map can be compared to the underlying map, which can show a satellite image, the topographic terrain, or a modern street map showing cities and current political boundaries (figure 6.52).

The map and the other components are tightly linked together: clicking on the wireframe in the interactive map displays metadata about the historic map it represents and shows a thumbnail of the full map in the image shelf. Likewise, the maps in the image shelf are scrollable and keywords are searchable. Clicking on a thumbnail will cause the interactive map to navigate to its position in the world, showing context.

Geometry versus Geography

Maps do not always need to be faithful reproductions of reality for purposes of navigation or location. Maps can also be used as illustrations, to communicate relative proximity, size, and relationships among the features drawn on the map to represent a sense of geometry rather than strict geography (Moretti, 2005).

An interesting example of maps as illustrations are *typographic maps*, which accurately depict streets and other features using type instead of lines. They weave together thousands of individual words in varying color, faces, and sizes until a realistic, but stylized image of a city emerges, such as the map of Manhattan in figure 6.53 with a magnified portion of the East River, drawn in blue words. Just as with a pointillist painting made of dots, these maps are highly realistic when viewed from a distance, but the areas give way to individual letters on closer examination.

8. Tile-based maps, such as Google Maps, send only the sections being viewed, making downloads faster.
9. www.viseyes.org/show?id=empire.xml

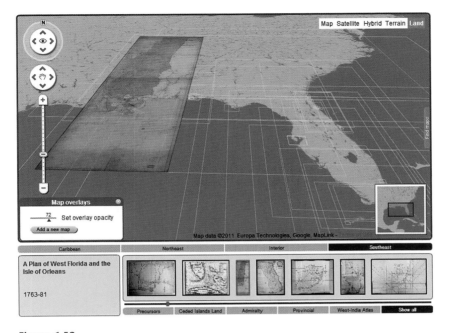

Figure 6.52
An interactive 3D Google map (image courtesy S. Max Edelson).

Maps can be effectively used to represent completely nongeographic information, such as this homage to Harry Beck's famous London Underground map (figure 6.54). Robin Richards depicts the software giant Microsoft's "trail" of investments and acquisitions over time. The subway format is successfully leveraged to provide context and insight into Microsoft's many financial investments using the line to represent an industry, and each stop a company. The transfer stations indicate where two industries overlap.

The Display of Animation

Animation can show movement through an area or a process unfolding over time or illuminate the construction of objects in ways that a static image cannot adequately convey. Anyone who has seen videos from Swedish data superstar Hans Rosling can appreciate the communicative value of animating data in a chart. In the sequence of images (figure 6.55) produced by his *GapMinder*[10] software, the bubble chart plots countries by their life expectancy on the vertical axis and income on the horizontal axis. Each frame represents a snapshot of the continuous animation of these factors

10. www.gapminder.org.

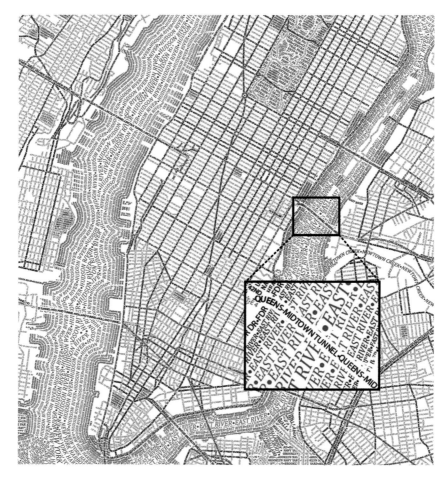

Figure 6.53
A typographic map of Manhattan (image courtesy Axis Maps, LLC: www.axismaps.com).

over time and graphically shows the progress in both factors as well as the increasing disparity of income and lifespan between countries.

The Hagley Museum created a VisualEyes animation[11] of early nineteenth century gunpowder sales (figure 6.56) by tracking each sale, found through the painstaking research efforts in the DuPont company archives by historian Randi Lewis. She tracked each invoice of a powder sale with an image of a gunpowder keg and animated it moving from Wilmington, DE, to where it was sold, over time. The result is a clearer picture of the proliferation of the spread of gunpowder within the growing nation, from 1804 leading up to the War of 1812.

11. www.hagley.org/library/exhibits/brandywine.

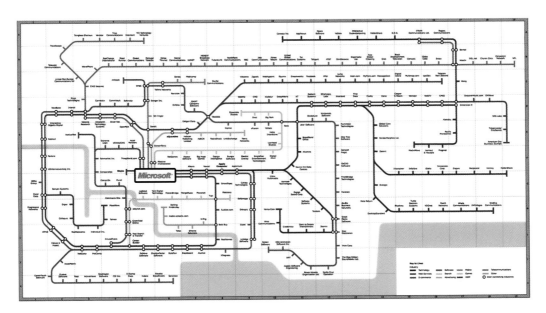

Figure 6.54
A variation on Harry Beck's subway map (image courtesy Robin Richards http://ripetungi.com).

Figure 6.55
Animating the health and wealth of nations (image courtesy www.gapminder.org).

There is some research that suggests that not all uses of animation are beneficial to better communication and understanding, and it may actually impede goals. Researchers have suggested two principles be considered when employing animation. The *congruence principle* states there should be a natural correspondence between the animation and the conceptual basis of the information being visualized. Second, the *apprehension principle* suggests that animation needs to be slow and clear enough for the user to comprehend the phenomenon being represented and comprehend the interrelations of its various parts (Tversky, Morrison, & Betrancort, 2002).

The Display of Text

Text displays are a useful way to present narrative or data-intensive information via pop-ups and dialog boxes. Text can be used as a display element itself by using a word

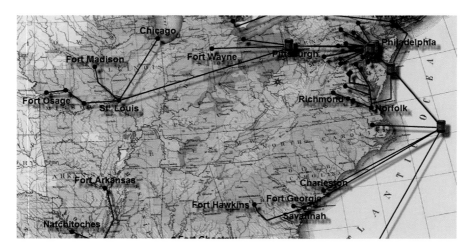

Figure 6.56
Animation of eighteenth-century DuPont gunpowder sales (image courtesy Hagley Museum).

cloud or other technique that uses word frequencies to communicate their relative importance.

Text can also be used as an aesthetic element that communicates less directly. The image in figure 6.57 was made using the *Wordle*[12] tool, which creates attractive *word clouds* from documents. The word is drawn larger in relation to the number of times it appears in the document, suggesting its relative importance to other words.

The Display of Media

Media such as video, audio, screen-casts, and animation clips can be easily added to visualizations and can be viewed passively or used in conjunction with other representational elements such as text displays (i.e., for transcripts), charts, and images. One interesting way to think about media is by its temporal nature: a media clip is a series of images and sounds that starts at a point in time and ends at another, just like a timeline. The act of traversing that time span is analogous to moving a timeline's slider and can be used to trigger collateral elements as appropriate.

The example illustrated in figure 6.58 links a video of a classic high-school science lab experiment and connects the video clip's current time as it plays to data displays. These include a graphical widget displaying the air pressure and a graph showing the temperature, allowing students to instantly make the connections among pressure, temperature, and real-world results in the visualization. All elements are synched

12. www.wordle.net.

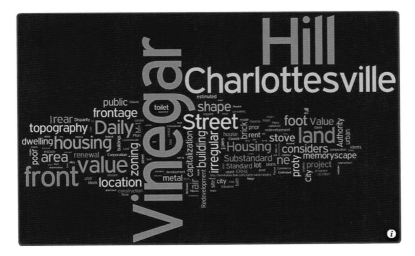

Figure 6.57
Word chart of terms found in city assessment reports (image courtesy wordle.net).

together by the movie clip's current time as it plays or searched with the timeline bar.

Pan and Zoom Displays

The filmmaker Ken Burns did not invent the process of panning and zooming through an image to tell a story, but he is perhaps the best-known user of this powerful visual technique in his documentary work on topics from the Civil War to baseball. Panning and zooming through a scene guides the viewer to focus on specific parts of the frame over time and, in the process, uses motion to communicate complex ideas.

For example, in this image of the 1895 University of Virginia Rotunda fire (figure 6.59), zooming in on the wheelbarrow, the bookshelves, and the books themselves can help tell the story of how the books were carried from the burning building and saved. This can be done in a continuous motion or as a series of frames, each representing a step in the sequence like a comic strip or storyboard.

A more exploratory version of zooming and panning a scene can be achieved using a technique called a *magic lens* (Spence, 2001) in which a virtual magnifier can be dragged by the user over the scene to zoom in on details. The magnification can be varied to zoom in and out at different levels to facilitate detailed inspection of small parts of the image within the context of the whole scene.

A variation on a magic lens is an *x-ray lens*, where the magnifier acts like a kind of revealing widget to expose a different version of the image beneath, as in the example of figure 6.60, where a 2000 aerial photograph is shown in the background, and the

Figure 6.58
A digital version of the classic egg-in-bottle experiment.

inside of the virtual magnifier lens shows what was there in 1948 by revealing an earlier aerial photo as the user drags the mouse over the base image.

The Display of Dimensionality
The world we inhabit is dimensionally rich, but the means of rendering those dimensions in visualizations, such as paper or a computer screen, are strictly flat. To better depict that richness, it can be useful to simulate real world three-dimensionality on these two-dimensional surfaces by using a number of rendering techniques that convey this dimensionality. Edward Tufte (1990) refers to this process as *escaping flatland*, an allusion to the classic 1884 mathematical satire.[13]

Plans, Elevations, and Perspective
Architectural and engineering drawings have long used the technique of showing multiple views of a three-dimensional object, such as a building, by drawing a bird's eye view, called the *plan*, and a front-on drawing known as an *elevation*. The dimensionality of either alone is flattened, but when they are presented side by side, a better

13. *Flatland: A Romance of Many Dimensions* by A. Square (Edwin Abbott).

Figure 6.59
Pan and zoom into 1895 University of Virginia rotunda fire photo (image courtesy University of Virginia Special Collections Library).

sense of the dimensionality emerges. This effect can be heightened when the drawings are rendered to the exact same scale and are aligned so tracing the lines on the plan that convey width and length connect with parts of the elevation that convey height (figure 6.61). These cross-relationships can be further made obvious by adding an isomorphic, perspective, or 3D representation of the object. This technique is often used in engineering, CAD,[14] and architectural drawing tools.

Cross Sections

A cross section makes an imaginary slice through an otherwise opaque three-dimensional object to reveal its interior space (figure 6.62). These can be computer generated or hand drawn or, in the case of the ship, a photograph of a hand-built model.

Axiometric

Axiometric projection drawings provide a stylized way to draw dimensionally rendered drawings used in such games as "The Sims" and "SimCity." There is no foreshortening to reflect perspective, so the vertical lines are always perfectly vertical (figure 6.63). They are not geometrically accurate but offer a different way to express dimensionality.

14. Computer-Aided Design.

Figure 6.60
X-ray lens display of Vinegar Hill showing 1948 aerial image within 2000 aerial image.

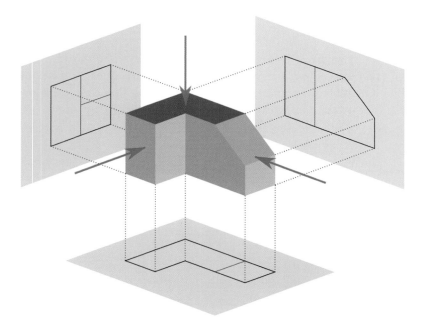

Figure 6.61
Elevation, plan, and perspective views (image courtesy Emok/Wikimedia Commons).

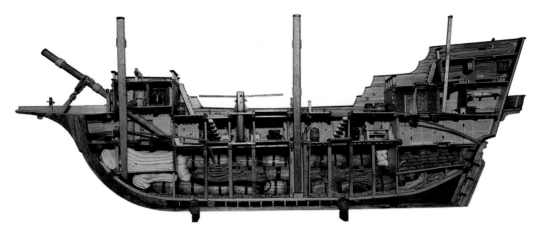

Figure 6.62
Cross section of a seventeenth-century merchant ship (image courtesy Musphot/Wikimedia Commons).

Figure 6.63
Axiometric view drawing (image courtesy Electronic Arts: www.ea.com).

Figure 6.64
LIDAR laser-scanned 3D aerial map (courtesy Geotechnologies Inc: www.web-demographics.com).

3D Rendering

The ability to realistically render a three-dimensional scene has been a mainstay of games, architecture, and simulations for almost two decades, but outside of scientific visualization, 3D rendering is currently an underutilized representational technique in visualizations for two main reasons. 3D models are difficult and time consuming to create, and, second, there are currently few effective technologies that enable the display of 3D objects in a web environment (figure 6.64).

That said, the ability to navigate in three dimensions offers interesting possibilities for the future. Adobe has plans to introduce a 3D version of *Flash*, and the Web3D standard is beginning to be adopted by HTML 5–based web browsers. A number of developers are using the Google Earth plug-in to render 3D scenes within their projects, but the rendering quality is not yet competitive with custom-programmed 3D engines, which take full advantage of fast graphics chips found on modern computers. Developers are typically creating digital movies and playing them on their web sites as other options begin to emerge.

The University of Maryland Baltimore Campus's Imaging Research Center took historic maps and drawings to create a 3D model of Washington, DC, as it appeared in the early nineteenth century. *Visualizing Early Washington*[15] recreates the true topography of the landscape as it appeared then as a fully navigable 3D model.

The model was created using maps between 1791 and 1800, historical elevation drawings generated by the US Coast and Geodetic Survey published in 1888, Pierre L'Enfant's city plans, and Benjamin Latrobe's drawings of Capitol Hill (figure 6.65). Buildings were modeled from historic drawings, and the completed 3D model was

15. http://visualizingdc.com.

a.1791 topographic map

b. Painting of Capitol Hill

c. 3D model with topography

d. Plan view of US capitol location

e. Constructing 3D from the 2D map

f. Fully rendered 3D version of capitol

Figure 6.65
Visualizing early Washington (images courtesy Dan Bailey: http://visualizingDC.com).

compared with historical drawings and artwork to triangulate the likely state of the city and landscape.

Physical Dimensionality

The display of dimensionality does not have to be limited to a two-dimensional plane. New York University student Mike Knuepfel created a playful sculpture (figure 6.66) that shows the frequency of letter use in a graphic and tactile manner as a physical bar chart. The height of each key on the keyboard is represented by the frequency of its use in the English language. We can assume William Playfair[16] would have been pleased.

16. Playfair was the eighteenth-century inventor of the bar chart.

Figure 6.66
Keyboard sculpture (image courtesy Mike Knuepfel: www.spike5000.com).

Search and Dynamic Queries

Search is more of a navigational tool than strictly a representation technique, but the results of a search can trigger many of the representations previously discussed. Because of its free-form nature, search is an important element in allowing users to use the visualization generatively—to find potentially meaningful relationships that the originally designer did not plan for.

Dynamic Queries

The display can graphically reflect changes in the data being requested in response to interaction from the user. This interaction can be a text search, selection of a checkbox or radio button, or movement of a slider and is particularly insightful when multiple dimensions can be changed together to see how they react with one another.

This map from the Vinegar Hill project (figure 6.67) looks at the data from a Charlottesville, VA, urban renewal project in the 1960s. Clicking on various options can shade the houses involved according to their assessments, condition, if they were owner occupied, and so forth. Multiple dimensions can be compared by controlling the interior and the edge colors of the house. Highlighting a combination of the interior color and the house's edge color graphically shows the interaction between factors.

An interesting example of a dynamic query is Martin Wattenberg's *Name Voyager*[17] (figure 6.68), which shows an ever-changing chart of first names popular between 1880 and 2010 as more letters of the name are typed. Developed to accompany his wife's book on finding baby names, the tool instantly searches names mined from the

17. www.babynamewizard.com.

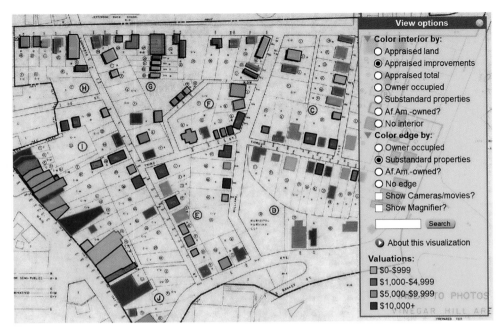

Figure 6.67
Dynamic queries of Vinegar Hill poperties.

Social Security Administration's database and displays them by year. My parents were apparently a decade behind the times, as the popularity of my name seems to have peaked in the 1940s.

Faceted Search

Faceted search is a useful technique for graphically enabling a Boolean[18] search by making the search terms more menu driven but still retaining their open-ended nature (figure 6.69). Originally developed by Berkeley researcher Marti Hearst in the Flamenco Project for browsing large image collections, it has become a staple in e-commerce web sites such as Amazon.com and Best Buy.

These systems work by having a dynamically generated menu of possibilities that are populated by a traditional textbox query. Each possibility has the number of subcategories printed, and clicking on one will spawn its own set of subpossibilities. Other controls can further reduce the number by limiting search by one or more additional factors.

18. Boolean searches allow users to combine combinations of terms to finely filter the results.

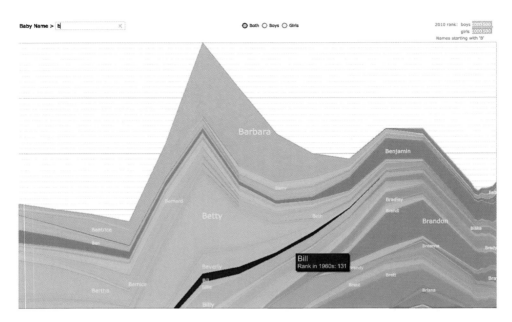

Figure 6.68
Baby Name Voyager (image courtesy Laura and Martin Wattenberg).

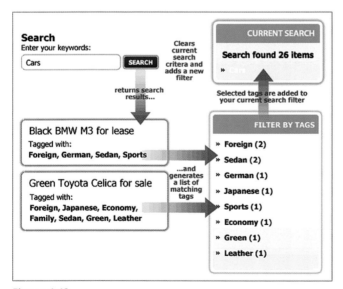

Figure 6.69
Faceted search (image courtesy Acquia, Inc.: www.acquia.com).

Links

Links to other web sites and web applications can connect a visualization to a broad collection of collateral sites such as Google Maps and Earth to provide rich context. They can be seamlessly integrated so the user experience feels cohesive and unified. Many web applications have the ability to be remotely controlled, so their capabilities can be exposed within another application. For example, the University of Virginia First Library project[19] contains a listing of 6500 books in the 1828 University of Virginia Library. Any of those books can be automatically searched in a number of sites, including Google Books, without the need to type the search parameters in, to see a full text copy directly overlaid on the screen.

Visualization Tools

There are many tools available for creating web-based interactive visualizations. Some are programming environments that require programming expertise; some are libraries providing programmers with capabilities that make it easier to create data-driven projects, and others provide online capabilities to create visualizations using online tools without extensive programming skills required.

Tools for Programmers

The following is by no means an exhaustive list but represents the range of tools available for people with a medium level of programming skills. Some are implemented as Application Programming Interfaces (APIs) to web services, whereas others are provided as libraries for languages such as Java, JavaScript, Python, Ruby, and PHP, and others such as *Flash* are complete development environments.

Adobe Flash *and* Flex

Adobe's *Flash* authoring tool provides a robust environment for developing visualizations. It is a commercial product, but projects done using *Flash* are freely accessible online to anyone using the free *Flash Player* browser plug-in. Final projects created in *Flash* are cross-platform,[20] small to download, and stable. There are two ways to use *Flash*—as a vector graphics animation authoring tool requiring minimal programming knowledge and as a more powerful but programming-intensive environment using the ActionScript language. The VisualEyes tool was developed using ActionScript: www.adobe.com/flash. Adobe's *Flex* environment is similar to *Flash* but comes with great data-charting capabilities and other features useful for developing visualizations. *Flex* comes in both commercial and free versions and requires a medium amount of programming skill: http://flex.org.

19. www.viseyes.org/show?base=library.
20. With the poignant exception of Apple's iPad, which Apple refuses to support.

Google Tools

The Google Maps API can create web-accessible geographic-based projects with little programming skill involved, and it provides direct access to most functionality from programming languages such as JavaScript, Java, ActionScript, and PHP. Google provides a browser plug-in that makes the rich 3D world views of Google Earth available for embedding into visualization projects. Access to the API is free, but Google has reserved the right to embed advertising within the maps in the future: http://code .google.com/apis/maps/index.html.

The Google Chart Tools/Visualization API is a collection of components useful for visualizations developed in JavaScript and requires a medium amount of programming skill: http://code.google.com/apis/chart/.

OpenLayers

OpenLayers provides much the same functionality as Google Maps but provides its JavaScript library as open source and can use customized tiles to create historic and customized maps: http://openlayers.org.

Prefuse/Protovis

Prefuse and Protovis are freely available visualization libraries for programmers developed by the Stanford University Visualization Group that support high-level data-driven projects using table, graph, and tree data structured and dynamic queries. Prefuse has libraries for Java and ActionScript, and Protovis supports interactive visualizations using JavaScript: www.prefuse.org and http://mbostock.github.com/ protovis.

Processing

Processing is a powerful and open-source programming language developed by Ben Fry and Casey Reas for Java and more recently, JavaScript. There is wide support in terms of books, online forums, and groups for Processing: www.processing.org and http://processingjs.org.

Tools for Nonprogrammers

There has been a proliferation of tools, most of them web-based and freely available, that can create sophisticated interactive visualizations with little or no programming expertise required.

Adobe Flash

Adobe's *Flash* authoring tool provides a robust environment for nonprogrammers to create interactive visualizations in its role as a vector graphics animation authoring tool: www.adobe.com/products/flash.

Gephi

Gephi is a free desktop application for Windows and Macintosh computers that provides a platform for exploring and displaying large sets of hierarchical and network data. It has tools for cluster, link, network, and social network analyses: http://gephi.org.

Google Fusion Tables/Chart Editor

Google Fusion is web-based tool that makes it easy to upload data and create sophisticated interactive visualizations of charts, maps, and timelines: www.google.com/fusiontables/public/tour/index.html. The Google Chart Editor has also provided a wizard-based online interface to create charts from Google's powerful Chart/Visualization API that can be easily embedded into web pages and blogs without any programming required: http://imagecharteditor.appspot.com.

ManyEyes

The work of IBM Research's Martin Wattenberg and Fernanda Viégas (now working at Google), ManyEyes allows users to share and visualize their own datasets using simple web-based tools, requiring no programming knowledge, that publicly reside on the ManyEyes web site: http://www-958.ibm.com.

NodeXL

NodeXL is a 5+ year collaborative effort, initially supported by Microsoft External Research with participation from the University of Maryland's HCIL. It continues to be developed and distributed by the Social Media Research Foundation (www.smrfoundation.org) as a freely available plug-in to Microsoft's Excel spreadsheet for Windows to display network graphs of tabular data with no programming required: http://nodexl.codeplex.com.

Tableau Public

Tableau Public is the freely available web-based version of the popular *Tableau* commercial desktop visualization software. It uses a drag-and-drop interface to create complex data-driven visualizations that publicly reside on *Tableau*'s web site: www.tableausoftware.com/public.

VIDI

The Jefferson Institute's VIDI web-based tool makes it easy to create powerful data-driven interactive visualizations of time lines, maps, and comparative data displays that can be easily embedded into web pages and blogs without any programming required. They also make available modules that allow for easy visualization integration into Drupal[21]-based web sites: www.dataviz.org.

---

21. Drupal is a popular web site content management system (CMS).

VisualEyes

VisualEyes is a freely available interactive visualization environment developed by the author at the University of Virginia. An authoring tool (VisEdit) scaffolds the creation of XML-based scripts that provide nonprogrammers the ability to rapidly create data-driven projects online: www.viseyes.org.

Wordle

Wordle will automatically generate well-designed word clouds from almost any source of text. There are a number of options to customize the shape, fonts, style, and colors used to create free word clouds: www.wordle.net.

Summary

This chapter discusses the elements that present the visualization to the user and allow them to interact with it. These elements are organized in three parts: *science*, *art*, and *display* techniques.

The *science* component has discussed Don Norman's interaction research about the dance between *affordances* and *constraints* and his iterative description of the *action cycle* of user-centered goals from formation, execution, feedback, and evaluation.

Perception is a critical part of the way we interact with visualizations, and people are more sensitive to visual sensations that appeal to the subconsciously processed *preattentive perceptions*. The *Gestalt laws* of pattern recognition provide some useful guidance on how to group objects for maximum communicative value.

Cognition is the complicated process of learning and making sense of the world, and the fact that short-term memory is limited to *seven items plus or minus two* is absolutely critical in designing visualizations. The channel structure in which information is encoded in the brain is also a useful way to design visualizations that are in synchronicity with our biology.

Don Norman had provided a five-point list of important issues to consider from a user-centered usability standpoint: provide *consistent models* of the project to the users, make *all features visible* and accessible, provide *good mappings* between controls and the things they control, offer *good feedback*, and *design for humanity*. The need for visualizations to be pleasurable to use can be enhanced by looking at the research into fun, flow, and video games.

The *art* component consists of the key role that *visual aesthetics* play in visualizations, and issues of *color, color schemes, spatial arrangement*, and the *fourth dimension* of screen design are discussed. An important goal of interactive visualization is to effectively communicate information to the user in an understandable and persuasive manner. This persuasion should not ideological, political, or self-serving (e.g., advertising) but an opportunity to effectively communicate a story using data to provide the evidence

The *display* technology delivers the ultimate embodiment of the visualization in the eyes of the user. The recent advances in computer and Internet technologies have opened up a wealth of possibilities that are just now being explored as new software tools are developed and made available to visualization designers. The display of charts, graphs, images, animation, maps, text, networks, and media can be marshaled and driven by data to create a compelling user experience. Finally, a number of tools useful in creating interactive visualizations are discussed.

The next chapter explores the value of telling a story with the visualization and discusses some models to use and some good examples of projects that effectively employ storytelling to communicate their message.

7 Tell a Story Using Data

A story has no beginning or end: arbitrarily one chooses that moment of experience from which to look back or from which to look ahead.

—Graham Greene

Storytelling is one of the primary ways we make sense of the world. A good visualization answers a question using primary source evidence to tell a story. That story should be meaningful and able to address the significant criteria (the *so what?*). The elements of effective storytelling have been studied from multiple disciplines including psychology, literature, theater, and cinema. A common set of principles has emerged and is instructive as a guide in developing interactive visualizations.

This chapter explores the following topics:

- Schemas
- Narrative structure
- Kaleidoscopic narrative
- Examples of storytelling in visualizations
- Misleading representations
- Validity threats
- Design tensions

Schemas

"Knowledge is stories" according to psychology researcher Roger Shank, and stories are how people make sense of the world. Stories are used *to chunk* information into more memorable units, thereby avoiding some of the limitations of short-term memory. By chunking the information in a compact and structured format, people are able to generalize and compare experiences in ways not possible if the details were unorganized sets of unrelated information. Stories provide *scripts* or *schemas* in which people interpret new information from previous experiences or portrayals. Shank has identified a number of these schemas in terms of their communicative

intent, and these archetypes can be useful in structuring the stories in visualizations (Shank, 1990):

• *Distillation* is a two-phase process in which the constituent events are condensed into a set of simpler propositions, called the *gist* of things. The gist contains all the important data needed to tell the story. The second phase involves the *translation* of the raw facts into a natural language. In terms of an interactive visualization, the natural language is the visual representation of the data.

• *Combination* integrates elements from multiple stories by either the *suppression* or *conjunction* of elements identified from the gist into a new story whose main point may not be those of the constituent stories.

• *Elaboration* is the process of focusing attention on one or more aspects through *detail addition*, the adding of more in-depth information and the addition of *commentary* that offers a subjective and/or descriptive perspective on the data.

Narrative Structure

Stories typically follow a structure that describes the action over time, called its *narrative* or *dramatic arc*. In *The Poetics*, Aristotle thought of the dramatic arc as a structure in which to "imitate life" through the device of the theater, in which that imitation (the plot) moves through time from the *beginning*, through the *middle*, to an *end* (Meadows, 2003).

The goal of the narrative arc is to move the viewer from *possibility* to *causality*, using *complication* to provide context and add interest, until a *resolution* is reached. The German theater critic Gustav Freytag in 1863 offered a triangular-shaped model of the narrative arc (figure 7.1), starting at the bottom with the *introduction*, the *rising action* on the way to the *turning point* at the top of the triangle, followed by the *falling action* on the downward slope to the conclusion.

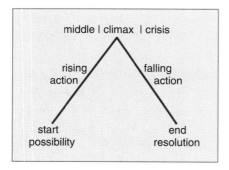

Figure 7.1
Gustav's triangle of narrative flow.

The introduction and rising and falling actions represent the informational attributes. The timing of these phases can vary greatly, typically skewing the climax more toward the end than the absolute middle. Other models use such terms as *exposition, initiation, complication, climax,* and *resolution* or *discovery, surprise,* and *reversal* to essentially describe that same narrative arc (Laurel, 1991).

Ben Shneiderman's famous visualization mantra, *"overview first, zoom and filter, then details-on-demand,"* follows the spirit of the narrative arc, the *overview* acting as the introduction, much like an establishing shot in a feature, *zooming* in on items of interest while *filtering out* extraneous features, amplified by the ability to show additional *details-on-demand,* providing context.

The role of perspective is an important element to consider as it shapes the story being told. Perspective can be a conscious act or simply reflect the values and life experiences that have shaped the visualization designer's frame of reference. Visualizations based on qualitative data may seem objective and without obvious perspective, but note that the designer chooses the specific data to represent and determines how it is represented. The more those decisions are expressly made with the designer's self-awareness of the perspective(s) being represented, the stronger the communicative value of the visualization (Meadows, 2003).

Other ways to structure a story than using a narrative arc structure include the LATCH scheme for organizing elements (location, time, and hierarchy), which can be used to organize narrative elements as a vehicle to move through the story in a visualization. Time and location are particularly useful dimensions to exploit and powerful when used together (Eccles, Kapler, Harper, & Wright, 2008).

The Kaleidoscopic Narrative

Janet Murray (1997) offered the kaleidoscope as a metaphor to view the narrative elements in the emerging digital environments that may be useful in the narrative component of interactive visualization. Just as the physical kaleidoscope divides the linear view from its lens into a nonlinear *mosaic*[1] of portions of that world, interactive visualizations are a mosaic patchwork of interconnected views of data that can be infinitely recombined and viewed.

This is not to say there is or should not be any organization to the parts, as we would be overwhelmed by the apparent chaos. In past media, we have used conventions to bring order. In newspapers the grid format of headlines and story sections provides us with a way to organize the information in a meaningful manner. Similarly, the editing conventions first introduced by Sergei Eisenstein's 1925 film, *Battleship Potemkin,* established a language to make sense of the discontinuous images being

1. The term was used by Marshall McLuhan (1964) to describe its nonlinearity.

flashed across the screen. These media conventions became polished and tacit over time and continue to provide a structural base to build understanding on.

Murray suggests there are a number of essential qualities that digital environments should possess to facilitate narration and move them from *additive*, where they merely mimic earlier media conventions, to more *expressive* forms:

1. Digital environments are *procedural,* in that the computer follows rules that guide the user through the experience.
2. Digital environments are *participatory,* and the procedural guidance provided is not fixed and is reflexive to the user's input.
3. Digital environments are inherently *spatial* because of the interactive nature of the navigational process.
4. Digital environments are encyclopedic and can deliver an almost boundless amount of information, both in scope and in particularity.

Left off her list is the *temporal* property critical for historical visualization, but all five are germane to interactive visualizations.

Computers, digitization, and the Internet have sought to ingest many of the conventions of the media that it has so rapidly embraced: the *spatial* mosaic of newspapers and magazines, the *temporal* mosaic of film, radio, television, and theater, and the *participatory* mosaic of interaction with the television remote. It has added some new conventions, such as *Googling* to search for new web pages, social media interactions, and other structures that combine older conventions to yield new experiences: "On the computer we can lay out all the simultaneous actions in one grid, and allow the interactor to navigate among them. We can have the expansiveness of the novel with the rapid intercutting of the film" (Murray, 1997).

The conventions for interactive visualizations are still evolving, but as in all the media that have come before, they are based on adaptations and combinations of their progenitors. The kaleidoscope is a useful metaphor for thinking about novel permutations. Because computer-based interactive visualizations are less constrained by the conventions of earlier media, innovative mixtures of space, time, perspective, and dimensionality can be experimented with.

Some Examples of Storytelling in Visualizations

• Swedish physician and data analyst Hans Rosling uses his *GapMinder* interactive software to play dynamic animations using OECD[2] datasets, which can map the correlations among factors such as infant mortality, births per family, and economic

2. *Organization for Economic Co-operation and Development*, an international economic policy group.

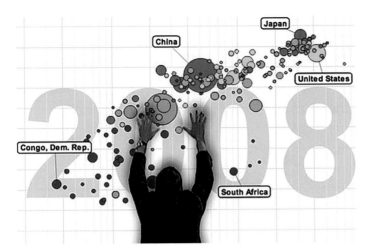

Figure 7.2
Hans Rosling's "animating" data (image courtesy www.gapminder.org).

income. He weaves fascinating conclusions by animating pairs of factors over time, providing a sportscaster's "play-by-play commentary" analysis to graphically understand the relationships between them. The software can slice up the data by continent, country, and country region to show nuances that can be lost in a aggregated view (figure 7.2). Rosling's now famous TED talk can be viewed from the *GapMinder* web site.[3]

• Charles Minard's 1869 drawing graphically tells the story of the of Napoleon's 1812 campaign into and out of Russia showing a steady loss of troops en route to Moscow in one color and an equally declining count on the return (figure 7.3). The chart shows multiple sets of information at once: size of the army, their location, the dates, and the temperature, creating a compelling story about the environmental hardships and their devastating effect on troop numbers. *"Minard made this because he hated war,"* design guru Edward Tufte said. The map was not about Napoleon, the war's surviving hero, who is mentioned nowhere on the page, Tufte explained, but of the quiet, anonymous misery of tens of thousands of French soldiers. *"This was meant as an antiwar poster"* (Jaffa, 2011; Tufte, 1983).

• The University of Maryland's Human Computer Interaction Lab's *SocialAction*[4] tool uncovers the latent structures in social networks over time. In one project, researchers plotted the correlation between the number of times U.S. senators voted with each

3. www.gapminder.org.
4. www.cs.umd.edu/hcil/socialaction.

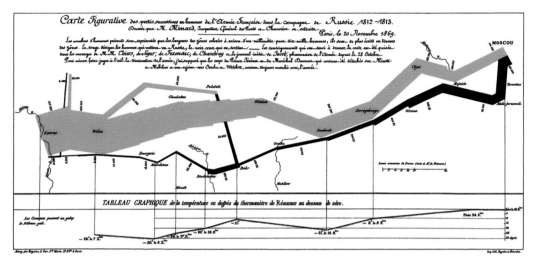

Figure 7.3
Charles Minard's map of Napoleon's march to Moscow.

other (figure 7.4). When all senators were plotted together, the map of their social network was uninformative because there was much common voting between the parties, in contrast to popular thought. When common votes were filtered to show only those with a 60 percent voting coincidence, strong political partisanship began to emerge.

• Stanford University's *Mapping the Republic of Letters*[5] project provides an interactive way to view the 55,000 letters in the seventeenth-century Electronic Enlightenment[6] database developed at the University of Oxford. The developers have mapped each of the letters according to sender and recipients and their locations (figure 7.5) and are able to visually track who communicated with whom and when. This information could be painstakingly gleaned from reviewing the letters themselves with much manual effort, but the graphic nature of the web application Stanford developed makes relationships instantly obvious. In the visualization of the network that the French Enlightenment writer Voltaire created through his correspondence, it is interesting to see that he did not often communicate with English correspondents, even though the French greatly admired the political and religious thinking of the English Enlightenment.

• Artist and historian Alice Cannon[7] owns a house in central Virginia that was once a plantation, and she actively researched the identities of the approximately 54 enslaved people who had lived there at one time. She used *progressive disclosure* to tell

5. https://republicofletters.stanford.edu.
6. www.e-enlightenment.com.
7. www.alicecannon.com.

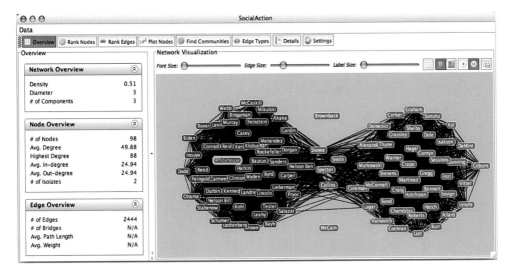

Figure 7.4
SocialAction map (used with permission of University of Maryland Human–Computer Interaction Lab).

Figure 7.5
Voltaire's letters (image courtesy of Mapping the Republic of Letters).

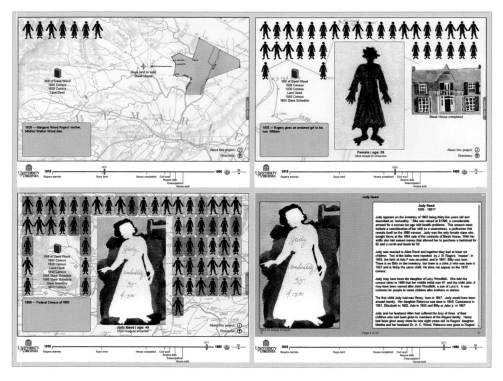

Figure 7.6
Progressive disclosure of Bleak House Slaves (image courtesy Alice Cannon).

the story of the personification of slaves over time by modulating the information known about them as the timeline progresses from antebellum through emancipation.[8] Initially, only their sex and age are known, but as time moves forward, more information is disclosed sequentially, revealing the first names, last names, their family connections, and finally full biographies (figure 7.6). The rendering of the artwork of the depiction of the people also progresses, from a crude iconic representation, to beautiful watercolor "negative space" drawings that hope to further reveal the humanity of these people.

• University of Virginia Tibetan studies student Kate Hartmann spent a summer living in the culturally Tibetan village of Karsha, in northern India, where she lived with the nuns at the Khachoe Drubling nunnery. From the copious notes she took, Hartmann created a map of the nunnery and plotted where each of the 21 nuns was at any given time. Each nun is represented by a colored dot that moves from room to room when

8. www.viseyes.org/show/?id=bleak.xml.

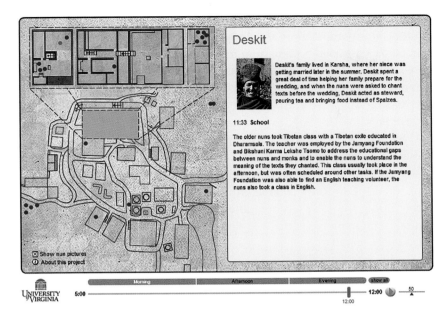

Figure 7.7
The daily life of the nuns at Khacloe Drubling (image courtesy Kate Hartmann).

the timeline is animated, tracking their movements. Hartmann's visualization paints a compelling picture of the day in the life of the nunnery, where and what the nuns do, and how they interact with one another. Clicking on a nun's representative dot colors it green to make tracking her easier, and more information is shown in real-time about her life and greater detail about her current activity in the yellow screen (figure 7.7).

Misleading Representations

Mark Twain popularized the saying, "There are three kinds of lies: lies, damn lies, and statistics." It is all too easy to use graphs and other kinds of visual representations that favor one interpretation of the data over another, either unwittingly or as a conscious effort. The following are some common examples of misleading representations:

• *Inappropriate representations*   Certain representational techniques can distort the true relationships between data elements and suggest an attenuated or exaggerated interaction that may not really be there. The starting points and ranges of graphs are especially sensitive to this kind of misrepresentation.
• *Correlation is not causation*   There are many possible explanations to explain why two datasets are related: set A may cause a change in set B, but set B may actually

cause set A to change. The changes may be the result of factor C, be within the normal range of possibility, or any number of alternative explanations.

• *The average is not the individual*   A common mistake is to assume that an individual data item will conform to the average. That the average height of a population may be five foot ten does not mean that people who are two feet and eight feet tall do not naturally exist. Statisticians have a joke about a man being boiled alive with an ice block on his head who boasts: *"On average, I feel just fine."*

• *Data do not represent the population*   Selecting sources for their convenience or through purposeful selection or omission of sets or subsets (called *cherry picking*) may lead to conclusions that cannot be generalized to other populations. A famous example of this occurred when the Chicago Tribune erroneously printed the headline "Dewey Defeats Truman" during the 1948 election, after basing their polling on a sample of voters that was not representative of the U.S. electorate and by using an inappropriate technique called *quota sampling.*

Validity Threats

Using data to support research questions and arguments requires a heightened awareness of a new class of potential problems called *validity threats*. Validity threats can hamper the reliance on conclusions made from the data and compromise the credibility of a data visualization. The social-science research literature has long identified a number of issues that can weaken research designs, all of which fall into two basic categories:

• *Internal validity threats,* which are flaws in the project's design that call into question the way the data have been selected, structured, or tested, such as history, instrumentation, and statistical methods chosen.

• *External validity threats,* which question the ability of the data to be generalized beyond the sample data chosen. This can happen due to selection bias or from working with too small a sample of data (Kazdin, 1982).

Tamara Munzner (2009) has identified some additional validity threats that are specific to visualizations:

• The *validity threat*, in which the visualization's base problem is mischaracterized.

• The *abstraction threat*, in which the visualization does not properly convert the data from the problem domain into the visualization and therefore does not realistically represent the underlying phenomena

• The *encoding threat*, in which the representation of the data does not accurately reflect its true nature.

• *Algorithm threats,* which transform the data using some statistical or mathematical process that fails to reflect the underlying process.

• *Mismatch threats,* which distort the data's contribution to the argument because the representation does not actually reflect that aspect.

Design Tensions

In all design projects, decisions must be made that sacrifice one goal for another. The following are some common tensions that arise in creating interactive visualizations. The ideal in resolving these conflicts is finding a "middle way" that combines appropriate and best features from both of the extremes or at least finds an optimal point within the continuum:

• *Narrative versus exploratory*   Narrative visualizations feature the voice of the designer as a prominent element and are common in historical and educational projects. They provide a curated path that leads the viewer through the primary source material toward insights and conclusions that benefit from the designer's subject matter expertise. Exploratory visualizations provide a virtual "sandbox" where information is made available for search and discovery by the viewer, with little guidance provided by the designer, allowing the viewer to construct his or her own understanding directly. Each approach has advantages and disadvantages for a project. Highly exploratory visualizations often lack the context to properly understand the issues, and overly narrative projects often eliminate the ability of viewers to find relationships from that data that the designer did not implicitly plan for. Good visualizations often have both.

• *Functionality/usability versus aesthetics*   The guidelines for creating usable visualizations (good models, visibility, mappings, and feedback) are often at odds with attractive design, so a concerted effort at merging the two will reward viewers with a usable project that they will enjoy working with.

• *Functionality/usability/aesthetics versus time*   Creating an effective, compelling, usable, and attractive interactive visualization takes time, and often one or more of these important factors is sacrificed in the name of time.

Summary

This chapter discusses the importance of the storytelling component of an interactive visualization. A good visualization answers a question using primary source evidence to tell a story. That story should be meaningful and able to address the significant criteria (the *so what?*).

The psychologist Roger Shank believes that most of human knowledge is stored internally as stories in the form of *scripts* or *schemas* that abstract the actual facts into idealized and connected elements through the processes of *distillation, combination,* and *elaboration.* Storytellers since Aristotle have identified the structure of the *narrative arc*. Gustav Freytag created a triangular drawing in 1863 that showed the structure of a narrative from rising action to climax to falling action.

The chapter presents some examples of effective storytelling in interactive visualizations: Hans Rosling's *GapMinder* software and his energetic presentation of it, the iconic 1869 Charles Minard map of Napoleon's march to Moscow, the University of Maryland's *SocialAction* tool showing partisanship in U.S. Senate voting patterns, and, finally, Stanford's Mapping the Republic of Letters project that maps letters of the Enlightenment.

Care should be taken to ensure that visual representations do not favor one interpretation of the data over another, either unwittingly or as a conscious effort. This can result from inappropriate representations or from wrongly assuming correlation means causation, ascribing the average to the individual, or cherry-picking data. A number of *validity threats* can also lead to inaccurate data representations due to internal, external, validity, and abstraction issues.

Finally, decisions during the design process must be made that typically sacrifice one goal for another. The following common tensions arise in interactive visualizations: a narrative voice versus an exploratory sandbox, overall functionality and usability versus aesthetic issues, and overall functionality, usability, and aesthetics versus time.

8 Visualization in the Classroom

Just in time instead of just in case.
—John Mergendoller

The ASSERT model has been developed in the context of teaching undergraduate students over the course of 5 years at the University of Virginia. Visualization seminars (VSEM) provide digital interactive visualization to a broad community of faculty, scholars, and students across multiple disciplines of study. The ability to visualize primary sources and information presents a new opportunity for digital scholarship using data to support inquiry and argument.

A visualization seminar is an innovative team-taught seminar that invites students working with faculty across departments and disciplines to develop highly interactive visualizations while they advance a broadly collaborative research agenda (figure 8.1). It combines the best of liberal arts and discipline-specific education with training in visual thinking and the application of new technologies. As importantly, it offers undergraduates an opportunity to present original research for peer review and online publication, adding value and purpose to their work.

Each seminar of 10 to 20 students is designed and taught by a content instructor, whose scholarly interests frame the course and help to define the research agenda, and a visualization instructor, who sets the visualization portion of the curriculum and helps to realize the project's goals in a digital form. In the first third of the semester, students are introduced to the core subject matter through readings, lectures, field trips, and videos (figure 8.2). Guest lecturers and project participants from outside the university are invited to interact with students via telecommunication technology such as Skype.

In the second third of the course, students are encouraged to define/refine their research questions and identify/locate primary source materials that can be used to answer them. In the final third of the course, students work closely with the instructors and their peers to organize their data and create visualizations that can reveal new insights and support arguments. At the end of the course, students make final

Figure 8.1
Students in a visualization seminar.

presentations of their work to project partners and invited guests—a dynamic, interactive version of a "poster session" at a conference.

Over the course of the semester, students gain mastery of the course content, an understanding of basic academic research methodologies, and a proficiency with visualization technologies. The seminar's collaborative research environment encourages faculty mentoring and hands-on learning. For prospective graduate students, it offers a glimpse of new educational models that are transforming our disciplines and the world of academic scholarship.

We see the VSEM as a great use of an educational model called *Project-Based Learning* (PBL) and rewarding to all involved (figure 8.3). Students learn the course content within the context of developing a project, in this case an interactive visualization. PBL encourages *just-in-time* learning of the elements needed as opposed to *just-in-case* instruction.

Students have an opportunity to work closely with senior faculty members across disciplines to do authentic research using next-generation tools to make real contributions to the literature. Faculty members are able to advance their research agendas in innovative ways, and the collaboration with scholarly partners enhances the university's relationship in the community. The Buck Institute of Education[1] provides a great source of information to assist instructors in using PBL in their classrooms.

We have seen undergraduate students benefit greatly from this type of classroom structure. Rather than passively ingesting knowledge from lectures, demonstrating

1. www.bie.org.

Figure 8.2
Student presenting work in final presentation.

Figure 8.3
The steps involved in Project-Based Learning (image courtesy of Buck Institute of Education).

recall on tests and papers, and promptly forgetting the information, the learning tends to be more authentic and constructive in nature.

Students are actively engaged in inquiry with direct and constant interaction with faculty members and each other. They are encouraged to seek the help of outside scholars and to make use of special collections, archives, and other information sources of data beyond "The Google."

In short, *they learn how to do research.*

The seminars promote what are often referred to as *twenty-first-century learning skills*: the pursuit of knowledge through inquiry; the ability to collaborate with peers and outside sources; the effective use of technology and media; the use of new models of communication and group interaction; and critical thinking skills that are often absent in lecture-style instruction and important to students' eventual careers and to the twenty-first-century world.

Case Study: The University of Virginia's First Library

This case study explores a visualization project undertaken by undergraduate students in a class at the University of Virginia whose goals were to teach basic historical research skills. This was done in the context of a project-based learning seminar in which the students looked at the books found in the university's first library in 1828, which was housed in the Rotunda.

The project is significant because all of the books were personally chosen by Thomas Jefferson, the university's founder. The Rotunda and the library it contained constituted Thomas Jefferson's last great act of scholarship, both in terms of his archi-

Figure 8.4
Opening panel of the library project.

tectural design and his broad selection of humanist and scientific books of the period, reflecting his deep understanding of Enlightenment principles in a lifetime of personal book collecting.

The library opened in the winter of 1826, 6 months after Jefferson's death, and was ranked among the great university libraries, holding over 7000 volumes with 3000 unique titles, a large number for the time.

The overarching goal was to analyze the books Mr. Jefferson chose to see if we could learn something from his choices and organization and to communicate in a visual manner something about the intellectual environment in the early days of the American experiment (figure 8.4).

The seminar of 12 first- and second-year students was team taught by religious studies professor Kurtis Schaeffer and the author. Professor Schaeffer suggested the library as a project to study and took primary responsibility for historical and bibliographic issues, whereas I focused on the ways we could organize and communicate the information using VisualEyes.

Data Sources

Doing research on early nineteenth-century subjects can be daunting because of the dearth of materials that have survived the test of time, and in this case, a tragic fire in 1895 destroyed much of the Rotunda and its contents. The most important resource was a printed catalog of all the books in the library: *Catalogue of the Library of the University of Virginia. Arranged Alphabetically under Different Heads, with the Number and Size of the Volumes of Each Work, and Its Edition Specified.*

This was essentially a bound version of the card catalog containing a limited amount of information about each book, divided into chapters corresponding to the way Jefferson organized his own library at Monticello. It was also the initial organizational structure of the Library of Congress collection, which was founded on the purchase of Jefferson's library in 1815. The books were organized into 29 chapters, which were in turn divided into three parts that mirrored the way of viewing knowledge espoused by Francis Bacon and falling within the three-part scheme of Diderot and d'Alembert's *Encyclopedia: Memory, Reason, and Imagination.* The 1828 catalog did not contain these three headings, but the subordinate chapters were consistent with that organization, so we were able to use it as an overarching theme consistent with Jefferson's view:

[I. History/Memory]
1. School of Ancient Languages
2. Modern History
3. Modern Geography
4. Modern Philology and Literature
5. Mathematics and Natural Philosophy
6. General Natural Philosophy
7. Agriculture and Horticulture
8. Botany
9. Zoology
10. Mineralogy and Geology
11. Chemistry
12. History of Medicine and Medical Biography
13. Hygiene
14. Materia Medica and Pharmacy
15. Medical Jurisprudence and Toxicology
16. Anatomy, Sound and Morbid
17. Physiology
18. Pathology and Therapeutics
19. Operative Surgery
20. Obstetrics
21. Veterinary Medicine
22. General Medicine
[II. Philosophy/Reason]
23. Mental Philosophy and Ethics

24. Political Economy
25. Politics
26. Law
27. Religion (Christian, Ethnick &c.) and Ecclesiastical History
[III. Fine Arts/Imagination]
28. Architecture, Designing, Painting, Sculpture, and Music
29. Miscellaneous, Including Poetry, Rhetoric, Education, &c.

Each book was represented by seven consistent categories of information, although some entries contained information about editors and translations. The ones we chose were these:

1. Author
2. Short title in English
3. Date of publication
4. Language, if not English
5. City of publication
6. Number of volumes
7. Size of book (i.e., quarto, folio, etc...)

Here is an example, the first entry in chapter 27 on Religion:

"Adam's Dictionary of Religions, Boston, 1817—(vols.) 1 (size) 8"

that yielded the following information, split into the seven fields:

Author: *Adams*
Title: *Dictionary of Religions*
Language: *English*
Place published: *Boston*
Date published: *1817*
Volumes: *1*
Size: *Octavo*

Structuring the Data

A transcribed version of the catalog existed in the university's eText collection, but the seven basic categories were not separated into individual fields, so a graduate student painstakingly structured the data into a spreadsheet with 7000 rows and seven columns: one book per row and one field per column.

We wanted to do some analysis on a country rather than a city basis, so an additional column was added to hold that information. A student went through each row and identified the country from its city name and populated that eighth column on a one-by-one basis.

This spreadsheet became the primary data source for the visualization, but some secondary resources became useful. The university's special collections librarian mentioned an additional source that proved useful. When the library burned in 1895, only 10 percent of the books survived the fire, and those books were noted in a document that was made available. A ninth column was added to the spreadsheet to reflect whether or not the book entered had survived the fire.

Research Questions

One particularly skeptical young man expressed his doubts that we would be able to provide anything interesting in such a boring dataset, and Kurtis and I took this as a challenge to show that even this limited dataset could yield some interesting insights.

Several classes were devoted to unstructured discussion on what questions we might ask about the origins, organization, and content of the library, using the catalog as guide. Among them were the following:

- Who are the authors?
- How many authors are represented by multiple titles?
- Where were the authors from?
- When did they live?
- What languages were represented in the library?
- How many books are in each language?
- What are the relative numbers in each language?
- Where are the books published?
- What are the relative numbers of books published in particular places?
- What are the date ranges of the particular chapters?
- How many multivolume works are there?
- How many distinct types of volumes are there?
- What are the relative numbers of the different sizes of volumes?
- Are there discernable trends in publishing across Europe? America?

Kurtis suggested creating a matrix among the eight things we knew about each book and seeing what kind of questions the relationships between the factors might present. This yielded a number of additional questions, such as the relationship between the language the book had been written in relative to the country where it had been published.

Envisioning the Project

The finite time of a semester course forced us to choose a few questions we wanted to investigate and visualize with the data we had. The class voted on the following questions:

1. What is the relationship between the books organized by chapter and their languages?
2. What is the relationship between the books organized by chapter and countries of publication?
3. What is the relationship between the books organized by chapter and those that survived the 1895 fire?
4. How many books were published in each location?

In addition, we wanted to provide access to the books in a number of ways:

1. Allow structured search by field of all the books in the library.
2. Provide access to digitized versions of the books.
3. Show the books in a "virtual bookshelf."

Representing the Project

VisualEyes supports a notion of tabbed panels to organize aspects into discrete sections. We opted to set up three panels: an introductory panel, one dedicated to the questions concerning the organization of the books with respect to their language and country of publication, and, finally, a panel dedicated to exploring the books themselves and their place of publication in the world.

The first panel introduced the project and showed a historic photo of the library's interior that was stylized by using a grain effect created in Photoshop. The project's title was overlaid in a "digital-style" typeface to contrast the historical image and hint at the visualization elements within the project.

A student had identified a series of historic photos of the library in the special collections library, and we discussed how to present them. If we were to show them too small, detail would be lost or require a click to zoom in, and they would take up too much screen space if larger. We decided to present them in a manner similar to the Macintosh program bar, so the images automatically grew in size when the mouse was over them (figure 8.5).

Buttons provided access to popup dialogues that introduced the project in a short narrative as well as a simple timeline (figure 8.6) that graphically highlighted key events in the library's history.

The second panel focused on exposing the relationship between the organization of the books according to the Memory, Reason, and Imagination scheme and the books' languages, places of publication, and whether or not they survived the 1895 Rotunda fire using a stacked horizontal bar chart. Each bar represented a chapter, the overall length giving information about the total number of books in that chapter, with the primary grouping shown in brackets (figure 8.7).

A set of radio buttons controlled what kind of information was displayed in the bar: the language, country of publication, and fire survival data. For example, the

Figure 8.5
Historic photos of the library in image dock.

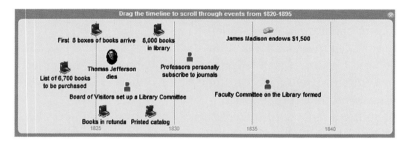

Figure 8.6
Timeline of library events.

various languages were drawn in different colors so it was easy to see the distribution within a given chapter.

We placed the chart atop an image of a page in Jefferson's own handwriting describing the organization of his retirement library at Monticello. The image was blurred so that it would not distract from the information display, and it gives a graphic sense of the historical period of the library.

One student found a list of overdue book fines in the university's special collections library, and a button brings up a dual-paned document viewer that shows a zoomable digitized view of the original page on the left and a transcription of the page on the right (figure 8.8). It turned out that Edgar Allen Poe was a two-time offender, owing the library $5.20 in book fines!

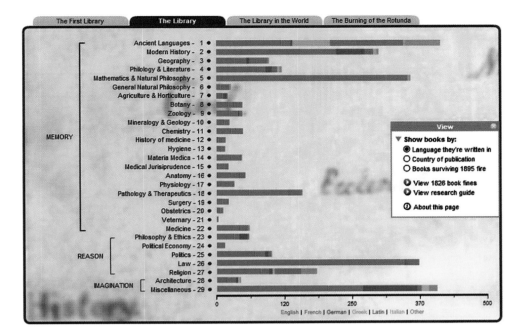

Figure 8.7
The books in the library.

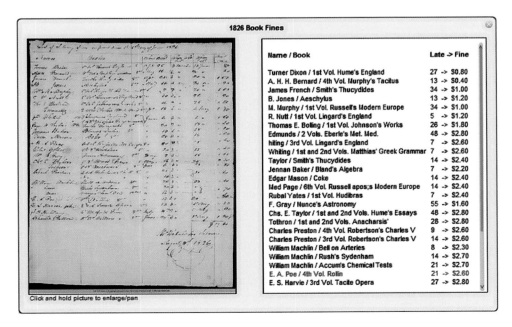

Figure 8.8
Document showing overdue fines.

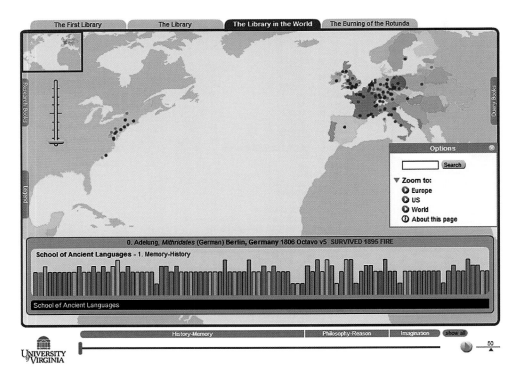

Figure 8.9
The books in the world.

The third panel explored the books in the world and the effect of geography. The goal was to represent each book individually while still giving a sense of their number relative to other books. A colorful vector-based map of the Atlantic corridor that showed the countries as filled areas was chosen to provide geographic context (figure 8.9). We tried using historical maps, but the rich annotation distracted from the expository role of the map to simply provide relative location.

Each of the books was represented as a circular red dot centered on its place of publication. We tried various techniques to represent the number of books at each location, including changing the size and color of the dot relative to the number of books published there, but found those techniques lacking. Changing the size caused smaller publishers to be occluded by more prolific cities. We ultimately chose to draw each dot with the transparency set to 15 percent. As more books were published in a single location, those cities became more saturated, correctly giving the cue that more books were published there (figure 8.10). Nearby towns with fewer books published showed as an aura that did not occlude other towns and cities.

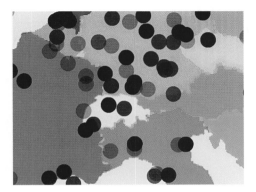

Figure 8.10
Dots highlighting where books were published.

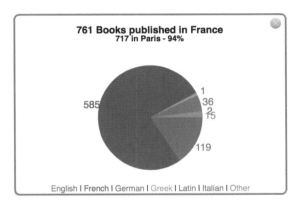

Figure 8.11
Popup dialog showing languages books were written in.

To show more information about the books published in any location, a pop-up dialog box appeared when a city was clicked that contained a pie chart that showed the relative distribution of the languages the books were written in for that country (figure 8.11).

The best way to visually represent such a large number of books in a usable manner became a challenge. We investigated using various structures, including hierarchical trees, tree maps, and radial maps. We decided to simulate a virtual bookshelf using a schematized representation of each book as a rectangle in a scrollable shelf (figure 8.12). The books were colored by the languages they were written in, and the height reflected the size of the book (ocatavo, folio, quarto, etc.).

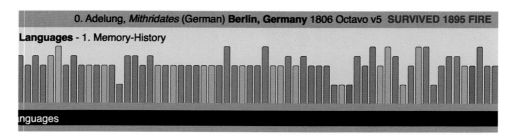

Figure 8.12
The virtual book shelf.

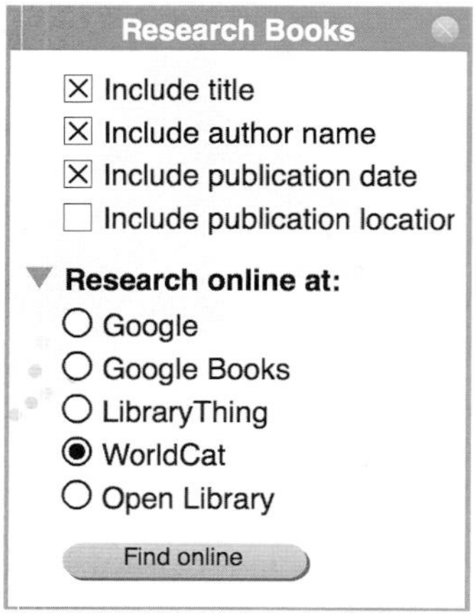

Figure 8.13
Boolean search panel.

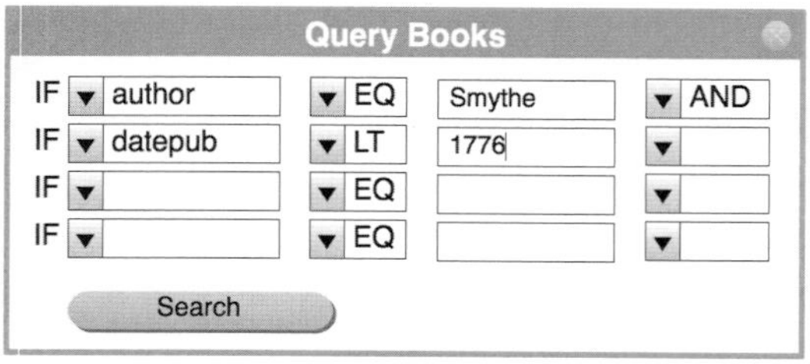

Figure 8.14
Finding digitized copies of books.

The books were arranged in their order by chapter, and colored bands were run beneath the books to indicate the chapter those books appeared within. To help further reduce the number of books to scroll through, a menu below limited the display to only books in the *Memory*, *History*, and *Reason* divisions when clicked.

Clicking on a book shows its information above the bookshelf. Because the shelf is directly interactive with the map, clicking on a book causes the city it was published in to become highlighted, and the map zooms to the side of the Atlantic it originated from. An animation control automatically scrolls through the books from left to right, highlighting the book, its information, and its location in the world in a compelling manner.

A search box made structured searching on the catalog easily done, providing up to four compound Boolean AND/OR queries. A second dialogue box provided pre-populated search queries using the current book in digitized repositories such as Google Books, Open Library, Library Thing, and WorldCat (figures 8.13 and 8.14). When found, the original text comes up in a separate window.

Telling a Story

The final visualization takes a rather limited collection of data—a library card catalog using a limited number of fields—to interactively explore an example of early eighteenth-century American scholarship.

It was immediately clear from the mapping that England, France, and Germany dominated the library's holding and how few American books were a part of it. The English and Americans were much more provincial about writing only in English when publishing books, as compared to the French and German publishers, with the Germans supporting the widest range of languages other than German.

Seeing which books had survived the 1895 Rotunda fire prompted questions as to why those books were targeted for escape. Was it that the locations of those books were convenient to the exits, or were some volumes valued more than others?

9 The Internet

The Internet is not a big truck, but a series of tubes.
—Senator Ted Stevens

The Internet and the World Wide Web are arguably the most important innovations impacting interactive visualization today. They are the source of a wealth of data that drive visualizations and the mechanism that delivers compelling user experiences anywhere in the world. Although the actual mechanisms are complicated, the overall concepts of how the Internet works are quite simple. This chapter introduces these basic ideas to help demystify this important tool.

Clients and Servers

The World Wide Web is an interconnected collection of devices that connect computers to computers. Some of these computers are personal computers (PCs) controlled by people, called *clients*. Other computers, not all that different from your own laptop, deliver web pages to a client computer in response to its electronic requests. These larger and more powerful computers are called *servers*. This system of *client/server* computing describes the current state of networked computing. A simplified drawing of this is shown in figure 9.1.

When you type a web address into your web browser, your computer sends some instructions via the router or modem to your Internet service provider (ISP), who then forwards it to the Internet. Those instructions are sent to a server also connected to the Internet. The appropriate web page you requested is sent back along the same path to your computer, where it is displayed by the web browser.

Clients

A client computer is pretty much synonymous with a PC or laptop but can include PDAs and even smart phones like the iPhone. These all consist of the actual hardware, the operating system (i.e., Windows or MacOS or Linux), and whatever programs or

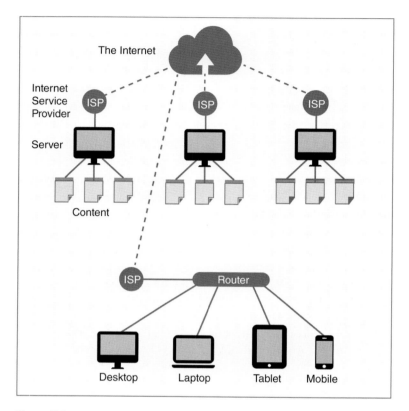

Figure 9.1
A simplified map of the Internet.

applications you want to run on the computer. A web *browser* is simply another application that allows you to access web-based resources.

Browsers

The browser is an application program that runs on your computer and gives you a graphical way to view web pages from servers. Most computers come with a default browser. For example, Windows-based computers come with *Internet Explorer*, whereas Macintosh computers come with *Safari* already installed. Other good alternatives for both platforms are *Firefox* and *Google Chrome*, which are available for most kinds of computers.

The web browser is really a remarkable piece of software. It can interact with a web page such as a web form, which allows you to send a request to a server to retrieve specific web content. A web browser also can show movies, display documents, and play music. When the web was young, the content retrieved was typically a static page of information, but new technologies sometimes called Web 2.0 or AJAX make browsing web pages a highly interactive experience.

Browsers can accept small pieces of software written by third parties, called *plug-ins,* to support additional functionality. This software is often written to allow different forms of media to play within the browser rather than in a separate window. Popular plug-ins include Adobe *Flash* (formerly Macromedia's *Flash*) for interactive content, Adobe *Acrobat* for PDF documents, and *QuickTime* media player to play movies. *ActiveX controls* are similar to plug-ins but extend functionality in *Internet Explorer.*

Servers

Servers are typically more powerful computers that have hardware and software specially designed to deliver or "serve" software resources and data to you, the client, in the fastest, most efficient way possible. At the heart of things, servers are really no different from your PC but typically have more storage space, memory, and additional processors.

The Internet and the World Wide Web make extensive use of client/server computing, and over the years, both the client side and server side of the computing process have grown quite robust and therefore complex.

At its heart, a server is simply a computer that shares the contents of its hard disk with the world via the Internet. A server uses a modem to connect to an Internet Service Provider, that in turn is connected to the other servers that form the Internet.

Server Software

A very powerful combination of software that provides robust delivery and development of web-based products and services is LAMP. LAMP consists of the Linux operating system and the *Apache* server software, which provide the delivery of web-based resources. Linux is an operating system (just as Windows and MacOS are), and *Apache* is the web application software that runs on Linux servers. *Apache*'s name was derived from its open-source roots, having been developed from "a patch of" software code written by different developers in the open-source community. This combination of software runs over half of the world's web servers (Microsoft's IIS system is second at 34 percent). MySQL is a robust database application, and PHP is a powerful server-based programming language popular for writing web-based applications. All of this software is open source and free for downloading.

Networks

The ability of computers to physically communicate with one another is accomplished by using a *network*. A network can take many forms and can be a combination of these. Connections can be made wirelessly, such as using Wi-Fi (802.11), through cables, or by fiber optics. A typical system might contain all three forms to connect your computer to the Internet.

Your computer has a piece of hardware inside it called *the network interface adapter* (NIC) that physically connects your computer to the network. A wireless NIC has an antenna to receive information via radio waves, whereas a wired NIC has a jack to accept an Ethernet cable. Whether wired or wireless, your information is sent to a *router* or hub, which connects all of the computers on your network together in a *local area network* (LAN).

LANs consist of two or more connected computers that are normally in close proximity to each other but may be expanded and connected together to form a larger cluster of networks. The router connects to the Internet via a modem that may use direct wiring or fiber optics to connect to the Internet service provider as shown.

Internet Service Provider

An Internet service provider (ISP) is a company that provides computers access to the Internet. Both servers and clients require some connection to the Internet via an ISP. Early ISPs include America Online and CompuServe, who provided dial-up access to millions of people, but now there are a myriad of ways people connect to the Internet. Connectivity can be established through cable companies, satellite services, and phone companies via DSL. Universities and other large organizations have direct connections to the Internet without the need for an ISP.

Files and File Systems

The web and computers in general have adopted a document-and-folder metaphor to represent how information is stored. Just as papers can be stored in manila folders, digital files are stored in directories. Folder and subfolder structures have a relative "parent-child" relationship that can be established several layers deep. This makes it easy to organize large amounts of information on web sites and computers.

Files

A file is the atomic unit of the scenario, with each element being represented by a named file. For example a JPEG file containing an image of my picture might be called MyPicture.jpg, and a PDF document with my resume might be called MyResume.pdf. Files are named in two parts: the name (MyPicture) and the extension (jpg) separated by a dot. The extensions help tell the computer what kind of file it is (i.e., a JPEG picture or PDF document).

There are some restrictions on what you can name files, and a number of characters, such as " * / : < > ? \ |, are not permitted. In addition files on web servers are typically case sensitive (i.e., mypicture.jpg and MyPicture.jpg are different files) cannot have spaces in them, which is why you see MyPicture.jpg instead of My Picture.jpg. Personal computers do not have any problems with spaces in filenames.

Directories (a.k.a. Folders) and Paths

Directories and folders allow you to group and organize files in a meaningful way. Writing the names of these folders from left to right, where each folder and subfolder is separated by a forward slash (/), describes the *path* to the resource. This hierarchy of containers and subcontainers allows you to use the same filenames on the same server without conflict. For example, if I were organizing my photo album on the web, I might have a folder called 2010. Inside that folder there might be a number of files including one called MyPicture.jpg. I might take a different picture, also named MyPicture.jpg but shot in 2009, and place it into a folder called 2009. Although these two files have the same name, this works because they are in two different folders.

Folders can have an unlimited number of subfolders, which makes them useful in organizing your computer or web site. I could access the picture by following the path of folder/subfolder names before the file name. As shown in figure 9.2, for example, you could follow the MyComputer/MyStuff/Photos/2010 path to access MyPicture.jpg shot in 2010. The process of placing child subfolders or files within a parent folder is called *nesting*.

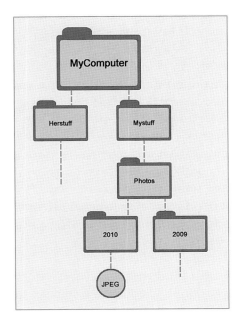

Figure 9.2
Folders.

The Internet

Even though most of us use the Internet on a daily basis, describing just exactly what the Internet is can be difficult. People often see the Internet as a resource like electricity without really understanding what is going on behind the scenes.

The Internet was started in the late 1950s by a small group of university researchers using military-sponsored grants to develop a system in which computers could talk to one another using telephone lines. Its use was limited until the 1990s, when easy-to-use browsers were developed, and a critical mass of people began using the Internet. The rest is history. Just a side note: although Al Gore did not invent the Internet, he was instrumental in providing funding that encouraged its success.

What started out as a half-dozen university sites has grown to millions of computers, all connected to one another. They connect to the Internet in a number of ways, using fiber-optic cables, wired connections, satellites, microwaves, and even still telephone lines.

Internet Protocol

The foundation these researchers set in place over 50 years ago has guided its growth. The biggest idea was that the Internet be decentralized and grow organically. There is no head office for the Internet anywhere. It began with a few university computers interconnected by telephone lines. These researchers developed a format, called the *Internet Protocol* (IP), to make sure the computers in the network could send and receive information, and although a number of other protocols have been added on top of it to provide new features, the IP protocol has remained the backbone of how computers on the Internet communicate with one another.

The second big idea is that rather than making direct connections between sites that want to talk in the manner that telephones do, information would be broken up into little packets, and a system was devised for routing these packets to their destinations.

To identify the various computers on the network, each computer was assigned a number, not unlike a telephone number, that uniquely identifies it on an IP-based network. This *IP address* is usually shown as four numbers separated by dots, for example, *128.143.22.100*. These numbers are assigned by an international organization called Internet Corporation for Assigned Names and Numbers (ICANN), which represents the only centralized authority of the Internet.

The Domain Name System

As more and more *computers* joined the Internet, the simple idea of a number to identify web sites became too cumbersome, so ICANN developed a directory service not unlike a digital telephone book, where people could use names to identify particular computers on the network. This *domain name* consists of two parts: the name of the site and *the top level domain*, which can be *.com, .net, .gov, .org, .edu,* or country names such as *.uk, .ca,* etc. When you type a domain name into your browser, a domain name system (DNS) server on the web looks up the domain name and connects you to the IP address that is registered with it via ICANN.

Uniform Resource Locator

A uniform resource locator (URL) provides an address for your browser to load a specific page from the Internet. There are three parts to a URL: the service, the hostname, and the path to the page itself. This service is typically *http*, so your browser will automatically add that part if you do not type it. The hostname is the DNS domain name of the server the page is sitting on, followed by the page itself. For example, the address http://www.viseyes.org/video/VisEditOverview.htm looks for the page called *VisEditOverview.htm* in the *video* folder on the server at www.viseyes.org.

If you do not specify a page, the server will typically send back one called *index. html*. URLs are unforgiving, and you must type the exact address. One misplaced or misrepresented letter, space, or slash will prevent your browser from finding the wanted resource. Generally speaking, upper- and lowercase letters matter.

Web Services

It has been well over a decade since the web first gained popularity, and we are poised to enter a new era of increased interactivity that may indeed deliver on the promise of early Internet evangelists. The computer maker Sun Microsystems's then CEO Jonathan Schwartz has called this the "Age of Participation," where people are not passive consumers of linear information but actively construct their own meaning from a wide variety of available sources. People contribute to the dialogue through comments, blogs, reviews, newsgroups, ratings, and more organized efforts such as Wikipedia.

Although this person-to-person discourse is exciting and will greatly enrich both personal experience and the collective good, a second kind of conversation has tremendous potential to increase the level of digital history scholarship—computer-to-computer interaction. This interaction is evident when one web page relies on another page for information, such as getting weather information, maps, stock prices, and so forth.

Receptive When Asked

This cooperation occurs when the user-facing web page sends a message, called a *web service request,* to another web page for some information, such as the current weather. The "invisible" page responds by sending that information back to the user-facing page, which then displays it.

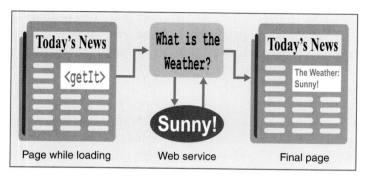

Figure 9.3
How web services work.

When the user clicks on a page that contains a call to a web service, the page will begin to load from the page's server. When the server reaches the part of the page where it wants to find the current weather, the server will ask a second server that contains a web service, in this case the weather server, to provide some information that will be inserted into the page (figure 9.3). This automated dance occurs because the makers of both pages agreed on a common format to facilitate this interaction. The REST and SOAP specifications are often-used formats. The main page asked for the information, and the weather page was receptive to being asked.

Flash

Adobe's *Flash* is a popular plug-in for web browsers that makes it easy to add highly interactive and graphical elements to web pages. *Flash* started out as a way for graphic designers to add animated openings and splash pages to their web sites but quickly grew into a rich environment for interactivity on the web. It is hard to get an understanding of *Flash* because of this evolution and the very different ways people use it today.

At its heart, *Flash* is a program that is able to display files that have been created in a format called *SWF* (pronounced *swiff*). When *Flash* first started out, these SWF files contained animated movies that played in high quality within a web page. Up to that point, web pages typically only displayed text and still images. Even though *Flash* has evolved beyond just movies, the moniker stuck, and SWF files are still often referred to as *Flash* movies.

Vector Graphics

Flash uses a technique similar to hand sketching called *vector* graphics, which results in high-quality drawings. Rather than storing every point in the image as

JPEG images do, Flash stores the image as a series of commands such as draw a line from here to here or fill this area in red. This technique enabled *Flash* to create graphics that were of extremely high quality, could be easily animated, and were very compact in size—an important asset in the days before broadband became popular.

Cross-Platform

Because Adobe provides plug-ins for most of the major computer platforms and web browsers, SWF files are inherently cross-platform and do not require special tweaks or even completely new versions for particular computers the way that other solutions require.

Flash and *Flash*

Macromedia, the original developer of *Flash*, used a clever business strategy to promote its success. Rather than charge people to view *Flash*'s SWF files on their web browsers, Macromedia gave it away as a free download and provided a robust animation tool (unfortunately also called *Flash*) to create the SWF for a fee. The strategy worked, with over 90 percent of the world's computers having the *Flash* plug-in installed in their web browsers.

When people talk about *Flash*, they really mean one of two things: the interactive tool for creating SWF movies that Adobe (which acquired Macromedia) sells or the free *Flash* plug-in Adobe provides to play those SWF files.

How *Flash* Works in the Web Browser

When you browse to a page that contains *Flash* content, HTML instructions on that web page ask the server to load the SWF file directly to the *Flash* plug-in. The instructions on the web page also save a spot on the screen to display the *Flash* content when it has loaded.

ActionScript

Flash grew more sophisticated as time went on, and a language was developed called ActionScript that added interactive capabilities to *Flash* movies. ActionScript started with humble beginnings and was little more than a scripting tool to enable very simple interactions with buttons and timers in *Flash* movies. Over time, the language grew in sophistication into a real programming language with capabilities that rival any of the traditional contenders such as Java.

It is the power of this new language that threatens to put a dent in Microsoft's hegemony of the desktop because there are few applications that cannot be effectively programmed in ActionScript. With ActionScript, *Flash* has come a long way since making annoying splash screens that people clicked through anyway.

Flash and XML

Flash makes it easy to import XML-formatted text files to add content to or control a *Flash* web application. This has created the ability to have very flexible data-driven applications that can change their behaviors by getting information from anywhere on the web, which makes it easy to have very rich web applications that can perform better than desktop applications because the information is live.

For example, a *Flash* application that searches through movie reviews can dynamically load the most recent reviews, information about the actors, and links to trailers and pictures without having to be reprogrammed. Simply changing the XML file that contains that information will update the application automatically.

Because images, XML, media, and other elements can be dynamically loaded into a *Flash* application, it is not necessary to have all the elements on one server. Through the use of web services and a wealth of publicly available images, such as the Library of Congress archives, *Flash* applications can deliver an almost unlimited collection of content.

10   Statistics

Lies, damn lies, and statistics.
—Mark Twain/Benjamin Disraeli

This section gives a very brief overview to some of the key concepts and tools that statistics can offer designers of information-driven visualizations. Statistics is one of the most dreaded subjects in all levels of education, from high school to graduate studies. The reality is that the basic ideas in statistics are actually pretty simple, and taking the time to understand them will enrich one's effectiveness as a designer of interactive visualizations and a citizen in a democracy. Statistics are used more and more as instruments of political persuasion, and a good grasp of just a few simple ideas can create a more informed electorate (Huff, 1954).

It is not necessary to understand the mathematics underlying how statistics are calculated, just as one can remain blissfully ignorant of the wiring that supplies a houses' electrical current, but knowing how to turn on a light is useful. It is also not necessary to use specialized, expensive, and difficult-to-use statistics tools such as SPSS for most of the analysis used in information visualizations. Modern spreadsheets such as Microsoft's *Excel* and Google *Docs* have powerful and easy-to-use tools for most of the needed statistical functions. The following chapter has detailed information about using modern spreadsheets for statistical analysis.

What Is Statistics?

Statistics is the process of converting data into information that is usable to people. Collections of numbers are difficult for people to make sense of directly. Statistics is a collection of tools that help people understand the meaning of quantitative data. These tools can compare datasets to see how similar they are to one another, how internally consistent the data are, and the characteristics of the data.

Populations and Samples

The data used in statistics consist of two basic groups, *populations* and *samples*, and the distinction between them is important to understand how to use statistics to explore. The US Census is an example of a population group because it theoretically includes everyone in the country. Samples are subsets of populations, where a representative sampling of the population is selected, such as in election polls.

Populations

Populations are groups of numbers that represent *all* of the objects of interest. By including all the members, we can derive some definitive statements about that population, such as averages, biggest, smallest, and so forth, but those statements are only true of the group itself and cannot be generalized to other groups.

For example, if our interest is in a classroom of students, all of the students in the classroom must be included in the study. The analysis performed on this data can yield insights on the entire class. If our interest was only on the boys in the class, we could ignore the girls, but the analysis results would be limited only to the boys. Simply because we studied just one class, it would be impossible to say with any certainty that a different classroom would have similar characteristics.

Samples

Samples are a subset of the full population. This is done because it is difficult or impossible to include the entire population, and the same issues of generalizations about the objects of interest from populations apply.

To be useful, a sample should be representative of the population. For example, if there are 56 percent women in the population, the sample should also have 56 percent women. There are many ways to fairly reduce the size of the dataset. The most common method is *random sampling,* in which each element should have an equal probability of occurring in the sample. Other techniques such as *quota sampling* and *stratified sampling* try to take advantage of previous knowledge of the population's makeup and try to include members according to some attribute, such as gender or race.

The size of a sample will have a large impact on how the results of the analysis can be generalized. Assuming the sampling method created a representative subset of the population data, a larger number of elements, called its *sample size,* will ensure that random variations in the samples will not distort the overall characteristics of the data.

Descriptive and Inferential Statistics

There are two basic divisions in the statistics. *Descriptive statistics* describes and summarizes the characteristics of a dataset, such as its range of values, its average, and how much individual elements vary from that average, called its *variance*.

Inferential statistics is used to draw conclusions and make predictions on the population, based on a sample of that population. Descriptive statistics can make definitive

Table 10.1
Heights of a group of people, in inches

40	45	50	55	60	65	70	75	80
					x	x		
					x	x		
				x	x	x	x	
			x	x	x	x	x	
			x	x	x	x	x	
		x	x	x	x	x	x	
	x	x	x	x	x	x	x	x

statements about the dataset's nature, whereas inferential statistics gives us probabilities about the dataset's makeup. These techniques can be quite powerful and are more abstract than the simpler descriptive statistics, but all provide means to suggest that two or more sets are similar to one another.

Statistics' One Big Idea: The Normal Curve

If there is only one big idea to understand in statistics, it is the *normal distribution* or *normal curve,* sometimes also known as a *bell curve,* which shows how a group of numbers are distributed. It turns out that natural phenomena such as age, height, and pretty much any other attribute have similar distributions of values. There are a few small ones, lots of ones in the middle, and a few large ones.

For example, if we want to see how a group of people vary in height, we would measure each one and put an *x* in the column corresponding to a person's height as in table 10.1. What would emerge would begin to resemble a bell curve like the one in figure 10.1.

At the extremes, there are not too many people shorter than four feet or taller than seven feet, with most people around the middle. How these numbers vary from low to high is called their *distribution*. More precisely, it is a distribution of their *frequency*, or number of times they occur in the dataset. The average of all these heights is between 65 and 70 inches, and the majority of the *x* marks cluster there.

If we were measuring people in Sweden, we would expect to see more people on the right, and if we measured in Peru, we would see more people to the left, but the overall shape would be similar: less on the ends and the majority around the middle. Because so many natural attributes follow this distribution shape, we can use the curve to predict values.

The Standard Deviation

The standard deviation (SD) is a measurement of how much variability there is in a dataset. This is measured by seeing how far each individual value is from the mean

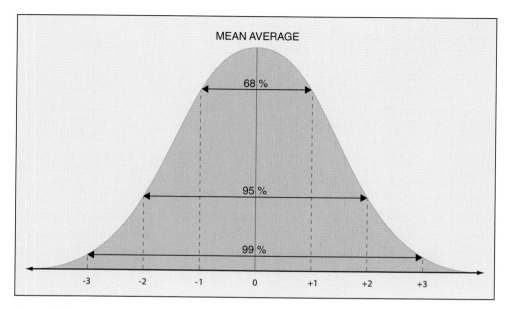

Figure 10.1
The normal curve.

average (figure 10.2), and it gives a good clue about whether the average is representative of all the members of the dataset.

A high SD means there are a lot of values higher and/or lower than the average, and knowing the average's value will not be as helpful in predicting any particular value. A low SD means that all the values are close to one another, and the mean average is likely to be close to any given value.

For example, if we were to measure the SAT scores of a group of Ivy League students, we would expect their scores to be close to the average and the standard deviation to be low. The SAT scores of a high-school class are likely to be more varied and to diverge from the average, yielding a high SD.

Knowing the SD and the mean average of a dataset makes it easy to get a sense of the data if they follow the normal curve. Values that are between 1 SD to the left and 1 SD to the right of the average make up 68 percent of the values. Two SD on either side make up 95 percent of the values, and 3 SD comprise a full 99.7 percent of the values.

As an example, intelligence quotient (IQ) tests have a mean average score of 100 points and a standard deviation of 15 points. This means that 68 percent of people scored between 85 and 115 on the tests (±1 SD), that 95 percent of people score

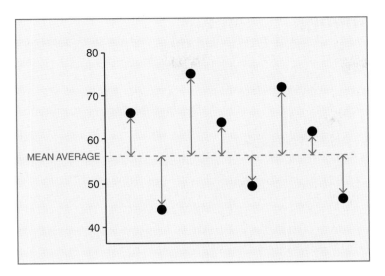

Figure 10.2
Deviations from the mean that form the standard deviation.

between 70 and 130 on the tests (±2 SD), and 99.7 percent of people score between 55 and 145 on the tests (±3 SD). This means that there is a 0.3 percent chance that someone will score under 55 or over 145, making these people rare indeed.

Descriptive Statistics

Descriptive statistics *describes* a dataset in declarative terms and provides a summary view of the dataset that is often more revealing than looking at the data directly. These kinds of statistics describe the distribution of values (*range*) in the dataset, their tendency to cluster around the middle values, called the *central tendency* (*mean, median, and mode*), and how the values are dispersed around the middle values (*variance* and *standard deviation*).

Distribution: Range
Looking at the range (the lowest and highest values) in relation to individual members of the information can offer information about the scale of the data. For example, if we had a dataset of pine trees offered for use as the national Christmas tree in Washington, DC, one might expect a range from 20 to 40 feet. If the range were 10 to 100 feet, we might wonder why a small 10-foot tree had been offered and if the 100 foot tree represented a data-entry error. Histograms and stem and leaf graphs can help visualize distributions.

Central Tendency: Mean, Median, and Mode

These are basic statistics that take a group of values and offer a single number that represents the group. The *mean* will say what the average data values are, the *median* is the middlemost value by quantity, and the *mode* is the value that occurs the most. Looking at the three together can offer clues about the nature of the dataset. If the mean and median are close, that suggests a *normal* distribution of values in the set.

Dispersion: Variance and Standard Deviation

The variation (measured by the SD) is how much any given data value varies from the average curve of what we usually would expect. Values may be clustered around a certain level, suggesting that something is behind the grouping (i.e., number of pimples at age 15). Value may be evenly distributed along a bell curve, suggesting the data represent the normal range of naturally occurring phenomena, or be erratic, suggesting no underlying factors behind the values.

Inferential Statistics

Inferential statistics goes beyond describing the characteristics of datasets and uses probability and the nearly universal nature of normal distributions to make predictions and draw conclusions from the dataset that go beyond what the numbers directly indicate. These techniques are useful in telling whether two groups are similar to each other and, if so, to what degree. Inferential statistics is used to test how likely it is that an individual is a part of another population and whether a particular factor has an impact on some other factor. An almost unlimited number of different inferential statistical tests have been developed to analyze data, but the most commonly used are listed below.

Correlation

Correlations are useful to see how any two factors in a dataset are related to one another. This is most often visualized by a scatter plot, where one factor is plotted on the *x*-axis and the other on the *y*-axis. The shape of the distribution of dots will reflect the relationship between the factors. If they are unrelated, it will appear as a cloud, and the extent to which they form a straight line shows their degree of relation. If the relationship is positive (i.e., cigarettes and emphysema), then more of one will be accompanied by more of the other, and the line will slope upward (figure 10.3, left). If the relationship is negative (i.e., income and crime), then more of one will be accompanied by *less* of the other, and the line will slope downward (figure 10.3, right). This is expressed by a statistical test such as the *Pearson correlation* as a number from –1 (a negative correlation) through 0 (no correlation) to +1 (a positive correlation).

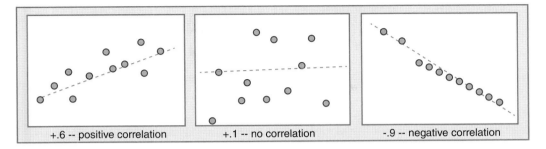

Figure 10.3
Correlation.

Regression

Regression is another test that can see if two or more factors in a dataset are related to one another and additionally can interpolate one value of a one factor from a value for the other that is not actually in the dataset. Suppose we have a dataset containing two factors, education level and income. A correlation test yielded a coefficient +.5, meaning that the two factors are positively correlated. We want to know what the income might be if a person had 7 years of schooling, so we run a regression test to interpolate an income from all of the other pairs of education and schooling in the dataset.

Z-Test, T-Test, and ANOVA

These tests all provide a way to determine if the mean averages of two data sets represent the same population. Suppose we had two classes of students, and we gave textbook A to the first class and textbook B to the other and then gave each a test to see how well they had learned the material. All of these tests can tell us which group performed better on the test.

The simplest of these is the *t*-test: the result is a number (the *t-value*) that can be used to look up in a table the probability of the two groups being the same. The analysis of variance (ANOVA) test is similar to the *t*-test but can handle more than two datasets and returns the probability directly without a need to look it up. This *p-value* indicates the *significance* of the test. This is a little confusing, as rather than saying $p = .95$ to mean there is a 95 percent chance of this being true, it is expressed as $p = .05$, meaning there is a 5 percent chance of it not being true and simply a matter of chance.

11 Using Spreadsheets

It is better to travel well than to arrive.

—Buddha

The modern spreadsheet is one of the best tools available for structuring information for use in visualizations. It can be successfully used as a method for simply storing the right item in its proper category, but it also has the ability to transform and analyze the data in ways that can offer insight into underlying phenomena. Spreadsheets do the latter by providing simple tools and functions for people to use to make the data dynamic and reactive to other pieces of information.

For example, a spreadsheet might be used to see if a person could afford purchasing a house by examining all the possible variable costs. The spreadsheet would automatically recalculate the total cost for the house if the price or interest changed. This makes it easy for the user to test various combinations of rates to see what might be affordable. The dynamic ability for a spreadsheet to instantly react to item changes makes it such a powerful tool for the inquiry and structuring of data.

The most popular spreadsheet available is Microsoft's *Excel*, but other options include the freely available *Open Office*[1] and Google *Docs*[2] and the spreadsheet applications found in Apple's *iWork* and Microsoft's *Works* suites. All these tools work very much in the same general manner and are descendants of the groundbreaking *VisiCalc* program developed by Dan Bricklin and Bob Frankston in 1979, which inspired competitor *Lotus 1–2–3* to earn the title as the "killer application" for the nascent personal computer.

Modern spreadsheets include the ability to generate sophisticated charts and graphs that can facilitate a deeper understanding of the data through rudimentary visualization techniques. These spreadsheets can even do relatively sophisticated statistical analyses, such as correlations and regressions, that can highlight trends between

1. www.openoffice.org.
2. http://.docs.google.com.

datasets, thereby eliminating the need for purchasing expensive and difficult-to-use statistical analysis applications such as SPSS.

"Cloud-based" spreadsheets such as Google *Docs* make real-time collaboration on projects radically easier to manage. Because cloud-based applications store their files on a mutually accessible server in the Internet, any number of people can simultaneously edit data on a single file without engendering the inevitable confusion that develops with people working on multiple versions of the same project. Some tools, including VisualEyes, can access the online spreadsheet for use as a simple database of data for visualization.

Spreadsheet Overview

A spreadsheet is like a simple table in a word processor. It keeps information organized in a gridlike collection of boxes called *cells*. Each cell can be filled in with numbers or letters to organize information according to columns and rows. It is easy to fill in a cell by clicking on it and typing directly into its box, or pasting text from your clipboard into the *formula bar* at the top of the page/screen.

At the top, the *columns* are labeled with letters from A to Z, and the *rows* are labeled on the left with numbers. The combination of a column and row will uniquely point to a particular cell and forms its *address*, just as a real world street address appears. For example, in table 11.1 the address **B2** refers to the second row in the B column, which in this case has the number *40* in it.

This ability to refer to cells by their position in the grid (called *relative addressing*) is a little abstract to grasp at first but makes the spreadsheet a very powerful tool for structuring information because we can easily apply operations to cells based on formulas.

Formulas

Formulas are similar to simple arithmetic statements like the ones 1+2=3 or 4*5=20. The formula itself appears in the *formula bar*, a box above the cell grid, and the results

Table 11.1
A spreadsheet table

	A	B
1	**name**	**age**
2	Manny	40
3	Moe	50
4	Jack	60

Table 11.2

Simple formulas

fx	=1+2		
	A	B	C
1	3		
2	20		

Table 11.3

Referencing cells

fx	=B1+C1		
	A	B	C
1	3	1	2
2	9	4	5

of a formula show up in the cell itself (table 11.2). The spreadsheet knows it is a formula rather than text or a number because it starts with an equals sign. All the usual arithmetic operations can be used in formulas: add (+), subtract (–), multiply (*), and divide (/). Parentheses can be used to group the order of these operations properly. In addition to these basic math operations, there are literally hundreds of specialized functions (described below) that can perform more sophisticated operations such as averaging and statistical operations.

Formulas are more useful when they refer to the contents of other cells rather than to specific numbers. The example in table 11.3 returns the same results in the **A1** cell as the previous example but gets the number 1 from the contents of cell **B1** and the number 2 from the contents of cell **C1** by using the formula **=B1+C1** instead of having to specify the numbers explicitly.

Suppose we wanted to compare the weights of two groups of people, but the French group was in kilograms and the English group in pounds. We would need to put the data into one system or another. We could convert the English pounds into kilograms by dividing each entry by 2.2 using a calculator, but that would be time consuming. The ability of the spreadsheet to do this simple calculation simplifies our task by adding a new column that references the kilos cell and multiplies each weight by 2.2 using a simple formula.

Spreadsheet formulas begin with an equals sign, as in **=A2*2.2**, which tells the spreadsheet to look at the number in the cell located at **A2** (*52* in this case), multiply

Table 11.4
Converting kilos to pounds

	A	B	C
1	**kgs**	**lbs**	
2	52	114	
3	60	132	
4	63	139	

it by 2.2 and write the result, 114, in the grid (table 11.4). The formula itself shows up in the text box at the top of the grid, but the result appears in the cell. We only need to write the formula once and then copy and paste it to the other cells we want to convert. The spreadsheet will automatically advance the address as appropriate (i.e., A3, A4, A5, etc.).

Absolute Cell Addresses

The feature of automatically advancing the cell addresses is very convenient for multiplying by a constant value, but there are times when we want to control all the calculations from single cell. Putting a dollar sign before the column and/or row indicator (table 11.5) will prevent the spreadsheet app from advancing the column letter or the row number when copy and pasting cells.

For example, when a person is deciding whether to purchase a house of a given price, the rate of interest will be an important deciding point. Isolating the interest rate in its own cell makes it easy to see the effect on the cost by simply changing the contents of cell **B5**; then the cost column will be recalculated instantly to reflect the new interest rate's effect.

Naming Cells

As an alternative to absolute addressing of cells, most spreadsheets permit naming a cell with a unique name, such as "InterestRate." Instead of referring to the cell by its address, we associate that name to the cell. This feature is found in the *Name* item in *Excel*'s *Insert* menu and in the *Named Ranges* item from Google *Docs*'s *Edit* menu. Once defined, we can use that name as a variable in formulas: **=A2*B$5** becomes a more understandable **=A2*InterestRate**.

Cell Ranges

A cell range is similar to a regular cell address but refers to a block of cells rather than just one cell. The range is specified by the top left and bottom right corners separated

Table 11.5

Absolute cell addresses

fx	=A2*B$5		
	A	B	C
1	**price**	**cost**	
2	50,000	2,000	
3	60,000	2,400	
4	70,000	2,800	
5	**interest**	4%	

Table 11.6

Cell ranges

	A	B	C	D
1	**name**	**age**	**sex**	**grade**
2	Bob	22	M	100
3	Ted	50	M	80
4	Carol	34	F	45
5	Alice	43	F	100

by a colon. The range **B2:C3** refers to the cells located at **B2, B3, C2,** and **C3** (table 11.6). Ranges are used in functions such as those that average a group of cells.

Lists

A spreadsheet can simply contain a series of items arranged horizontally or vertically, but more commonly they are arranged in a *list* format. This format is useful in its own right as a clear way to organize information for later representation in a visualization.

Most spreadsheet applications need the data in the list format for graphing and other advanced functions.

In a list, the vertical columns are used to group like things together (i.e., attributes), and each horizontal row is dedicated to enumerating those attributes for a particular entity. The top row, called the *header*, is usually dedicated to a list of names that describes the attributes, called *fields*. In table 11.7, the rows contain individual people,

Table 11.7

Lists

	A	B	C
1	**name**	**age**	**sex**
2	Bob	22	M
3	Ted	50	M
4	Carol	34	F
5	Alice	43	F

and the columns contain attributes about each person (name, age, and sex) under the appropriate field names.

Freezing of Columns/Rows

In larger datasets, it is useful to know what field name you are currently viewing once the top header line that defines them has scrolled out of view. You can "freeze" the rows or columns at some point so they do not scroll with the rest of the cell matrix to provide a constant reminder of their meanings. In *Excel*, this is done by highlighting the cell below or to the right of those whose column or row you wish to retain and then selecting *Freeze Panes* in the *Window* menu. In Google *Docs*, this is accomplished by selecting the *Freeze Rows* or *Freeze Columns* item in the *Tools* menu.

Paste Special

When you copy a cell to the clipboard for later inclusion into another cell, *Excel* has to make some hard choices: Does it need to copy the formula or the end result of that formula? For example, if a cell contained **=A1+B1**, there may be times when we want to duplicate that formula for use in calculating different cells and other times when we want to copy the number value generated when **A1** and **B1** were added.

By default, *Excel* copies the formula, but if we want the value, *Excel* has a very useful item called *Paste Special* in the *Edit* menu that offers some options to the way cells that have been copied into the clipboard can be pasted into new cells. This brings up a dialog box with some options under *Paste*, including one called *Values* that will only copy the results of the formula's calculation and not the formula itself.

Transposing Columns and Rows

Sometimes the cells are arranged in the right direction for the immediate task, but we may need the cells to run horizontally instead of vertically, or vice versa. The *Paste Special* dialogue box has a checkbox that facilitates this.

Formatting Cells

Most spreadsheet applications offer a number of ways to change the appearance of the cells in terms of changing the text font, size, and color and the cell's internal and external color. From the data's point of view, when used in a visualization this graphical formatting is largely ignored as window dressing, but in more complex sets of data, the ability to graphically group items by color can shed insight into the nature of the data and make it easier for the user to navigate through larger datasets.

Cell Data Formats

The native value of a cell falls in three primary categories: *Text,* which represents letters and numbers as a stream of characters; *Numbers,* which represent whole and fractional numbers; and *Dates,* which reflect the idea of time. Within these three basic categories, spreadsheets do offer some ways to format the data that make the data more understandable, such as adding a comma to separate thousands in large numbers. This formatting does not change the underlying value of the cell, just how it is displayed.

For example, *0.045* and *4.5 percent* represent the same number mathematically, but the latter can more understandably express value to people without sacrificing accuracy. Likewise, consciously limiting the display to a number of decimal places (1.73346643 to 1.73) can help to remove the appearance of complexity and increase understanding again while it does not sacrifice the accuracy of the base value. Likewise, the *Number* and *Currency* formats, which add commas to thousands and $ symbols, help to clarify the data.

Forcing a Number as Text

By default, *Excel* formats cells in a format called *General*, which is a hybrid of the text and number formats. If you type a number into a General cell, it will be treated as a number for calculation purposes, and if you type text, Excel will treat those characters as text.

There are some circumstances where you actually want to treat a number as text. If you were storing an archive record number such as *000623.0*, the spreadsheet would assume you wanted the value of that number and simplify it to *623*. You can tell the spreadsheet to treat the cell as a text value by setting its format to Text or by preceding the number with an apostrophe (i.e., *'000623.0*) to force it to be considered as text. One visual cue that spreadsheets offer as to the formatting is the alignment: numbers are right-justified, and text is left justified.

Dates

Spreadsheets handle dates in a more complicated manner, so some of the results from formulas and calculations may come out differently than expected. There are numerous ways to store dates (i.e., 1800, 5/1800, 5/2/1800, May 2, 1800, etc.), but they all reflect the same moment in time. Most spreadsheets convert that complex representation to a simpler native format when doing calculations on dates, by storing dates internally as the number of days (plus or minus) from January 1, 1900.

This allows for the proper sorting of dates, with *11/2/1800* showing up after *4/2/1800* instead of before if it were alphabetically sorted, and it also makes arithmetic operations such as finding the number of days between two dates possible. For example, the formula **=11/2/1800–4/2/1800** would result in 214 days (7 months) to be returned to the cell. There are a large number of built-in functions that make it easy to tease out the days, weeks, months, and years from dates.

Sorting

Sorting the data can be an excellent way to get some insight into the underlying phenomena they are representing. For example, if we wanted to get a quick idea of how many times the lunch menu had tacos on Tuesday, we would sort the list by the *weekday* field, followed by a secondary sort by the *entree* field. This would cause all the rows in the list to first be grouped by the day, so all of the Mondays would be grouped together, as would all of the Tuesdays, and so forth. The second sort would sort the entrees alphabetically *within* the daywise groupings to make a clump of taco entries stand out from the rest.

Clicking on the *Sort* item in the *Data* menu in *Excel* (in the *Tools* menu from Google *Docs*) will bring up a dialogue box with the options to sort the list by. It is easy to can sort the data up or down by column and then further sort the information based on the order in other columns. The sort can be alphabetically ascending (i.e., A–Z) or descending. Because the sort is alphabetical, dates and numbers can sometimes be incorrectly sorted. If your data have a header row, be sure to click on the button so that row does not get sorted with the rest of the data.

Formula Functions

There are hundreds of built-in *functions* in the modern spreadsheet that can be performed between cells, not just simple arithmetic but a wide variety of functions ranging from simply adding a series of numbers together to sophisticated statistical and financial operations. Each function has a number of parameters within its parentheses and returns the results of their calculations back to the cell or as a parameter to another function.

Table 11.8

Formula functions

fx	=SUM(B2:B4)	
	A	B
1	**name**	**weight**
2	John	150
3	Paul	180
4	George	140
5	**Total**	470

The number and kind of parameters for each function are dependent on that particular function. In *Excel*, all of the available functions are listed by their type, grouped by category, by clicking on the *fx* button to the left of the formula bar. Choosing one will bring up its description and how to use it. Google *Docs* has many of the same functions available by clicking on the *Function* item in the *Insert* menu.

For example, you could use the **SUM** function to add up a column of numbers by using the formula **=SUM(B2:B4)** and place the result in cell B5 (table 11.8). The parameter to the SUM function is the range of cells to add up, which was specified by the range B2:B4 to include B2, B3, and B4. The result from the **SUM** function could be just as well used in another operation, say to create an average: **=SUM(B2:B4)/3**, although there is an **AVERAGE** function built in for this common operation.

Commonly Used Functions

The following functions are commonly used in visualizations and are grouped by the general category they appear in. There are literally hundreds of functions available in most spreadsheets, so it is worthwhile to look at the help screens to see if a more appropriate one is available than the one listed below:

Math
- **ABS** (number)   Returns the absolute value (nonnegative) of a number
- **AVERAGE** (range)   Returns the average (mean) of a range of numbers
- **CEILING** (number, 1)   Returns the rounded-up integral part of a number
- **FLOOR** (number, 1)   Returns the lower integral part of a number
- **MAX** (num1, num2, . . .)   Returns the largest of two or more numbers
- **MIN** (num1, num2, . . .)   Returns the smallest of two or more numbers
- **SUM** (range) Returns the total of a range of numbers

Date and Time
- **DATE** (year, month, day)   Returns the date based on year, month, and date
- **DAY** (date)   Returns the day number (1–31) from a date
- **HOUR** (date)   Returns the hour number (0–23) from a date
- **MINUTE** (date)   Returns the minute number (0–59) from a date
- **MONTH** (date)   Returns the month number (1–12) from a date
- **WEEKDAY** (date)   Returns the day text (Sunday-Saturday) from a date
- **YEAR** (date)   Returns the year number (1900–9999) from a date

Text
- **CLEAN** (text)   Returns the text cleaned of any nonprintable characters
- **CONCATENATE** (text1, text2, . . .)   Returns the union of two or more strings
- **LOWER** (text)   Returns the text in all lowercase letters
- **PROPER** (text)   Returns the text in title case (first letters of words in caps)
- **TRIM** (text)   Returns the text with extraneous spaces removed
- **UPPER** (text)   Returns the text in all uppercase letters

Lookup
- **HLOOKUP** (value, range, index)   Returns the matching value for value found in a horizontal lookup table (see section below on lookups)
- **VLOOKUP** (value, range, index)   Returns the matching value for value found in a vertical lookup table (see section below on lookups)

Statistics
- **FTEST** (range1, range2)   Returns probably of two means being the same
- **AVERAGE** (range)   Returns the mean of a range of numbers
- **MEDIAN** (range)   Returns the median of a range of numbers
- **MODE** (range)   Returns the mode of a range of numbers
- **PEARSON** (range1, range2)   Returns the correlation between two ranges
- **STDEV** (range)   Returns the standard deviation of a range of numbers
- **TTEST** (r1, r2, tails, type)   Returns probably of two means being the same
- **VAR** (range)   Returns the variance of a range of numbers

Graphing

The ability to visually represent data is as valuable to the designers of interactive visualizations as it is to their consumers. Spreadsheets make it easy to quickly create charts and graphs to visually explore the data relationships. This can lead to insights into the underlying phenomenon that can direct the kind of visualizations that will be most effective.

Excel and Google *Docs* have excellent charting capabilities and work in a similar manner. We select the table you want to chart by highlighting the cells that define it and click on the *Chart* icon in the tool bar. A dialogue box will offer a number of chart styles, and you can instantly see a preview of that style using your data.

Choosing the Right Kind of Graph

The various styles are useful in exploring different kinds of relationships among the data:

• **Time-series** relationships, where the values of data are plotted vertically as time marches across, are most fruitfully rendered by line and area styles.

• **Quantitative** relationships between items in a dataset are best drawn using bar, area, and line charts.

• **Part-to-whole** relationships, in which the relative value of one item is compared with the group, are well represented by pie or stacked bar/area charts.

• **Correlation** relationships, where a number data points are plotted using two variables, are best drawn using scatter and bubble charts.

• **Hierarchical/organizational** relationships between individual members can yield insight using organization maps, network diagrams, and trees.

There is a simple-to-use template for *Excel* that makes it easy to explore, analyze, and visualize network node-link data. NodeXL[3] was developed at the University of Maryland's HCIL group and is freely available for download.

Trend Lines

A trend line is a line overlaid on a chart that "smoothes out" the data and gives you an overall sense of the trend the data are taking; it is useful in seeing whether, in general, the values are increasing or decreasing over time. For more information, see the section on *Trends in Time-Series Data* in chapter 10. In *Excel*, you click on the *Add trendline* option in the *Chart* menu.

Importing Data

Although it is certainly possible to manually type data into a spreadsheet, most people choose to import it from some existing source, which can be a text file or a structured table from a database or web site page.

Data from Text Files

The goal of putting data in a spreadsheet is to organize the data in some meaningful way using fields that have been defined. Unfortunately, many primary sources of data

---

3. http://nodexl.codeplex.com.

come from largely unstructured sources, such as letters, documents, and other largely prosaic styles of organization.

It can be useful to use a word processor such as Microsoft *Word* or Google *Docs* to prepare the text prior to import into the more rigid constraints of a spreadsheet by creatively using the *Find and Replace* functionality to rearrange the data into the columns and rows required. The text can be easily reformatted so that it will slot into the proper columns and rows when pasted into the spreadsheet by making sure each row of data is listed on its own line, with tabs between fields.

To aid in this process, Word has some special characters that allow you to search for and insert characters as new lines (**^p**) and tabs (**^t**). The *Special* button, exposed when the *More* options button is active, will show all the available characters. For example, the following find-and-replace combination would look through the text for any double-line feeds following a *Title:* as the delimiter to a record and replace it with a simple line feed:

Find what: | *Title:*^*p*^*p* | Replace with: | ^*p* |.

If the field values are separated by commas or some other separator, you will need to put tabs so the spreadsheet recognizes them as distinct fields with a following combination like this:

Find what: | , | Replace with: | ^*t* |.

Finally, *Excel* has an option in the *Data* menu called *Text to Columns* that will parse some unformatted text in a cell or range of cells and distribute the contents into columns based on one or more defined delineators such as a tab or comma.

Data from Web Pages

Existing web sites are a great source of data for visualization projects. Many web sites, such as the U.S. Census,[4] OECD,[5] and ManyEyes,[6] make it easy to directly download data files in one or more formats for editing within a spreadsheet. Some of these sites offer the data in *Excel*'s native format (.XLS), but comma-separated values (.CSV) and tab-delineated (.TXT) formats are more common. Most spreadsheets and Google *Docs* can load these formats easily.

Screen Scraping Table Data

It is still possible to capture the data from web pages even when no download option is provided by the page's author through a process sometimes called *screen scraping*.

---

4. www.census.gov.

5. www.oecd.org/statsportal.

6. www-958.ibm.com/software/data/cognos/manyeyes.

Scraping is the process of pulling data directly from a fully formatted web page on the Internet and extracting the raw information for use in a spreadsheet.

Modern web browsers make it easy to copy a table of data directly from a web page using the familiar copy-and-paste functionality. Once you have found a table of data you want, select the entire table and copy (CTRL-C key or the *Copy* item in the *Edit* menu) it into your computer's clipboard. Paste (CTRL-V) these data in an open *Excel* spreadsheet. You will probably need to clean up any extraneous bits and pieces and most likely need to reset the formatting carried over from the web page to match your spreadsheet's formatting.

The Windows versions of *Excel* have a table-scraping option built in that loads a web page in a dialogue box, automatically identifies the data tables on the page, and allows you to select one. A number of useful options are available that help import the data in the format desired, and these are found in the *Data* menu, in the *Get External Data/New Web Query* option.

Lookup Tables

A lookup table is a method to use one list to provide one or more items of information for another. An example of this would be a price list's relationship to a catalog. We may want to keep all the prices in a single list and look them up based on the item's description. To do this our spreadsheet would contain both lists like the spreadsheet of table 11.9. The first two columns are the catalog, and the last two are the price list. The formula for the **B** column uses the **VLOOKUP** function to look through

Table 11.9
Lookup tables

fx	=VLOOKUP(A2,D$2:E$5,2)				
	A	B	C	D	E
1	**item**	**cost**		**item**	**price**
2	shoe	$40.99		pants	35.99
3	sock	$12.99		shirt	24.95
4	pants	$35.98		shoe	40.99
5	shirt	$24.95		sock	12.99
6					

the price list (located at **D2:E5**) for the item in the **A** column and insert the price for each item from the **E** column.

The actual formula looks complicated but is simple once it is broken down by the three parameters required, the *value*, *range*, and *index*:

=VLOOKUP(**A2**, D$2:E$5, 2)

A2 The cell of the item to look up (in this case "shoe")
D Starting column of lookup list's range
$ Hold the row number constant when we copy and paste
2 Starting row of lookup list's range
: Range separator
E Ending column of lookup list's range
$ Hold the row number constant when we copy and paste
5 Ending row of lookup list range
2 Which column in lookup list to return (the second with the price)

The HLOOKUP function works in very much the same way, but the lookup occurs horizontally instead of vertically, and the index parameter refers to the row rather than the column.

Pivot Tables

Excel also has powerful mechanisms for selecting and displaying data tables into more understandable forms, called *pivot tables*. Because of the complexity involved in using them, this section focuses on filters to perform similar tasks. But see the link for an excellent article on the use of pivot tables within *Excel*.[7]

Filtering Data

Excel has a feature that allows the user to search through a data list and extract only the rows that meet certain criteria. This is useful from both the data-structuring and data-exploration perspectives. In the former, filtering can be used to create smaller subsets from larger ones, for example, make a list that only contains males between the ages of 18 and 30. Second, filtering is useful in the exploratory phase to graph or view selected subsets within categories

The implementation of filtering in *Excel* is as inelegant as it is powerful, with unfortunately very few supports to guide the process. The basic idea is that some criterion is applied against a list of data, and any rows that meet that criterion are copied to a

---

7. http://www.timeatlas.com/5_minute_tips/chunkers/learn_to_use_pivot_tables_in_excel_2007_to_organize_data.

Table 11.10

Filtering data

	A	B	C	D
1	**item**	**cost**	**size**	
2	shoe	$40.99	S	cost
3	sock	$12.99	M	>30
4	pants	$35.98	M	
5	shirt	$24.95	S	
6				
7	**item**	**cost**	**size**	
8	shoe	$40.99	S	
9	pants	$35.98	M	

new list in the spreadsheet (table 11.10). To do this, the user must identify three cell ranges:

1. The *list range* that will be filtered from. This is a typical *Excel* list, where the top row defines the fields and each row below it contains the data.

2. The *criterion range* specifies the criterion that needs to be met before a row is included in the rows that are selected (in column D). In this case, any row whose cost is greater than $30 will be chosen.

3. The *extract range* is where the rows that met the demands of the criterion will be copied to (the lower table beginning on row 8 of table 11.10).

Filtering in *Excel*

Clicking on the *Advanced Filter* option in the *Data* menu will bring up a dialogue box in which to tell *Excel* where on the spreadsheet's grid those three areas are located. The *List range* button will select the list to be filtered from, and the entire list, including the header row, should be selected.

The *Criterion range* button is used to select the cells that define the criterion for inclusion in the new list. The criterion contains pairs of cells, with the topmost one specifying the field being examined (cost in this case) and the criterion below it (>30). Possible operators include less than, less than or equal, equal, not equal, greater than, and greater than or equal (<, <=, =, <>, >, >=).

Although it is possible to filter the results in place, typically we want to create a second list to hold the results, so make sure the *Copy to another location* radio button is checked and that a single cell is selected using the *Copy to* button. Clicking the OK button will copy any rows that meet the criterion to that new range.

Advanced Filtering Criteria

The example above is the simplest case of using a filter to select a subset of rows from a larger dataset, but *Excel*'s filtering can create complex queries using multiple sets of criteria, more complex formulas, and wildcard searches to artfully tease out intricate relationships from the data.

Multiple-Criteria Cells

The example in table 11.10 used only one pair of cells to define the criteria for inclusion, the rows in which the cost field was over $30, but we define additional criteria to further refine or expand the rows selected. The criteria list can contain multiple columns, each one containing a field to search on.

If we wanted to search for items that cost over $40 *and* were size M, the criterion range in table 11.11 would search the data list and select only rows that met both criteria, in this case only *pants*. Because the criteria were on the same rows, both conditions would need to be met to be included.

If we wanted to search for items that cost over $40 *or* were size M, the criteria range in table 11.12 would search the data list and select only rows that met either one of the individual criteria, in this case *pants, shoes,* and *socks*. Because the criteria cells are on the different rows, either condition needed to be met for the item to be included.

Complex Formulas

Almost any of the formulas and functions available to normal spreadsheet cells can be used in evaluating the criteria for a field as long as the ultimate result of the cell

Table 11.11
Multiple criteria filtering

cost	Size
>30	M

Table 11.12
Multiple criteria filtering

cost	size
>30	
	M

returns a true/false answer. For example, **=ISNUMBER(A2)** would return *true* and cause that row to be included in the selected rows if the value found in cell **A2** was a number. The formula **=A2>A7** would include only rows where the value of cell **A2** was greater than the value in the cell at **A7**.

Wildcards

Finally, you can use a number of *wildcards* when specifying text to search on. *Wildcards* are characters that tell *Excel* that you want to broaden the acceptable value to find beyond what you have specified. For example, if we specified *shoes* as a search term, we would not get any results for *shoe* because it is not an exact match. If we specify *shoe?*, any character that comes after shoe would be included (i.e., *shoe*, *shoes*, *shoe1*, but not *shoe12*). Specifying *shoe** makes the search broader, allowing any number of letters following shoe to be accepted (i.e., *shoe*, *shoes*, *shoe12*, *shoelace*). Wildcards can be placed in any spot of the search term (i.e., *shoe*s*, would return *shoes* and *shoelaces*, but not *shoetip*).

Statistics Using Spreadsheets

Two basic kinds of statistics can be applied to a dataset: *descriptive statistics* and *inferential statistics*. Both *Excel* and Google *Docs* have a large number of these sophisticated techniques available as functions for inclusion into cell formulas. See chapter 10 for more information about using statistics.

Excel goes a step further than Google *Docs* (at least for now) by providing a menu-driven mechanism, very similar to those in statistical packages such as SPSS, that makes it very easy to add and view the results of the most commonly used statistical tests, such as correlations, regressions, descriptives, and *t*-tests.

Note: You may need to install the *Data Analysis add-in* (included on the *Excel* CD but not typically installed by default).

Descriptive Statistics

As the name implies, *descriptive statistics* provide simple summaries to begin to understand the nature of the data through the average value (the *mean*), the middlemost value (the *median*), the most common value (the *mode*), the largest and smallest values (the *range or min/max*), and the variance from the mean (the *standard deviation*) (table 11.13).

Using Formulas for Descriptive Statistics

The following formulas appear in cells **B7** to **B12** of table 11.13 to display the basic descriptive statistics for the ages in **B2** to **B5**:

- **=AVERAGE(B2:B6)**   The mean average age is 42.8
- **=MEDIAN(B2:B6)**   The middlemost person, age 43

Table 11.13
Descriptive statistics from formulas

	A	B
1	name	age
2	Bob	34
3	Ted	50
4	Carol	34
5	Alice	43
6	Larry	53
7		
8	Mean	42.8
9	Median	43
10	Mode	34
11	Min	34
12	Max	53
13	SD	8.8

- **=MODE(B2:B6)** Returns most common age of 34
- **=MIN(B2:B6)** Returns youngest person, at 34
- **=MAX(B2:B6)** Returns oldest person, Larry, at age 53
- **=STDEV(B2:B6)** Returns the standard deviation of ages of 8.81 years

From this limited set of data we know that ages range from 34 to 53, the average age is about 43, and, from the standard deviation, that 68 percent of the people in a set like this will be aged approximately between 34 and 52 (i.e., ±8.8 years from the mean/average of 43).

Descriptive Statistics Using Excel's Data Analysis
Clicking on the *Data Analysis* option in the *Tools* menu will bring up a dialogue box listing *Descriptive Statistics* as one of its Tools. The *input range* button selects the cell range in the data to analyze. Other checkboxes add additional descriptive statistics to the output, such as confidence levels. The *output range* button specifies the cells that the output will be written to. Table 11.14 contains just the descriptive statistical basics for the age dataset used by the formula method of generating them. See chapter 10 for more information about using these measures.

Table 11.14
Descriptive statistics table

Mean	42.8
Standard error	3.942080669
Median	43
Mode	34
Standard deviation	8.814760348
Sample variance	77.7
Kurtosis	−2.71915048
Skewness	0.043509564
Range	19
Minimum	34
Maximum	53
Sum	214
Count	5

Table 11.15
Inferential statistics

	A	B	C
1	**name**	**age**	**score**
2	Bob	34	80
3	Ted	50	70
4	Carol	34	90
5	Alice	43	56
6	Larry	53	76
7			
8	*t*-Test	0.002	
9	Pearson	−0.46	

Inferential Statistics

Inferential statistics builds on the information provided in descriptive statistics and enables a series of tests that attempt to infer whether two samples are from the same general population. There are a large number statistical functions available in both *Excel* and Google *Docs*, but only correlation and *t*-test are listed below to show the basic procedure (table 11.15). Again, look at the chapter 10 for more information about using these tests.

Using Formulas for Descriptive Statistics

• **=TTEST(B2:B6,C2:C6,2,1)**   The probability that the age and score are samples from the same data is 0.02 using a two-tailed *t*-test.
• **=PEARSON(B2:B6,C2:C6)**   The relationship between age and score is negatively correlated by –0.46 using a *Pearson Product Moment* test.

Descriptive Statistics Using Excel's Data Analysis

Clicking on the *Data Analysis* option in the *Tools* menu will bring up a dialog box listing the various tests that can be performed. Each test has its own options, but all will require defining the *input range* to select the cell range(s) of the data to analyze and the output range to which the output will be written.

12   Databases and XML

A place for everything and everything in its place.
—Benjamin Franklin

A database is a program that stores information in a structured format on a server so that you can easily request specific portions of it from a web browser. The purpose of this section is to present the big picture of how databases work. Although the details can be confusing, the overall idea is quite simple. In our travels on the web we come across many databases behind the scenes, and even Apple's *iTunes* is no more than a simple database.

The Role of Structure

A database is an application program (app) running on a server and similar to the servers that deliver web pages to your browser. This app contains the information stored in a *structured* format. Structured means that instead of the data and information being presented as a text document, particular kinds of data and information are grouped together. This makes it easier to find and retrieve specific data at a later time.

It is this structure that gives databases their value. For example, doing a library search involves going through a database of books in your library. The various aspects of the books such as the title, author, and subject are specifically identified so you can search all of the books in the library. Searching for books about Tiger Woods is more useful than a Google-style search, which would also bring up books about tigers, the animal.

The database app has an interface that Web pages use to search for information. A typical library search page has a simple HTML form that allows the user to keyboard in some words and select different options (figure 12.1). These choices determine how those words should be interpreted by the search process to give the user a more precise search result.

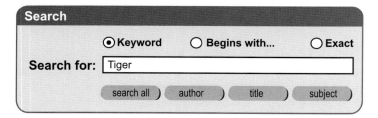

Figure 12.1
A typical library search box.

A database may consist of one or more files. Each file might include all novels in the library. Each file in turn includes records, which in this example are novels. One record is equal to one novel. All of the relevant information or data relating to the record are contained in fields. So fields make up a record, and a collection of records are included in a file. When the librarians entered the information about each book (record) into the database (file), they filled in pertinent information about the book such as the author, title, subject (fields).

In the above example, we are searching for a novel written by the golfer Tiger Woods. Typing "Tiger" and clicking on the author button would bring up books written by people named *Tiger*. Clicking on the title button would bring up books about *tigers* and about *Tiger Woods*.

When you click the button in the form, the information is sent to the web page which in turn queries the library database server. The web page's form waits to get the results from the database server and quickly returns any information it has found.

A Database's Structure

At the root of everything is the information that is actually stored—in this case, information about books. For the sake of simplicity let us say that we only want to store the title, the author, description, and a shelving number so we can go find the book in the stacks.

Databases store this information in tables, in which each row or *item* in the table contains the book, and each column contains one of the attributes or *fields* about the book. A very simple structure or *schema* might only have one table (table 12.1).

Queries

When we press the title button on the search page, the information typed was sent to a script on the web server, which converted the raw information into a *query* that the database understands. This query was sent to the database application using the *SQL* format, and the results were returned to the web page.

Table 12.1

A simple table

Title	Author	Description	ShelfID
My Life	Tiger Woods	The best book on me	G7678.W8
Waking the Tiger	Peter Leviathan	A treatise on ego	R8231.K8
. . .	. . .	. . .	. . .

The Tiger query, when we click on the author button, might look something like this: **SELECT * WHERE author = 'tiger'**. Simply translated, this query is saying: please return all entries in the database where the author is equal to "Tiger."

Real databases typically have multiple tables and can have complicated interrelationships among them, but the basics all work the same. SQL is very flexible, and its simple elements can be infinitely combined into very specific queries that can pull specific information from the database. For example, **SELECT * WHERE author = 'tiger' AND title = 'opus' AND date > 1960** would look through the database for any books for which the author was *Tiger*, the title was *opus,* and that had been written since *1960*.

XML

XML (eXtensible Markup Language) has become very popular as a way to request, retrieve, and show data in a web page. Because it is just plain text, people can write XML in almost any word processor or text editor. It is not a language but more of a storage format for exchanging information.

XML uses a tagged format and resembles HTML (the format of the World Wide Web) in its formatting and structure, but instead of a series of specific tags such as <b> to bold text, the tags are created by the person writing the XML to put the information into "slots," much like sorting the mail. The act of tagging the information into a format gives it structure so that a computer can read the document and know what is what.

Elements and Attributes

An XML document is made up of a number of *elements* that contain the information. Each element has a tagged name and begins with an opening tag enclosed in angle brackets, like <album>, and ends in a closing tag like </album>. Inside the opening tag, the node can contain *attributes* that define the properties of the information the user wants to store. For example, an album might contain attributes such as the title, the artist, and a year, for example:

```
<album title="Paper-cutting Blues" artist="Glen Bull" date="2010">
```

```
</album>
```

In this example, *album* is the name of the element; title, artist, and year are attributes. The information following the equals sign must be put in quotes. Attribute and element names cannot contain spaces, but people typically join the words together capitalizing the middle ones like this: aVeryGoodAlbum, called camelCase, because the capitals represented the humps on a camel to someone. Other elements or content can be written between the opening and closing of the attribute and element names. If there are no content or notes between the opening and closing, the opening and closing can be joined together.

```
<album title="Paper-cutting Blues" artist="Glen Bull" date="2010">

<song name="I Got the Blues"/>

</album>
```

Text

We can add some *text* to the node by encasing it in a <!CDATA[[. . .]]> wrapper tag, which allows the user to write any kind of characters within the brackets without worrying about disrupting the XML formatting.

```
<album title="Paper-cutting Blues" artist="Glen Bull" date="2010">

<song name="I Got the Blues"/>

<song name="Gina on my Mind"/>

<!CDATA[[This album was the was Bull's comeback in 2010]]>

</album>
```

There really is not that much more to XML than the simple ideas of *elements*, *attributes*, and *text*, but with these three ideas, we can describe very complicated relationships among things. The parent-child metaphor is often used to describe the relationship between elements and attributes. In the example above, we have an album (the *parent*) that contains two songs (the *children*) because the nodes for the songs are nested within the album. This kind of nesting can go on and on ad infinitum to simply represent very complex relationships among elements that are obvious to the naked eye and to the computer.

13 Accessibility

Information wants to be free.

—Stewart Brand

This chapter discusses the important role of providing accessibility into interactive visualization, both from the perspective of being inclusive and from being compliant with the US government laws under Section 508 of the 1998 Rehabilitation Act.

There is a continuum of ability in the human population, and different people have strengths and weaknesses in their three primary means of sensory perceptions: *visual*, *physical*, and *aural*. People can also have *cognitive* issues that impede their access to information.

There is a wide range of abilities among people. For example, human vision ranges from people with 20/20 vision to those considered legally blind. The goal of accessibility is to provide access to information at all points along the spectrum. As an ability becomes more impaired, accommodations can be made to communicate through an alternative sensory form, such as hearing or touch. In addition, approximately 8 percent of the world (mostly men) have some form of color blindness.

Interactive visualizations rely less on requiring a high ability to hear in order to communicate information unless audio and video files are used. Again, an alternative sensory form, such as captioning, can be employed (Mueller, 2003).

Section 508

Section 508[1] is an amendment to the Rehabilitation Act passed by the US Congress in 1998 to ensure that Americans of all abilities could enjoy access to information technologies, and it provides specific guidelines on how to achieve this.

1. www.section508.gov.

Who Needs to Comply?

The law dictates primarily that federal government–affiliated organizations comply with the Section 508 Act. A growing number of organizations and institutions are requiring compliance as a precondition to funding or purchase:

• *Government agencies*   The law specifically requires all government agencies and their employees (with the exception of the military and intelligence agencies) to use the guidelines when designing almost anything, from web sites to tables and chairs.
• *Federal contractors*   Contactors to the federal government and their subcontractors should comply with Section 508.
• *Private industry*   Accessibility compliance is required for the government or government contractors to purchase from larger companies.
• *Colleges and Universities*   There is much debate whether private and state academic institutions consider themselves obligated to comply with Section 508 under federal law, but most schools have adopted internal policies to comply with the Act.

Section 508 Rules for Internet-Based Applications

There are a number of different sets of rules, based on the application type (i.e., desktop software, Internet-based applications, mobile devices, etc.). The following rules apply to Internet-based applications, as most interactive visualizations will be delivered online (GSA, 2011):

a. A text equivalent for every nontext element shall be provided (e.g., via "alt," "long-desc," or in element content).
b. Web pages shall be designed so that all information conveyed with color is also available without color, for example, from context or markup.
c. Documents shall be organized so they are readable without requiring an associated style sheet.
d. Redundant text links shall be provided for each active region of a server-side image map.
e. Client-side image maps shall be provided instead of server-side image maps except where the regions cannot be defined with an available geometric shape.
f. Row and column headers shall be identified for data tables.
g. Markup shall be used to associate data cells and header cells for data tables that have two or more logical levels of row or column headers.
h. Frames shall be titled with text that facilitates frame identification and navigation.
i. Pages shall be designed to avoid causing the screen to flicker with a frequency greater than 2 Hz and lower than 55 Hz.
j. A text-only page, with equivalent information or functionality, shall be provided to make a web site comply with the provisions of this part when compliance cannot be accomplished in any other way.

k. The content of the text-only page shall be updated whenever the primary page changes.

l. When pages utilize scripting languages to display content or to create interface elements, the information provided by the script shall be identified with functional text that can be read by assistive technology.

m. When a web page requires that an applet, plug-in, or other application be present on the client system to interpret page content, the page must provide a link to a plug-in or applet that complies with §1194.21(a) through (l).

n. When electronic forms are designed to be completed on-line, the form shall allow people using assistive technology to access the information, field elements, and functionality required for completion and submission of the form, including all directions and cues.

o. A method shall be provided that permits users to skip repetitive navigation links.

p. When a timed response is required, the user shall be alerted and given sufficient time to indicate more time is required.

Adding Accessibility to Visualizations

Whether required to comply with Section 508 by law or not, accessibility is a valuable feature to increase the audience for an interactive visualization. The POUR principles provide some high-level guidance in designing accessibility, and Utah State University's Center for Persons with Disabilities WebAim project's Principles of Accessible Design offer some practical help in implementing accessibility.

The POUR principles of accessibility

The World Wide Web Consortium[2] (W3C), which sets the standards for the web, has developed a set of guidelines and an overarching framework for developing accessible web sites organized by the acronym POUR: *perceivable, operable, understandable,* and *robust*. POUR is a useful high-level set of goals that should guide whatever tactical steps are actually employed.

1. *Perceivable*   Information and user-interface elements should be presented in ways people can perceive them: nontextual elements should present a text-based alternative; audio and video should have transcriptions and other alternative representations; and background and foregrounds should be readily distinguishable.

2. *Operable*   The user-interface components and other navigational devices must be readily operable: all functionality should be able to be controlled from a keyboard or made time dependent; provide enough time to read and use the content; and provide ways to help users navigate and know where they are.

2. www.w3.org/TR/WCAG20.

3. *Understandable*   The content and navigational devices should be readable and easily understandable: language defaults should be programmable; pages should appear and operate predictably; and users should be guided from making errors during input.

4. *Robust*   Content should be robust enough to be reliably interpreted by tools such as assistive technology tools: Start and end tags should be consistently applied.

Principles of Accessible Design

The WebAim[3] project has developed a set of useful principles for accessible design in web sites that are equally applicable to interactive visualizations. The following text is courtesy of WebAim:

• *Provide appropriate alternative text*   Alternative text provides a textual alternative to nontext content in web pages. It is especially helpful for people who are blind and rely on a screen reader to have the content of the web site read to them.

• *Provide headings for data tables*   Tables are used online for layout and to organize data. Tables that are used to organize tabular data should have appropriate table headers (the <th> element). Data cells should be associated with their appropriate headers, making it easier for screen reader users to navigate and understand the data table.

• *Ensure users can complete and submit all forms*   Ensure that every form element (text field, checkbox, dropdown list, etc.) has a label, and make sure that label is associated to the correct form element using the <label> tag. Also make sure the user can submit the form and recover from any errors, such as the failure to fill in all required fields.

• *Ensure links make sense out of context*   Every link should make sense if the link text is read by itself. Screen reader users may choose to read only the links on a web page. Certain phrases such as "click here" and "more" must be avoided.

• *Caption and/or provide transcripts for media*   Videos and live audio must have captions and a transcript. With archived audio, a transcription may be sufficient.

• *Ensure accessibility of non-HTML content*   In addition to all of the other principles listed here, PDF documents and other non-HTML content must be as accessible as possible. If you cannot make it accessible, consider using HTML instead or, at the very least, provide an accessible alternative. PDF documents should also include a series of tags to make them more accessible. A tagged PDF file looks the same, but it is almost always more accessible to a person using a screen reader.

• *Allow users to skip repetitive elements on the page*   You should provide a method that allows users to skip navigation or other elements that repeat on every page. This is usually accomplished by providing a "Skip to Content," "Skip to Main Content," or

---

3. http://webaim.org.

"Skip Navigation" link at the top of the page, which jumps to the main content of the page.

• *Do not rely on color alone to convey meaning* The use of color can enhance comprehension, but do not use color alone to convey information. That information may not be available to a person who is colorblind and will be unavailable to screen reader users.

• *Make sure content is clearly written and easy to read* There are many ways to make your content easier to understand. Write clearly, use clear fonts, and use headings and lists appropriately.

• *Make JavaScript accessible* Ensure that JavaScript event handlers are device independent (e.g., they do not require the use of a mouse), and make sure that your page does not rely on JavaScript to function.

• *Design to standards* HTML-compliant and -accessible pages are more robust and provide better search engine optimization. Cascading Style Sheets (CSS) allow you to separate content from presentation. This provides more flexibility and accessibility of your content.

VisualEyes is web-based authoring tool developed at the University of Virginia to weave images, maps, charts, video, and data into highly interactive and compelling dynamic visualizations.

VisualEyes enables scholars to present selected primary source materials and research findings while encouraging active inquiry and hands-on learning among general and targeted audiences. It communicates through the use of dynamic displays—or *visualizations*—that organize and present meaningful information in both traditional and multimedia formats, such as audio-video, animation, charts, maps, data, and interactive timelines. The effective use of the visualizations can reveal and illuminate relationships among multiple kinds of information across time and space far more effectively than words alone.

VisualEyes projects consist of a tabbed-based collection of views of spatial and temporal events and data that can be interactively shown within a time period using the timeline tool. Views can contain event descriptions, primary source documents and imagery, maps, digital movies and audio, animations, and charts and graphs of data. These views can be fixed for demonstration purposes or left open for people to explore various relations among the elements provided, allowing for both purposeful and serendipitous discovery of complex interrelations.

There are three important aspects that make VisualEyes unique among other web-based techniques for visualization:

1. *Ease of creation* VisualEyes can be easily configured by nonprogrammers to create complex dynamic visualizations that were previously only possible by employing highly skilled (and expensive) computer programmers to develop single-purpose displays. VisualEyes is a generalized tool capable of representing a wide array of visualizations through the development of simple scripts that link resources and data into compelling, interactive, and instructive visual investigations.

2. *Dynamic generation* The value of connecting data and graphics has long been established in Geographic Information Systems (GIS), but current GIS systems have

very limited abilities to dynamically generate visualizations over the Internet. In contrast, VisualEyes visualizations are dynamically generated in real time in response to live data and requests for different views of those data and are not a static presentation of information.

3. *Access* Resources can come from anywhere on the web, such as the Library of Congress and other archives. Data can come from the census and a wide range of personal, public, and academic sources and be dynamically visualized.

The Anatomy of a VisualEyes Project

VisualEyes is a *Flash*-based online authoring system that uses the Internet to connect various resources, such as images, maps, video, and data, together in a seamless interactive presentation. It is a "virtual Lego set" containing a number of interactive features.

A VisualEyes project consists of information and images assembled into what are called *views*. The views are customizable and interactive, enabling users to change how the various *resources* interact (using *controls*). Often these views use a custom scripting language, called *GLUE,* to control the appearance and disappearance of various elements.

Views

Each VisualEyes project is divided into a number of views, with each view existing in a separate tab, accessible at the top of the window. Clicking on any of the tabs will bring up a different view.

Resources

Resources are the sources of information or media to be utilized in a project. The resources could be a map, some media, a table of data, or a graphic. Each resource item contains a URL to link the resource to the project. VisualEyes uses four basic types of resources:

• *Images* Digitized images of primary source documents from digital archives can be displayed and integrated into maps, animations, and other visualizations. These images can be in JPEG, GIF, or PNG format and can be dynamically sized and positioned. The image must be Internet accessible. The Flickr image-sharing site is a free and convenient place to store images online.

• *Movies* Video files can also be used, including *Flash* movies and animations. Video file must be available via the Internet or on Google's YouTube site.

• *Maps* VisualEyes contains a fully interactive geographic information viewer to display vector-based maps from GIS systems such as *ArcGIS*, Adobe *Illustrator*, and Adobe *Fireworks*.

• *Data*   A rich array of historical data can be imported into VisualEyes from a database as a table. These data can be supplied as a CSV, XML file, retrieved directly from Google *Docs*, or embedded directly in the project script.

Controls

Controls provide an opportunity for users to interact with a project with timelines, animation players, and control panels:

• *Control panels*   Views can have multiple pull-out areas docked to a side of the screen that can be expanded or collapsed as needed and contain a number of check boxes to toggle on and off various features of the map, such as data overlays, roads, town names, and so on. Various map features, such as the overview navigation insert and map legend, can be turned on and off here as well by assigning a GLUE script to be activated on clicking.

• *Timelines*   Each view can have its own timeline that can control the temporal aspect of the project. Sliding the cursor changes the view's date, which in turn can change the way in which information is displayed if it is time dependent.

• *Animation players*   The current time on the timeline can be animated over time, using a player control, allowing the project to animate any time-dependent elements from any point on the timeline to another.

• *Zoomers and overviews*   The screen can be controlled by a zoom slider and/or a small overview inset that facilitates panning through the screen.

Displays

Displays provide the means of showing data and information within a project to the viewer. They connect the raw data from tables into compelling representations that users can interact with, and include these features:

• *Text displays*   Text displays can be dynamically generated from databases, time from a timeline, settings of control panel items, or any combination of them.

• *Paths*   A series of positions on the screen (specified by pixel positions or latitude, longitude if a map) can be defined to appear at particular times. Each position can be marked by an icon, drawn shape, or an image file. Clicking on the position can call up a web page, draw graphical elements, or pop up a window to show some information. Lines can be drawn to connect these positions.

• *Graphs*   Various types of graphs (line, bar, pie, scatter, or others) can be drawn using dynamically generated data from data sources, time from a timeline, settings of control panel items, or any combination of them.

• *Concept and network maps*   A path can be arranged in a concept map format to help visualize relationships between/among objects shown in radial, hierarchical (i.e., an organization chart), or free-form shapes.

• *Timeviews and shelves*   These can be used to display interactive timelines and scrollable collections of images.
• *Widgets*   Widgets are a type of graph that graphically displays a single continuous value on the screen, such as a dial, clock, thermometer, and so forth.

GLUE

GLUE (The General Language to Unite Events) is a simple scripting language that connects the various resource elements with one another and controls how they are displayed. VisualEyes knows how to render a number of types of resources, such as tables, charts, text area, movies, audio clips, and vector and raster maps, and the GLUE language contains elements to cause them to display.

GLUE contains elements for linking user-generated actions, such as clicking on the screen, with on-screen actions. GLUE also provides an opportunity to calculate tables and fields in resources based on a simple script. Many common types of operations can be defined between these elements, so that VisualEyes is able to relate rich data relationships between them and visualize them on a spatial and temporal basis.

Elements and Attributes

VisualEyes uses a script format called XML to represent the projects internally. XML is a simple text format for storing information that a computer *and* a person can understand. If you use the *VisEdit* tool to create your project, you do not need to know how to format XML, but an understanding of its building blocks is useful.

Elements

Elements are building blocks in VisualEyes that are connected together to create a project. There is one *project* element, the element that contains your entire project. The *view* element requires additional elements to be nested within it.

The *project* element can contain multiple *view* elements, each one displayed as a separate tab in your project, each one containing elements itself, such as *resources*, *controls,* and *displays* (each box in the drawing represents an element).

Attributes and Values

The attributes control the details of how an element will look or what it will do. If the element were a person, its attributes would be eye color, weight, gender, and so on. An attribute is always paired up with a value, for example, *eyeColor* with "blue" and *weight* with "98." For example, the *view* element, aside from containing other elements, has an attribute called *title*, which causes the value assigned to it.

Creating VisualEyes Projects

Making a VisualEyes project involves gathering web-accessible resources and creating a script using the *VisEdit* tool to weave these resources into a presentation. You need to identify resources you want to use, such as images, movies, and data sets, and put them on the Internet so they can be accessed from anywhere. These can be stored on your own server, or a number of free or inexpensive services can be used:

- Images can be easily stored on sites such as Flickr or Picassa
- Videos can be stored on YouTube
- Data files can be stored on Google *Docs* or Dropbox.com

You will need to create an account using *VisEdit* where your project scripts and data files can be stored on our servers. The primary purpose of *VisEdit* is to guide you through creating a *project script* by allowing you to:

1. Add and/or modify elements to your project script
2. Save the revised script to the University of Virginia server
3. Display your project using that script
4. Rinse and repeat. . . .

The Structure of a Project

You can think of the *project* element as the main folder or tree trunk and the elements it holds as subfolders or tree branches. The project contains a number of subfolders called *views*. Each view manifests itself as a tab in your project. Each view can hold elements such as resources, displays, and controls.

The most basic elements of a *project* are created when you start a new project in *VisEdit*. These are *frame, textformat, logo, tab,* and *view*. These elements are required for all projects and can be customized as needed by adding or changing attributes. Many attributes have default settings, so if you do not explicitly set them, their default values will be used.

An Example: The Texas Slavery Project

The historian Andrew Torget, in his Texas Slavery Project (TSP), wanted to have the counties on the map shaded differently according to the enslaved population of that county. He connected the timeline's position to query the database containing the populations for the counties by year, and set the color of each county accordingly.

The data for the TSP project are in a mySQL database. The data were extracted according to the current year (gleaned from the position of the time timeline's slider bar), and the settings of the "Shaded by" radio buttons. In this case, we asked for the total slave population for 1837. Those data were used to color the map according to

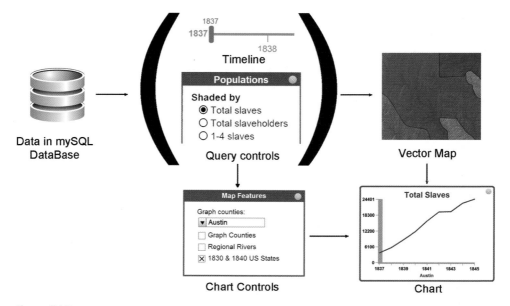

Figure 14.1
Structure of a VisualEyes project.

the population. Clicking on the "Graph Counties" checkbox caused those data to be further reduced to only the slaves from Austin County and graphed (figure 14.1).

This was easily accomplished by connecting the various resources (the data and the maps) and writing a simple XML script to connect them together. The fully interactive visualization can be found online.[1]

1. www.texasslaveryproject.org and www.viseyes.org/show?base=tsp.

Further Reading

Edward Tufte is considered by many the father of information graphics, and his books are as beautifully produced as they are enlightening to read: *The Visual Display of Quantitative Information* (1983), *Envisioning Information* (1990), *Visual Explanations: Images and Quantities, Evidence and Narrative* (1997), and *Beautiful Evidence* (2006). Cognitive psychologist Donald Norman has long been in the forefront of human-centered design, and if you only read one book on usability and human factors, it should be *The Design of Everyday Things* (1988).

Scott McCloud's *Understanding Comics* (1994) is a scholarly discussion of the art and design of the comic art form, done as a long-form comic. It is both insightful and entertaining. The designer of Al Gore's famous slide presentation for *An Inconvenient Truth*, Nancy Duarte, has an excellent book on presentation design, *Slide:ology The Art of Creating Great Presentations* (2008).

Stephen Few has presented the process of presenting quantitative data in a very pragmatic and directly applicable book, *Now You See It: Simple Visualization Techniques for Quantitative Analysis* (2009). Robert Harris's *Information Graphics* (1999) provides an encyclopedic reference to thousands of charts, graphs, and other visual tools for graphically communicating quantitative information.

The Craft of Research (2003) by Booth, Colomb, and Williams provides a good and practical guide to basic research methodology.

References

Alexander, C., Ishikawa, S., & Silverstein, M. (1977). *A pattern language: Towns, buildings, construction*. Berkeley, CA: Center for Environmental Science.

Arnheim, R. (1969). *Visual thinking*. Berkley, CA: University of California Press.

Baddeley, A. (1992). Working memory. *Science, 255,* 556–559.

Bateson, G. (2000). *Steps to an ecology of mind* (pp. 457–466). Chicago: University of Chicago Press.

Berners-Lee, T., Lassila, O., & Hendler, J. (2001). The semantic web. *Scientific American, 284*(5), 29–37.

Bertin, J. (1983). *Semiology of graphics*. Madison, WI: University of Wisconsin Press.

Booth, W., Colomb, G., & Williams, J. (2003). *The craft of research*. Chicago: University of Chicago Press.

Bransford, J., Brown, A., & Cocking, R. (2000). *How people learn: Brain, mind, experience, and school.* Committee on Learning Research and Educational Practice, National Research Council. Washington, DC: National Academy Press.

Brown, E., & Cairns, P. (2004). *A grounded investigation of game immersion* (p. 1297). Vienna, Austria: ACM/CHI.

Cairo, A. (2011). *Information visualization in the news* (unpublished). Retrieved June 12, 2011, from http://www.visualopolis.com.

Card, S., Mackinlay, J., & Shneiderman, B. (1999). *Readings in information visualization—Using vision to think*. San Francisco: Morgan Kaufmann.

Cawthon, N., & Vande Moere, A. (2007). The effect of aesthetic on the usability of data visualization. *11th International Conference on Information Visualization. IEEE*

Chi, E. (2000). A taxonomy of visualization techniques using the data state reference model. *Proceedings of the IEEE Symposium on Information Visualization* (p. 69). Washington, DC: IEEE Computer Society.

Coppock, J., & Rhind, D. (1991). The history of GIS. In D. J. Maguire, M. Goodchild, & D. Rhind (Eds.), *Geographical information systems: Principles and applications* (Vol. 1, pp. 21–43). London: Longmans.

Csikszentmihaly, M. (1991). *Flow: The psychology of optimal experience.* New York: Harper Perennial.

Duarte, N. (2008). *Slide:ology. The art and science of creating great presentations.* Sebastopol, CA: O'Reilly.

Eccles, R., Kapler, T., Harper, R., & Wright, W. (2008). Stories in GeoTime. *InfoVis, 7,* 3–17.

Fairchild, M. (1999). *Color appearance models.* Reading, MA: Addison-Wesley.

Few, S. (2009). *Now you see it: Simple visualization techniques for quantitative analysis.* Oakland, CA: Analytics Press.

Furnham, A. (2000). The brainstorming myth. *Business Strategy Review 11*(4), 21–28.

Frischetti, M. (1997). Blueprint for information architects. *Fast Company, 10*(August), 186.

Fry, B. (2004). *Computational information design.* Doctoral Thesis. UMI Order Number AAI0806331. Cambridge, MA: Massachusetts Institute of Technology.

Garrett, J. (2003). *The elements of user experience: User-centered design for the web.* Berkeley, CA: New Riders.

Gee, J. (2003). *What video games have to teach us about learning and literacy.* New York: Palgrave Macmillan.

Gordin, D. N., & Pea, R. D. (1995). Prospects for scientific visualization as an educational technology. *Journal of the Learning Sciences, 4*(3), 249–279.

Grimmer, J., & King, G. (2009) *Quantitative discovery from qualitative information: A general-purpose document clustering methodology.* Working Paper. Retrieved June 12, 2011, from http://gking .harvard.edu/files/abs/discov-abs.shtml.

GSA IT Accessibility and Workforce. (2011). *Resources for understanding and implementing Section 508.* Retrieved June 2, 2011, from http://www.section508.gov.

Harris, R. (1999). *Information graphics. A comprehensive illustrated reference.* New York: Oxford University Press.

Healey, C. (2007). *Perception in visualization.* Retrieved February 1, 2011, from http://www.csc .ncsu.edu/faculty/healey/PP/index.html.

Heer, J., Bostock, M., & Ogievetsky, V. (2010). A tour through the visualization zoo: A survey of powerful visualization techniques, from the obvious to the obscure. *Communications of the ACM, 53*(6), 59–67.

Huff, D. (1954). *How to lie with statistics.* New York: Norton.

Hung, P.-Y., & Pop, A. (2008). *Learning to do historical research: A primer. How to frame a researchable question*. Retrieved February 2, 2012, from http://www.williamcronon.net/researching/questions.htm.

Itten, J. (1970). *The elements of color*. London: Van Nostrand Reinhold.

Jaffa, Y. (2011). The information sage. *Washington Monthly Magazine*. May/June. Retrieved February 3, 2012 from http://www.washingtonmonthly.com/magazine/mayjune_2011/features/the_information_sage029137.php#

Johnson, S. (2006). *The ghost map*. New York: Riverhead.

Jordan, P. (2000). *Designing pleasurable products. An introduction to new human factors*. London: Taylor & Francis.

Kazdin, A. (1982). *Single-case research designs: Methods for clinical and applied settings*. New York: Oxford University Press.

Kelley, T. (2001). *The art of innovation*. New York: Random House.

Klein, G., Moon, B., & Hoffman, R. (2006). Making sense of sensemaking: Alternative perspectives. *Intelligent Systems, 21*(4), 71.

Kolko, J. (2010). Abductive thinking and sensemaking: The drivers of design synthesis. *MIT's Design Issues, 26*(1), 15–28.

Kolko, J. (2011). *Exposing the magic of design: A practitioner's guide to the methods and theory of synthesis*. New York: Oxford University Press.

Kosara, R. (2007). Visualization criticism—The missing link between information visualization and art. In *Proceedings of the 11th international conference on information visualization* (Vol. IV, pp. 631–636). Washington, DC: IEEE Computer Society.

Kosko, B. (1993). *Fuzzy thinking: The new science of fuzzy logic*. New York: Hyperion.

Laurel, B. (1991). *Computers as theatre*. Reading, MA: Addison-Wesley.

Lave, C., & March, J. (1993). *An introduction to models in the social sciences*. Lanham, MD: University Press of America.

Lee, B., Plaisant, C., Parr, C. S., Fekete, J., & Henry, N. (2006). Task taxonomy for graph visualization. *Proceedings of the 2006 AVI workshop on beyond time and errors: Novel evaluation methods for information visualization, BELIV '06*. New York: ACM.

Lima, M. (2011). *Visual complexity: Mapping patterns of information*. New York: Princeton Architectural Press.

Liu, Z., Nersessian, N., & Stasko, J. (2008). Distributed cognition as a theoretical framework for information visualization. *IEEE Transactions on Visualization and Computer Graphics, 14*(8), 1173–1180.

Lukić, B. (2011). *Nonobject*. Cambridge, MA: MIT Press.

Man, P. (2011). What data visualization can learn from game design. *Masters of Media Blog*, University of Amsterdam. Retrieved May 1, 2011, from http://mastersofmedia.hum.uva.nl/2011/04/19/what-data-visualization-can-learn-from-game-design.

Manovich, L. (2010) What is visualization? Retrieved October 1, 2010, from http://manovich.net/2010/10/25/new-article-what-is-visualization.

Mayer, R. E. (2005). *Multimedia learning*. New York: Cambridge University Press.

McCloud, S. (1994). *Understanding comics: The invisible art*. New York: Harper Collins.

McLuhan, M. (1964). *Understanding media*. New York: Mentor.

Meadows, M. (2003). *Pause and effect*. Indianapolis, IN: New Riders.

Mueller, J. (2003). *Accessibility for everybody: Understanding the section 508 accessibility requirements*. New York: Apress.

Miller, G. (1956). The magical number seven, plus or minus two: Some limits on our capacity for processing information. *Psychological Review, 63*, 81–97.

Mok, C. (1996). *Designing business*. San Jose, CA: Macmillan.

Moretti, F. (2005). *Graphs maps trees: Abstract models for literary history*. London: Verso.

Munzner, T. (2009). A nested process model for visualization design and validation. *IEEE Transactions on Visualization and Computer Graphics, 15*(6), 921–928.

Murray, J. (1997). *Hamlet on the holodeck: The future of narrative in cyberspace*. Cambridge, MA: MIT Press.

Norman, D. (1988). *The design of everyday things*. New York: Doubleday.

Norman, D. (2004). *Emotional design*. New York: Basic Books.

Oard, D. (2009). A whirlwind tour of automated language processing for the humanities and social sciences. In *Working together or apart: Promoting the next generation of digital scholarship* (pp. 34–42). Washington, DC: Council on Library and Information Resources.

Ogle, D. M. (1986). K-W-L: A teaching model that develops active reading of expository text. *Reading Teacher, 39*, 564–570.

Presnell, J. (2007). *The information-literate historian: A guide to research for history students*. New York: Oxford University Press.

Pylyshyn, Z. (2002). Mental imagery: In search of a theory. *Behavioral and Brain Sciences, 25*(2), 157–237.

Rapp, D. (2005). Mental models: Theoretical issues for visualizations in science education. In J. Gilbert (Ed.), *Visualization in science education* (pp. 43–60). The Netherlands: Springer.

Roam, D. (2008). *The back of the napkin: Solving problems and selling ideas with pictures*. New York: Portfolio.

Shank, R. (1990). *Tell me a story*. New York: Scribners.

Shedroff, N. (1999). Information interaction design: A unified field theory of design. In R. E. Jacobson (Ed.), *Information design* (pp. 267–292). Cambridge, MA: MIT Press.

Shneiderman, B. (1996). The eyes have it: A task by data type taxonomy for information visualizations. *Proceedings of the 1996 IEEE Symposium on Visual Languages*. Washington, DC: IEEE.

Shneiderman, B., & Plaisant, C. (2010). *Designing the user interface: Strategies for effective human-computer interaction* (5th ed.). Reading, MA: Addison-Wesley.

Spence, R. (2001). *Information visualization*. Essex, England: ACM Press.

Spieglhalter, D. (2008). Nightingale's "coxcombs." *Understanding Uncertainty*. Retrieved October 20, 2011, from http://understandinguncertainty.org/coxcombs.

Staley, D. (2003). *Computers, visualization and history*. New York: ME Sharpe.

Staley, D. (2007). H*istory and future: Using historical thinking to imagine the future*. New York: Lexington Books.

Stray, J. (2011). *A full-text visualization of the Iraq War logs*. Retrieved June 12, 2011, from http://jonathanstray.com.

Sweller, J. (2005). Cognitive theory of multimedia learning. In Mayer, R. E. (Ed.). *The Cambridge handbook of multimedia learning* (pp. 19–30). New York: Cambridge University Press.

Taylor, C., & Gibbs, G. (2010). How and what to code, *Online QDA Web Site*, Retrieved May 21, 2011, from onlineqda.hud.ac.uk/Intro_QDA/how_what_to_code.php.

Tory, M., & Moller, T. (2004). Rethinking visualization: A high-level taxonomy. *Proceedings of the IEEE Symposium on information* (pp. 151–158). Washington, DC: IEEE Computer Society.

Treffinger, D., Isaksen, S., & Stead-Dorval, B. (2006). *Creative problem solving: An introduction* (4th ed.). Waco, TX: Prufrock Press.

Treinish, L. (1999). A function-based data model for visualization. *Proceedings of the IEEE Computer Society Visualization* (pp. 73–76). Washington, DC: IEEE.

Treisman, A., & Gormican, S. (1988). Feature analysis in early vision: Evidence from search asymmetries. *Psychological Review, 95*, 15–48.

Tufte, E. (1983). *The visual display of graphic information*. Cheshire, CT: Graphics Press.

Tufte, E. (1990). *Envisioning information*. Cheshire, CT: Graphics Press.

Tufte, E. (1997). *Visual explanations: Images and quantities, evidence and narration*. Cheshire, CT: Graphics Press.

Tufte, E. (2006). *Beautiful evidence*. Cheshire, CT: Graphics Press.

Tversky, B., Morrison, J., & Betrancort, M. (2002). Animation: Can it facilitate? *International Journal of Human-Computer Studies, 57*(4), 247–262.

Twain, M. (2011). *Adventures of Tom Sawyer and Huckleberry Finn* (The NewSouth Edition, A. Gribben, ed.). Montgomery, AL: NewSouth.

van Ham, F., & Perer, A. (2009). Search, show context, expand on demand: Supporting large graph exploration with degree-of-interest. *IEEE Transactions on Visualization and Computer Graphics, 15*(6), 953–960.

Wang, J., & Brown, M. (2007). Automated essay scoring versus human scoring: A comparative study. *Journal of Technology, Learning, and Assessment, 6*(2). Retrieved June, 3, 2011 from http://www.jtla.org.

Ware, C. (2004). *Information visualization: Perception for design*. San Francisco: Morgan Kaufmann.

Ware, C. (2008). *Visual thinking for design*. Burlington, MA: Morgan Kaufmann.

Wijk, J. (2005). The value of visualization. *Proceedings of IEEE Visualization, 1*, 79–86.

Williams, R. (2004). *The non-designer's design book*. Berkeley, CA: Peachpit.

Williamson, C., & Shneiderman, B. (1992). The dynamic HomeFinder: Evaluating dynamic queries in a real-estate information exploration system. *Proceedings of the 15th Annual International ACM SIGIR* (pp. 338–346). Copenhagen, Denmark.

Wurman, R. (1989). *Information anxiety*. New York: Doubleday.

Wurman, R. (1996). *Information architects*. Zurich: Graphis Press.

Yi, J, Kang, Y., Stasko, J., & Jacko, J. (2007). Toward a deeper understanding of the role of interaction in information visualization. *IEEE Transactions on Visualization, 13*, 1224–1231.

Index